Industry Transaction & Profile Annual Report: Auto Dealerships—2010 Edition

BVR
What It's Worth

Business Valuation Resources, LLC
1000 SW Broadway St. Suite 1200
Portland, OR 97205
(503) 291-7963   Fax (503) 291-7955   www.BVResources.com

Copyright © 2010 by Business Valuation Resources, L.L.C. (BVR) except where otherwise noted. All rights reserved.

Printed in the United States of America.

No part of this publication may be reproduced, stored in a retrieval system or transmitted in any form or by any means, electronic, mechanical, photocopying, recording, scanning or otherwise, except as permitted under Sections 107 or 108 of the 1976 United States Copyright Act, without either the prior written permission of the Publisher or authorization through payment of the appropriate per copy fee to the Publisher. Requests for permission should be addressed to the Permissions Department, Business Valuation Resources, LLC, 1000 SW Broadway St., Suite 1200, Portland, OR, 97205, (503) 291-7963, fax (503) 291-7955.

Information contained in this book has been obtained by Business Valuation Resources from sources believed to be reliable. However, neither Business Valuation Resources nor its authors guarantee the accuracy or completeness of any information published herein and neither Business Valuation Resources nor its authors shall be responsible for any errors, omissions, or damages arising out of use of this information. This work is published with the understanding that Business Valuation Resources and its authors are supplying information but are not attempting to render business valuation or other professional services. If such services are required, the assistance of an appropriate professional should be sought.

ISBN: 978-1-935081-43-2

Table of Contents

Section 1
Valuing Auto Dealers in a Tough Economy
By Kevin Yeanoplos 1-1

Section 2
First Research® Industry Profile Automobile Dealerships 2-1

Section 3
Bizminer Auto Dealerships Report 3-1

Section 4
Business Reference Guide Rules of Thumb and General Information 4-1

Section 5
Pratt's Stats® Auto Dealership Report 5-1

Section 6
BIZCOMPS® Auto Dealerships Report 6-1

Section 7
Mergerstat Auto Dealerships Report 7-1

Section 8
Valuing Auto Dealerships July 29, 2010 BVR Webinar 8-1

Section 9
Data Sources 9-1

Section 1
Valuing Auto Dealers in a Tough Economy
By Kevin Yeanoplos

Copyright 2010, by Kevin Yeanoplos reprinted with permission

Valuing Auto Dealers in a Tough Economy

By Kevin Yeanoplos

Economic and industry factors could hardly be more negative for the auto industry. With the current economic slump, auto dealers are seeing declining demand for new cars. Still, the demand to value auto dealers remains strong, as these predominantly family-owned businesses gift shares of stock to the next generation, decide to sell out or require valuations for other needs.

For the last decade, the Asian imports have gained a significant portion of the U.S. market share, based on competitive advantages such as fuel efficiency, reliability, and affordability. Obviously, this is having a positive impact on dealership values for imports such as Honda, Toyota, etc. In 2006, Toyota dealerships averaged more than triple the new vehicle sales of the average Chevrolet dealership. GM has attributed this to having too many dealerships, and therefore, has started bundling their Buick, Pontiac, and GMC franchises into single dealerships.

Data gathering challenges

In the data gathering stage of an auto dealer valuation, it is particularly important to focus on prior offers for the dealership. Dealerships are bought and sold quite frequently and it's not unusual to find that a particular dealership has had a number of offers. The offer could be a good indicator of the value of the dealership even if it wasn't consummated, although we would want to look at the reasons for the deal not being consummated.

The next data-gathering issue relates to the compensation of officers. Many times you'll find that officers in a dealership will pay themselves a large bonus at the end of the year. Sometimes what will be recorded on the year-end dealer statement may not be what was ultimately paid to the officers. So there may be some discrepancy in what's appearing on the dealer statement and what actually shows up on the tax return. We also may find that there is compensation being paid to a prior owner as part of the transfer of the dealership. Questions on perks will be particularly important to discuss with management. It's just part of the normal business process with auto dealers.

We need to make sure that we understand the relationship between the dealership and the manufacturer. We need to ask about expansion plans or any plans to do major improvements on the dealership. These types of expected capital expenditures can significantly impact the value of a dealership.

It's not unusual to find that a dealer may have some offsite inventory. There may be another lot somewhere else that isn't readily apparent that needs to be included. So making sure that we get a complete description of the buildings and facilities is very important, as is a site visit. We can determine a number of things by doing a site visit—the condition of the facilities, the location, the competitors that exist in close proximity, etc. The best reason for doing a site visit is just verifying that a business exists. In litigation settings, that question always comes up—did you do a site visit?

And it's important to understand any restrictions on transferability. Keep in mind that it's a franchise operation typically, and generally speaking, franchisors are going to put some restrictions on transferring the franchise to another individual or a company. They just don't want anybody to be able to own the franchise.

Valuing Auto Dealers in a Tough Economy

Industry data

The wonderful thing about valuing auto dealers, and frankly, one of the reasons why I enjoy this area so much, is that there is a tremendous amount of information. It's one of the biggest industries worldwide and there is an abundance of available information.

Dealers are required to provide monthly statements to the manufacturers, including the 13th Month Statement, which is supposed to be the final statement closing out the end of the year. Now I say supposed because I have found on many occasions that there were some additional adjustments pertaining to a particular fiscal year that were actually made after that 13th Month Statement that would certainly impact the valuation. So just because we're getting a "final" dealer statement for a particular year doesn't necessarily mean that it reflects valuation reality. So we would need to make sure that we ask for both the dealer statements and any other type of reviewed or compiled or audited statement for the particular dealership, and then finally, the tax returns because we need to make sure that we're dealing with reality.

One reason that those dealer statements can be particularly effective is if we're doing a valuation in the middle of the year. We know that auto dealers are subject to seasonality, and if we have the monthly statements, we'll be able to actually compare how the dealership is performing relative to the prior year at any interim point in the year. And because there is seasonality, it's very helpful to be able to see how many total cars were sold, how many used vehicles were sold, how many new vehicles were sold and what the profitability was year-to-date. The monthly statements provide some good detail in terms of the numbers of employees, the numbers of vehicles sold, the average profit margin for new vehicles and the average profit margin for used vehicles.

Trade publications

- Automotive Executive
- Automotive News
- JD Power & Associates
- Manheim Consulting
- National Independent Automobile Dealers Association

A collection of businesses

It's important to understand that an auto dealership is really a collection of a number of different types of businesses. And when we value a dealership, we need to independently look at what the performance is for each one of these departments or businesses.

Valuing Auto Dealers in a Tough Economy

> **Typical departments**
> - New Vehicle
> - Used Vehicle
> - Parts
> - Finance & Insurance
> - Body Shop
> - Service
> - Lease & Rental Sales (primarily larger dealerships)

New and used vehicles typically represent front-end revenues. In contrast, back-end revenues would be something like the parts, body shop and service departments. Generally speaking, we get new customers at the front end when they come in to buy a new vehicle or a used vehicle. Once they have those vehicles, we would get revenues from them on the back end from those other departments.

Many dealerships are increasing the number of used vehicles that are sold and perhaps even setting up a separate used car lot to provide areas for more inventory. There's a reason for that. The used vehicles, in general, can provide more opportunities for higher margins than the new vehicles. In fact, I tend to think of new vehicles as a loss leader. The new vehicles generally have lower margins because the prices are more competitive. The used vehicles generally offer a little more negotiating room to provide for higher margins. And the sources of inventory are coming from different places as well. The new vehicle inventory is coming from the manufacturers. The used vehicles are coming from trade-ins, from auctions, from a number of different sources. So there are some very good opportunities for added profits with used vehicles. Dealerships are better able to withstand some of the cycles that the auto industry goes through because of these back-end departments. For instance, in times when new vehicle sales are down, we may find that used vehicle sales would be up or people would be taking their existing vehicle and repairing it or upgrading it.

The finance and insurance department can be the most profitable of all of the departments because it has very little overhead. It's basically commissions that are paid to the dealership based on contracts that are sold, insurance policies that are sold, and things like that. But even though it's the most profitable because it has the least overhead, it's generally the department that is managed the most ineffectively. So that might be a practice development opportunity to help the dealers actually improve their ability to manage that F&I department.

FIFO vs. LIFO

Dealership accounting has some nuances that we need to consider in performing the valuation. Because of the favorable tax benefits, dealerships typically use last-in, first-out (LIFO) inventory method, so a LIFO adjustment is needed when a valuation is done. The LIFO adjustment is not just important on the income statement but it's important to the balance sheet as well. Since the public auto dealers generally use first-in, first-out (FIFO) and the private auto dealers use LIFO, we know that we're going to need to make an adjustment to make those consistent to be able to value them.

The next area is liability for charge-backs. Dealers receive a front-end commission on finance and on insurance. If the person who originally bought the vehicle refinances it or trades it in, or for some other reason, they don't have the vehicle for the time period that was expected at the front end, the dealership has already been overpaid a commission for the entire period of the contract. So the company that has paid them the commission certainly is going to want some kind of a refund. What they do is charge back the dealership for the overpaid commission. Generally, some of the smaller dealerships will not record any kind of reserve, and an adjustment would need to be made.

Risk areas

You can imagine that handling so much oil and gasoline would potentially create some environmental issues that certainly need to be addressed. At the very least, we may determine that we know there is a liability, whether it's been quantified. We would consider the risk associated with the liability in developing our discount rate.

Franchise alignment is another risk. We know GM is trying to combat some of its struggles by allowing the bundling of different brands. This allows the dealer to appeal to a broader market and we may actually get customers coming in that plan to buy a particular brand and they come in and decide to buy something else. So being able to bundle creates some efficiencies, and the lack of bundling can create some additional risks.

Potential or existing litigation can exist with the franchisor because of some encroachment. Perhaps there was an additional dealer placed in an area that was too close to another dealership, and in essence, it wound up cannibalizing it.

Valuation methods

With the asset approach for dealerships, a key adjustment relates to LIFO. We know that in a period of rising prices, LIFO understates the inventory on the books. So it has to be adjusted to FIFO, net of tax. It's also very common to find a dealership that has real estate, airplanes and antique cars.

Some of the nuances with the income approach include the industry cycle, which historically has been about three years. Because auto dealers have good times and bad times, we're going to look at average historical earnings or cash flow as opposed to a weighted average. Because we're dealing with a cycle, any one of those years would be as representative as the next, and for that reason, it would make sense to look at just a simple average. Occasionally, you would do a discounted cash flow forecast, particularly for a dealership that has gone through some significant reworking. But generally speaking, if we have an established dealership, a simple average of historical cash flow will do.

Control vs. minority interest

If we're valuing a controlling interest, then the owner has the ability to make discretionary adjustments whereas the minority interest owner does not. In contrast, we handle discounts for lack of control by not making discretionary adjustments. In essence, our cash flow is less than it would be for a controlling shareholder, and therefore, because we have reduced cash flow to a minority shareholder, there is an implicit discount for the lack of control.

Valuing Auto Dealers in a Tough Economy

And for the most part, that's how most valuation analysts are handling the issues related to control or the lack of it—whether it's auto dealers or any other industry.

If you're doing the income approach, you may find that there is excess cash, for instance, or investments, but it may be that the manufacturer has required the dealer to deposit some additional cash reserves, and in return, they're giving them favorable flooring financing.

We want to look at non-recurring gains, losses, expenses or income. We've got a number of clients that after 9/11 saw very little activity. They had spent a lot of money on advertising to increase business. So if it was an expense such as advertising that was unusual, then that would potentially require an adjustment.

The dealerships get their inventory and finance it with something called flooring—flooring financing, which is a "glorified" payable. The financing on a particular vehicle is, in theory, paid off when the vehicle is sold. The dealership pays financing charges to the financing company, and that interest on flooring is considered an operating expense.

Common adjustments
- Rent
- LIFO
- Dealer and Family Member Compensation
- "Watered" Receivables and Inventories
- Real Estate and Fixed Asset Values
- Dealer Perks/Discretionary Expenses
- Non-Recurring Gains or Losses
- Assets and Liabilities Not Included on the Books

Finally, capital expenditures are certainly a key issue that we need to consider as part of the valuation because they can be a significant potential detriment to value if we know that the company is planning or needs to make some additional expenditures related to expanding or improving.

The wonderful thing about the market approach and the automobile industry is that we do have a very finite group of publicly traded companies. We can get a tremendous amount of information on those guideline companies, and of course, we would need to adjust them to make them appropriate to use with our private companies. The biggest adjustments would relate to size and potential growth. The growth for our subject company can vary significantly from one dealership to the next, based on the brand, location, the ability of the management and so on.

Valuing Auto Dealers in a Tough Economy

Public companies

- Asbury Automotive Group, Inc. (ABG)
- AutoNation, Inc. (AN)
- Group 1 Automotive Group, Inc. (GPI)
- Penske Automotive Group, Inc. (PAG)
- Sonic Automotive, Inc. (SAH)
- Lithia Motors, Inc. (LAD)
- Car Max, Inc. (KMX)
- America's Car-Mart, Inc. (CRMT)

We can use private comps in valuing auto dealers but it's extremely important to remember that the time period that you're using can have a significant impact on the value of the subject company. In fact, recently, we've had a number of deals where private dealerships were being purchased left and right by the public companies, and that actually inflated the multiples. So it's important to make sure that we're within the same time period that we're doing the valuation because those multiples can be all over the place. A nice source of information on market comparables is the 8-Ks of publicly traded companies.

References

A Dealer Guide to...Valuing an Automobile Dealership, National Automobile Dealers Association, June 2000

Guide to Valuing an Automobile Dealership, by David A. Duryee, MBA, T.S. Tony Leung, CFA, CPA, ASA, and Mark D. Schmitz, Ph.D., Published by the National Automobile Dealers Association, January 1989\

Short-Term Energy Outlook, Energy Information Administration, September 11, 2007 Release

Valuing Automobile Dealerships, by James L. (Butch) Williams, CPA/ABV, CVA, CBA, published in the Handbook of Advanced Business Valuation and Intellectual Property Analysis, 2000

Automobile Dealerships, First Research, September 17, 2007

Beige Book National Summary, Federal Reserve Bank of Minneapolis, September 5, 2007

Section 2
First Research®
Industry Profile
Automobile Dealerships

SIC CODES: 5511, 5521
NAICS CODES: 4411

First Research® Industry Profile Automobile Dealerships

INDUSTRY PROFILE

Automobile Dealerships

SIC CODES: 5511, 5521
NAICS CODES: 4411

QUARTERLY UPDATE **8/9/2010**

About First Research

First Research, a D&B company, is the leading provider of Industry Intelligence Tools that help sales and marketing teams perform faster and smarter, open doors and close more deals. First Research performs the "heavy lifting" by analyzing hundreds of sources to create insightful and easy to digest Industry Intelligence that can be consumed very quickly to better understand a prospect's or client's business issues. Customers include leading companies in banking, accounting, insurance, technology, telecommunications, business process outsourcing and professional services such as ADP, Bank of America, Merrill Lynch and Sprint. Used by more than 60,000 sales professionals, First Research can benefit any organization which has prospects in multiple industries.

Attention: This profile purchase is an individual license and is not to be distributed to additional individuals even within the same organization. For corporate or small business subscription information, visit www.firstresearch.com or call 866-788-9389.

About Business Valuation Resources, LLC (BVR)

Every top business valuation firm depends on BVR for authoritative market data, continuing professional education, and expert opinion. Rely on BVR when your career depends on an unimpeachable business valuation. Our customers include business appraisers, certified public accountants, merger and acquisition professionals, business brokers, lawyers and judges, private equity and venture capitalists, owners, CFOs, and many others. Founded by Dr. Shannon Pratt, BVR's market databases and analysis have won in the courtroom — and the boardroom — for over a decade.

BVR is the exclusive distributor of First Research Industry and State Profile single reports. To order, go to www.bvresources.com/firstresearch or call 888-287-8258.

First Research® Industry Profile Automobile Dealerships

Industry Overview

The US automobile dealer industry includes about 45,000 new and used vehicle dealers with combined annual revenue of $600 billion. Major companies include AutoNation, Penske Automotive Group, Sonic Automotive, and CarMax. The industry is **highly fragmented**: the top 50 companies generate less than 15 percent of revenue.

COMPETITIVE LANDSCAPE

Consumer spending and **interest rates** drive demand. The profitability of individual companies depends on the volume and mix of cars and services sold. Large companies can offer a wider selection of cars and have advantages in marketing, purchasing, and finance. Small companies can compete effectively by offering superior customer service or serving a local market. The industry is capital-intensive: annual revenue per worker averages nearly $600,000.

For vehicle sales, auto dealers compete with private market sellers, who are increasingly using the Internet to bypass traditional retail channels. Companies compete with various retail outlets, such as oil change centers, tire stores, and independent service shops and chains, for service revenue.

PRODUCTS, OPERATIONS & TECHNOLOGY

New cars account for 50 percent of industry sales; **used cars** make up 30 percent. Other products and **services** include **parts** and accessories, financing plans, extended warranties, and insurance.

New car dealers have **franchise agreements** with car manufacturers, which give dealerships non-exclusive rights to sell certain brands of cars and offer related parts and services within a specified market area. Franchise agreements typically impose various requirements for operations, including inventory levels, working capital, sales practices, showrooms, service facilities, and monthly reporting. Multiple franchise agreements with different car manufacturers allow dealers to offer a broad range of vehicles. The average new car dealership generates less than $30 million annually, according to the National Automobile Dealers Association (NADA).

Dealers acquire new vehicles from manufacturers through an **allocation system** based on historical sales, and typically have limited influence over the colors and features of cars received. Companies buy used vehicles from a variety of sources, including trade-ins, auctions, other dealers, leasing companies, and rental companies. To set a price for a trade-in, used dealers consider a car's age, mileage, and condition to develop an **appraisal**. Used vehicles may require reconditioning prior to sale; vehicles unfit for retail resale are generally sold through wholesale auctions. Some manufacturers allow dealers to sell **certified pre-owned (CPO)** vehicles with extended warranties.

Service and parts operations may offer repair, maintenance, body work, and warranty services. A typical service department has 18 service bays and handles over 13,000 repair orders annually at an average value of just over $200 per order. Car manufacturers may **authorize** dealers to perform warranty work.

Auto dealers rely on **computerized information systems** to store vehicle information, track vehicle movement, and process sales transactions. **Inventory management** systems help companies optimize the supply and mix of vehicles, and are especially useful for companies monitoring inventory across multiple dealerships. **Customer databases** store information on existing and potential customers and help dealerships develop marketing programs. **Radio frequency identification devices** (RFID) capture test drive information.

SALES & MARKETING

Marketing and promotional vehicles include newspaper, TV, radio, and outdoor (billboard) advertising and direct mail. Dealers benefit from **national advertising** from car manufacturers, which are among the largest TV advertisers. Manufacturers may offer consumer incentives, such as **cash rebates** and **low interest financing**, to drive sales.

With intense competition among dealers, **customer satisfaction** has become an important differentiator and a key tool in developing repeat sales. While most auto dealers rely on a commissioned sales force, negative publicity about **high-pressure sales tactics** has made **fixed-price selling, non-commissioned sales staff,** and **Internet sales** more popular. Good customer experiences in service departments help dealers develop ongoing relationships with customers.

Internet sites allow dealers to reach customers beyond local markets. Auto manufacturer and syndicated websites, such as

First Research® Industry Profile Automobile Dealerships

Autotrader.com or cars.com, help generate sales leads and drive dealership traffic. Dealer websites may let customers search inventory, review pricing, compare vehicles, calculate payments, and estimate trade-in values. Companies may allow customers to apply for financing and finalize purchases via the Internet.

The **average retail price** for a new car is about $26,000, according to Comerica Bank. Retail prices for used cars average $9,600, according to the NADA. Manufacturers establish the manufacturer suggested retail price (MSRP) for vehicles, but dealers usually discount the list price.

FINANCE & REGULATION

Sales are **seasonal**, with peaks during spring and summer. During the new vehicle model-year changeover period in the fall, dealers often heavily discount current year models. Inventories are a dealer's largest asset and are typically funded with **"floor plan financing"** through car manufacturers or commercial banks. **Inventory levels** range from 50 to 90 days sales: imported cars sell faster and can average about 50 days sales. Receivables are generally low, since most dealers provide customer financing through third parties. Most dealers receive **commissions** for arranging third-party customer financing, leasing, or insurance. Companies facilitate customer loans through the financial arm of car manufacturers or banks.

Gross margins are about 15 percent of sales. Because sales of new vehicles can be volatile, service and parts can account for a majority of operating profit. During tough economic times, dealers may barely break even on new vehicle sales. Used cars are generally more profitable than new cars.

Federal, state, and local laws regulate dealer advertising, sales, financing, employment, and repair operations. Consumer protection and truth-in-lending laws affect sales practices and customer financing programs. Environmental laws affect service operations, since repairs may involve disposal of hazardous materials and waste.

REGIONAL & INTERNATIONAL ISSUES

Average dealership revenue varies significantly nationwide, due to differences in sales volume and product mix. **Foreign brands** such as Toyota and Honda account for more than half of the US new vehicle market. The majority of imported vehicles come from Japan, Canada, Germany, Mexico, and Korea. Most Canadian and Mexican imports come from manufacturing facilities owned by US companies.

HUMAN RESOURCES

Typical jobs include sales associates, technicians, service and parts workers, and administrative staff. Average hourly industry wages are about the same as the national average, although employees of new car dealers tend to earn more than those of used car dealers. **Turnover** of experienced sales staff can be high. The industry injury rate is about the same as the national average.

Industry Employment Growth
Bureau of Labor Statistics

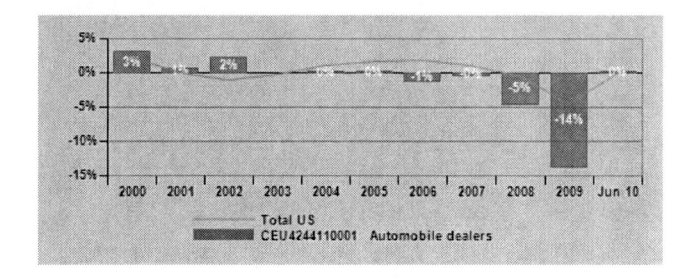

Average Hourly Earnings & Annual Wage Increase
Bureau of Labor Statistics

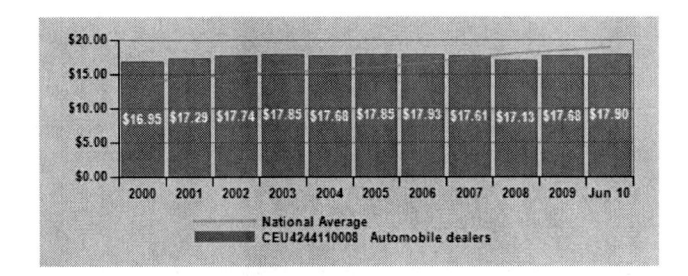

First Research® Industry Profile Automobile Dealerships

[Bar chart: National Average CEU4244110008 Automobile dealers, 2000–Jun 10: $16.95, $17.29, $17.74, $17.85, $17.68, $17.85, $17.93, $17.61, $17.13, $17.68, $17.90]

Quarterly Industry Update

Dealers Exempted from Financial Oversight Law - Auto dealers successfully lobbied for an exemption from a consumer lending bill passed by Congress in June 2010. The reform measures include the creation of a watchdog agency tasked with protecting consumers from deceptive lending practices. Many of the bill's supporters wanted car dealers, who write billions of dollars' worth of loans annually, to be under the agency's supervision. Dealers argued that current laws provide consumers with adequate protection, and increased regulation would have only raised auto lending costs, according to *The Detroit News*.

Chrysler's Reduced Ranks See Profit - About 80 percent of Chrysler dealerships reported a profit for first quarter 2010, compared to 70 percent who reported a profit in 2009. The increase could be a sign of recovery for the struggling automaker, but Chrysler's improved profitability has come at a cost to dealers. The company trimmed almost 800 outlets as part of its 2009 Chapter 11 reorganization, according to *The Wall Street Journal*. A number of dealers have used arbitration to appeal Chrysler's decision to sever ties, but most have been unsuccessful.

Tesla to Test New Dealership Model - Forgoing large inventories held by an extensive dealer network, Tesla Motors plans to use a just-in-time delivery system to make cars to order, according to *Greentech Media*. The company, which recently became the first American car manufacturer to go public in more than 50 years, plans to have only 50 dealerships worldwide by 2012. Tesla's success will likely determine what impact the company's business model will have on the industry. The maker of high-performance electric cars has lost money every year since its founding and does not expect profits for the foreseeable future.

INDUSTRY INDICATORS

US consumer spending on durable goods, an indicator of auto sales, fell 2 percent in May 2010 compared to the same month in 2009.

The bank prime loan rate, which indicates the finance rates available to dealerships and automobile consumers, remains at 3.25 percent as of the week of July 7, 2010, unchanged from the same week in 2009.

US retail sales for motor vehicle and parts dealers, a potential measure of demand for autos, increased 9.8 percent in the first six months of 2010 compared to the same period in 2009.

Business Challenges

CRITICAL ISSUES

Volatile Demand - Consumer demand for cars can vary significantly from year to year, due to a variety of factors, including changing economic conditions, consumer spending, inflation, and fuel prices. Sales for particular brands or styles are especially vulnerable to evolving consumer preferences. During a recent recessionary period, the number of autos sold declined, despite large financial incentives from car makers.

Interest Rates Affect Sales and Inventory Costs - Significant increases in interest rates can reduce consumer ability to buy cars and increase floor plan financing costs. Most customers buy vehicles with loans or leases. Dealer inventories are typically financed through variable interest rate loans. Increasing interest rates can reduce profits by affecting both sales

First Research® Industry Profile Automobile Dealerships

volume and dealer costs.

OTHER BUSINESS CHALLENGES

Dependence on Car Manufacturers - Dealers rely on car manufacturers for new vehicle inventory, financing, marketing, and warranty and service work. Companies have limited control over the colors and features of cars received, and often face the task of selling cars that may not be exactly what a customer wants. Financial distress can cause car manufacturers to cut marketing support or change floor plan or customer financing programs.

Vulnerability to Trade Disputes - Because foreign brands account for more than half the US car market, trade disputes, particularly with Japan or Germany, can affect dealership profitability. While many foreign manufacturers have established production plants in the US, imports of foreign cars and trucks still account for a large part of the market. Currency fluctuations, import duties, and trade restrictions can affect operations and costs for US car dealers.

Competition for Services - Car dealers face growing competition in the service segment from fast oil change outlets, tire stores, and independent service centers. Competitive chains specializing in a particular part or service often offer lower prices and more convenient locations. Increasing competition for services can considerably impact dealer profitability because services have strong margins and generate a greater percentage of profits than vehicle sales.

Periodic Skilled Labor Shortages - During periods of high demand, dealers have difficulty finding skilled service technicians. Cars have become more complex, making service jobs more challenging. Servicing sophisticated vehicle components requires technicians with math, electronic, computer, and analytical skills. Rapidly changing technology involves constant training to keep technicians current.

Changed Role for Local Dealers - Greater efficiencies in manufacturing, transport, and inventory management have reduced the strategic need for independent dealers. Now the big car companies can potentially produce cars by special order in as little as one week, which could lead to direct sales from car companies to consumers, with local dealers acting only as distribution and service locations.

Trends and Opportunities

BUSINESS TRENDS

Fluctuating Gas Prices - Drastic changes in gas prices are changing the auto industry. The retail price of gas surpassed $4 per gallon in summer 2008, dropped to below $2 in early 2009, and approached $3 in 2010. Such fluctuations have driven many consumers to seek fuel-efficient cars. Some car manufacturers, anticipating long-term reduced demand for low mileage vehicles, are scaling down or discontinuing production for certain SUVs and trucks. Weak demand for gas guzzlers has resulted in increased demand for small cars and hybrids and heavy discounting on new and used SUVs and trucks.

Industry Consolidation - Companies have been forced to grow through acquisition due to market contraction and increased efforts by car manufacturers to limit the number of franchise outlets. The number of small dealers declined by more than 20 percent between 1998 and 2008, according to the NADA; the number of large dealers grew 4 percent. With some domestic car manufacturers reducing brand lineups, single franchise dealerships will be unable to carry a full product line and may look to merge.

Customer Loyalty Declining - With a multitude of vehicle choices and heavy competition among dealers, car buyers are becoming more fickle and less loyal. The percentage of customers that repeatedly bought the same brands decreased from 49 percent to about 40 percent between 1998 and 2008, according to Experian Automotive. Consumers who were the most loyal tended to lease vehicles or finance purchases through car manufacturer programs.

INDUSTRY OPPORTUNITIES

More Convenient Services - Companies can offer customers better convenience by providing extended service hours and faster service. Over 70 percent of new car dealers offer weekend or evening service hours, according to the NADA. A growing number of dealerships have entered the quick oil change business by dedicating bays or erecting new buildings to handle quick service.

Aftermarket Sales - Dealers improve profitability by selling or installing high-margin aftermarket products, such as accessories, financing, insurance, and service contracts. Many consumers prefer to have accessories, such as audio systems, custom wheels, alarms, fabric protection, installed immediately after purchase. Income from financing, insurance, and service contracts accounts can help offset declining profits in new vehicle sales departments.

Certified Pre-Owned Cars - Sales of certified pre-owned (CPO) or used vehicles are growing, as more low mileage leased cars have become available. While most used cars are sold with a limited warranty, CPO vehicles typically carry extended warranties, which cover most major systems. While dealers have to invest more into inspection and reconditioning, they can often sell CPO cars at a higher price and generate greater profits. CPO customers are also likely to return to the dealer for service and their next new car purchase.

Nontraditional Sales Techniques - A growing number of dealers are implementing nontraditional sales tools to generate leads and appeal to consumers who dislike the traditional car buying process. Referral or manufacturer websites generate sales leads. Dealer websites allow consumers to search inventory for cars with desired features. Some third-party websites have partnered with dealers and allow customers to negotiate purchase terms and get financing online. Fixed prices and full disclosure of purchase terms creates a more honest customer transaction. Non-commissioned sales staff is less likely to pressure customers.

Leveraging Environmental Concern - Companies can take advantage of growing consumer concern about the environment by promoting hybrid vehicles and improving the environmental friendliness of customer-owned vehicles. While hybrids are a small segment of the market, sales are strong, even with temporary supply constraints limiting growth. Some hybrids qualify for tax rebates, effectively lowering the retail price to the customer. "Green" car checkups, which focus on components that have the greatest effect on fuel efficiency, can help drive traffic in service departments.

Call Preparation Questions

CONVERSATION STARTERS

How does the company perform during adverse economic conditions or periods of weak consumer demand?
Consumer demand for cars can vary significantly from year to year, due to a variety of factors, including changing economic conditions, consumer spending, inflation, and fuel prices.

How do fluctuating interest rates affect the company's business?
Significant increases in interest rates can reduce consumer ability to buy cars and increase floor plan financing costs.

How does the company rate its relationship with manufacturers?
Dealers rely on car manufacturers for new vehicle inventory, financing, marketing, and warranty and service work.

How can the company use convenience as a competitive advantage?
Companies can offer customers better convenience by providing extended service hours and faster service.

How important are aftermarket sales to the company?
Dealers improve profitability by selling or installing high-margin aftermarket products, such as accessories, financing, insurance, and service contracts.

How have the company's used car sales changed over time?
Sales of certified pre-owned (CPO) or used vehicles are growing, as more low mileage leased cars have become available.

QUARTERLY INDUSTRY UPDATE

How does the company keep track of proposed changes to federal and state lending rules that might affect its financing operations?
Auto dealers successfully lobbied for an exemption from a consumer lending bill passed by Congress in June 2010.

OPERATIONS, PRODUCTS, AND FACILITIES

How strong are the company's franchise relationships?
New car dealers have franchise agreements with car manufacturers, which give dealerships non-exclusive rights to sell certain brands of cars and offer related parts and services within a specified market area. Multiple franchise agreements with different car manufacturers allow dealers to offer a broad range of vehicles.

First Research® Industry Profile Automobile Dealerships

What difficulties has the company encountered in complying with franchise agreements?
Franchise agreements typically impose various requirements for operations, including inventory levels, working capital, sales practices, showrooms, service facilities, and monthly reporting.

What are the company's average annual sales?
The average new car dealership generates less than $30 million, according to the NADA.

How satisfied is the company with its vehicle allocations?
Dealers acquire new vehicles from manufacturers through an allocation system based on historical sales, and typically have limited influence over the colors and features of cars received.

What is the company's primary source for used vehicles?
Companies purchase used vehicles from a variety of sources, including trade-ins, auctions, other dealers, leasing companies, and rental companies.

How does the company develop appraisal prices for used vehicles?
To set a price for a trade-in, used dealers consider a car's age, mileage, and condition to develop an appraisal.

What process must the company follow to sell certified pre-owned vehicles?
Some manufacturers allow dealers to sell certified pre-owned (CPO) vehicles with extended warranties.

What is the company's main source of revenue?
New cars account for 50 percent of industry sales; used cars make up 30 percent. Other products and services include parts and accessories, financing plans, extended warranties, and insurance.

How big is the company's service department?
A typical service department has 18 service bays and handles over 13,000 repair orders annually at an average value of just over $200 per order.

How important is warranty work to the company's service department?
Car manufacturers may authorize dealers to perform warranty work

CUSTOMERS, MARKETING, PRICING, COMPETITION

What are the company's most effective marketing and promotional vehicles?
Marketing and promotional vehicles include newspaper, TV, radio, and outdoor (billboard) advertising and direct mail.

How important are national marketing efforts by car manufacturers?
Dealers benefit from national advertising from car manufacturers, which are among the largest TV advertisers.

How effective are manufacturers' programs as a dealer marketing tool?
Manufacturers may offer consumer incentives, such as cash rebates and low interest financing, to drive sales.

How would the company's customers describe the level of service they receive?
With intense competition between dealers, customer satisfaction has become an important differentiator and a key tool in developing repeat sales.

What role does the Internet play in the company's marketing strategy?
Internet sites allow dealers to reach customers beyond local markets. Auto manufacturer and syndicated websites, such as Autotrader.com or cars.com, help generate sales leads and drive dealership traffic.

How does the company's pricing compare to the competition's?
The average retail price for a new car is about $26,000, according to Comerica Bank. Retail prices for used cars average $9,600, according to the NADA.

What is the company's biggest competitive threat?
For vehicle sales, auto dealers compete with private-market sellers, who are increasingly using the Internet to bypass traditional retail channels. Companies compete with various retail outlets, such as oil change centers, tire stores, and independent service shops and chains, for service revenue.

REGULATIONS, R&D, IMPORTS AND EXPORTS

First Research® Industry Profile Automobile Dealerships

franchise dealerships will be unable to carry a full product line and may look to merge.

How has the environmental movement affected demand for the company's vehicles?
Companies can take advantage of growing consumer concern over the environment by promoting hybrid vehicles and improving the environmental friendliness of customer-owned vehicles.

Financial Information

COMPANY BENCHMARK INFORMATION

Automobile Dealers - (NAICS: 4411)

12 Month Rolling Data Period	Last Update March 2010
Small Company Data	Sales < $11,249,914
Table Data Format	Median Values

	US Private Company Data	
	Aggregate	Small Company
Company Count in Analysis	2502	626

Income Statement		
Net Sales	100%	100%
Gross Profit	16.9%	16.9%
Operating Income	1.6%	1.6%
Net Profit After Tax	0.9%	1.0%

Balance Sheet		
Cash	7.3%	5.7%
Accounts Receivable	4.0%	2.9%
Inventory	63.5%	65.0%
Total Current Assets	78.9%	76.4%
Total Fixed Assets	5.5%	5.7%
Other Non-Current Assets	15.5%	17.9%
Total Assets	100.0%	100.0%
Accounts Payable	2.8%	2.4%
Total Current Liabilities	21.8%	30.3%
Total Long-Term Liabilities	3.7%	3.1%
Net Worth	74.5%	66.6%

Financial Ratios		
(Click on any ratio for comprehensive definitions)		
Quick Ratio	0.21	0.2
Current Ratio	1.23	1.33
Current Liabilities to Net Worth	297.0%	224.0%

Current Liabilities to Inventory	108.0%	96.0%
Total Liabilities to Net Worth	343.0%	261.0%
Fixed Assets to Net Worth	26%	20%
Collection Period	3.6	3.8
Inventory Turnover	6.1	4.2
Assets to Sales	26.0%	39.0%
Sales to Working Capital	19.5	7.1
Accounts Payable to Sales	1.0%	1.0%
Return on Sales	1.0%	1.0%
Return on Assets	3.0%	3.0%
Return on Investment	20.0%	17.0%
Interest Coverage	2.2	1.5

Financial industry data provided by Fintel – offering leading benchmarking with a database of over 900 industries. Utilize financial analysis through profitability, liquidity, sustainable growth rate, business valuation, custom research, and other tools. Visit us on the web at www.fintel.us/firstresearch to find out how we can help you.

ECONOMIC STATISTICS AND INFORMATION

Annual Construction Put into Place - Census Bureau

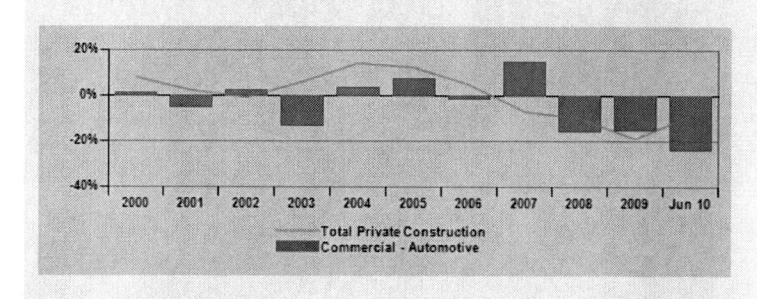

Retail Annual Sales Growth - Census Bureau

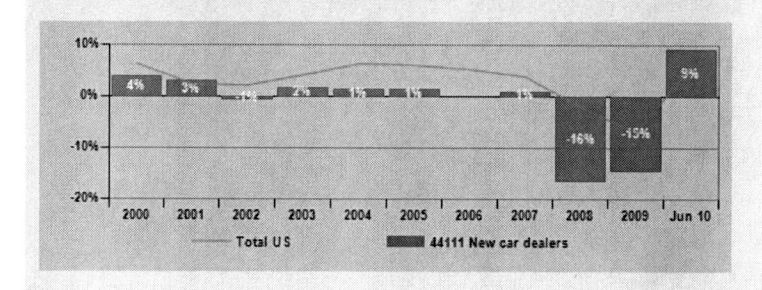

Change in Consumer Prices - Bureau of Labor Statistics

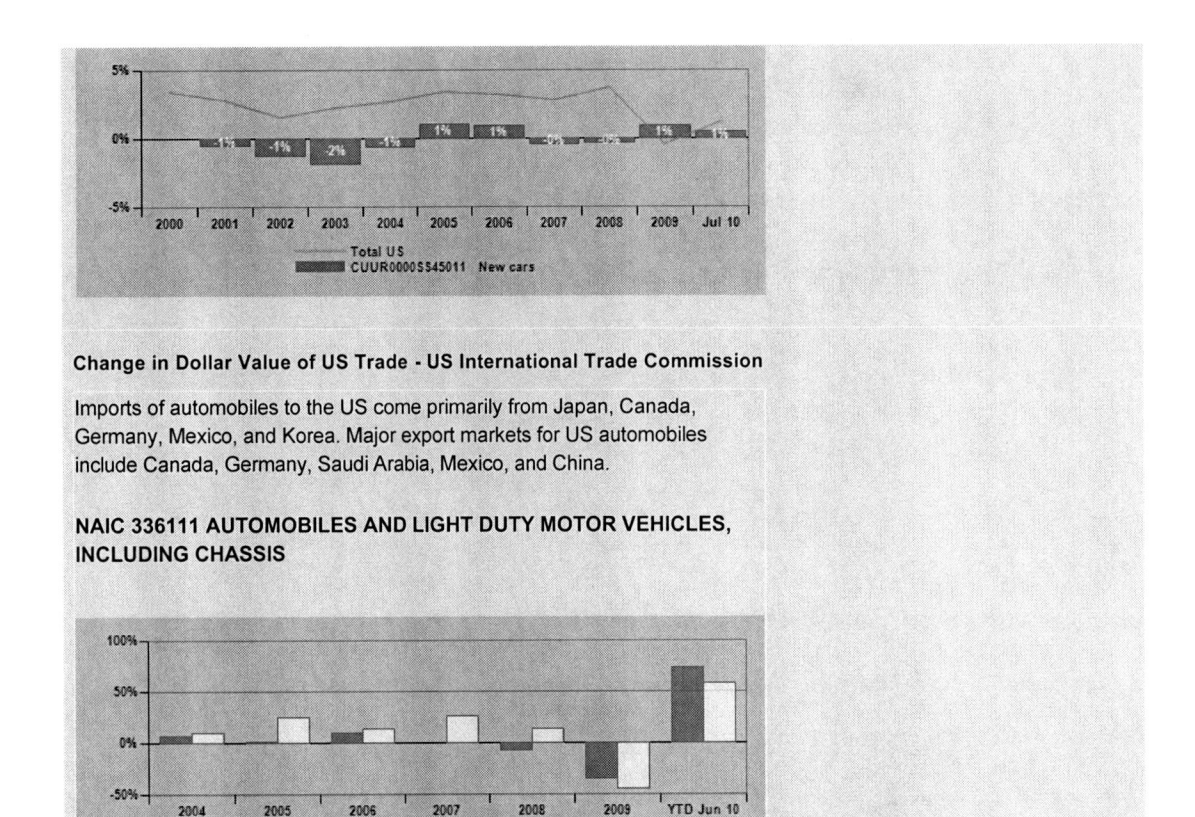

Change in Dollar Value of US Trade - US International Trade Commission

Imports of automobiles to the US come primarily from Japan, Canada, Germany, Mexico, and Korea. Major export markets for US automobiles include Canada, Germany, Saudi Arabia, Mexico, and China.

NAIC 336111 AUTOMOBILES AND LIGHT DUTY MOTOR VEHICLES, INCLUDING CHASSIS

VALUATION MULTIPLES

Automobile Dealerships

Acquisition multiples below are calculated using at least 8 private, middle-market (valued at less than $1 billion) industry transactions completed between 7/1997 and 5/2008. Data updated every six months. Last updated: March 2010.

Valuation Multiple	MVIC/Net Sales	MVIC/Gross Profit	MVIC/EBIT	MVIC/EBITDA
Median Value	0.3	1.5	8.4	7.6

MVIC (Market Value of Invested Capital) = Also known as the selling price, the MVIC is the total consideration paid to the seller and includes any cash, notes and/or securities that were used as a form of payment plus any interest-bearing liabilities assumed by the buyer.
Net Sales = Annual Gross Sales, net of returns and discounts allowed, if any.
Gross Profit = Net Sales - Cost of Goods Sold
EBIT = Operating Profit

EBITDA = Operating Profit + Noncash Charges

SOURCE: Pratt's Stats™ (Portland, OR: Business Valuation Resources, LLC) To purchase more detailed information, please either visit www.BVMarketData.com or call 888-287-8258.

Industry Forecast

US personal consumption expenditures of new and used autos and other motor vehicles are forecast to grow at an annual compounded rate of 7 percent between 2009 and 2014. Data Published: October 2009

Volatile Consumer Spending Growth on Motor Vehicles

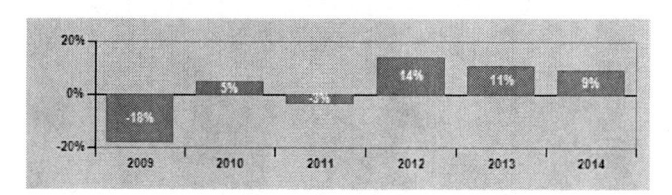

First Research forecasts are based on INFORUM forecasts that are licensed from the Interindustry Economic Research Fund, Inc. (IERF) in College Park, MD. INFORUM's "interindustry-macro" approach to modeling the economy captures the links between industries and the aggregate economy.

First Research Industry Growth Rating

LOW

The First Research Industry Growth Rating reflects the expected industry growth relative to other industries, based on INFORUM's forecasted average annual growth for the combined years of 2010 and 2011.

Industry Websites

American International Automobile Dealers Association
Advocates free trade and addresses industry issues and news affecting dealerships with foreign manufacturers.

AutoExec magazine
Dealer news.

Automotive Industries Association of Canada
News and links.

Automotive Service Association (ASA)
Magazine, news, events, and links.

Canadian Automobile Dealers Association
News, events, and information.

JD Power and Associates
Consumer information and forecasting about the auto industry.

National Association of Minority Automobile Dealers (NAMAD)
Schedules, directories, and legislative updates.

First Research® Industry Profile Automobile Dealerships

National Automobile Dealers Association
News, industry information, and more.

National Highway Traffic Safety Administration
Recalls, crash tests.

National Independent Automobile Dealers Association (NIADA)
State association information, government watch, events, and magazine.

Ward's Dealer Business
Dealership news.

Glossary of Acronyms

CPO - certified pre-owned

CRM - customer relationship management

MSRP - Manufacturer's Suggested Retail Price

NADA - North American Dealers Association

RFID - radio frequency identification

"The purpose of the Profiles is for sales call preparation and general business and industry analysis. Profiles provide general background information only and are not intended to furnish detailed information about the creditworthiness of any individual borrower or purchaser or to be used for making any loans, leases or extension of credit to any individual borrower or purchaser. First Research, Inc. is not an investment advisor, nor is it in the business of advising others as to the value of securities or the advisability of investing in securities, and the Profiles are not intended to be relied upon or used for investment purposes."

© Copyright 2010, First Research, Inc. All Rights Reserved. This data cannot be copied, sold, or distributed in any manner without the written permission of First Research Inc.

Section 3
Bizminer
Auto Dealerships Report

Copyright 2010, by Bizminer reprinted with permission

Bizminer Auto Dealerships Report

Industry Financial Profile (5 year)
release date: June 2010

[96-511] Sector: Retail

New and used car dealers

Sales Class: industry-wide

Firms Analyzed: 17,058

Contents
- P1: Income- Expense statement- dollar- based
- P2: Income- Expense statement- percentage- based
- P4: Balance Sheet- dollar- based
- P5: Balance Sheet- percentage- based
    Cash Flow Analysis
- P6: Financial Ratios - Cash Flow- Solvency
- P8: Financial Ratios - Profitability
- P10: Financial Ratios - Efficiency- Debt- Risk
- P13: Financial Ratios- Turnover
- P15: About the Data

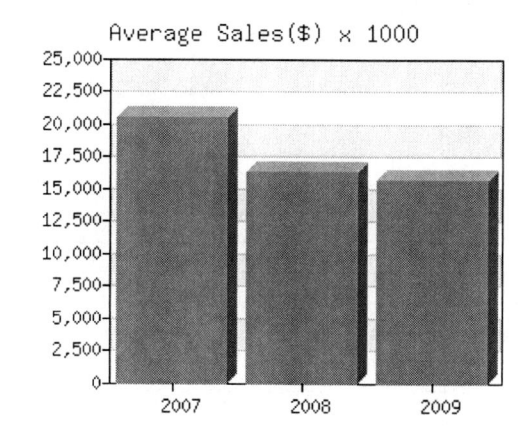

See P2 notes on Business Receipts for financial industry exceptions.

Income and Expense- Profit and Loss ($)	2005	2006	2007	2008	2009
Business Revenue	20,689,806	20,523,225	20,490,180	16,259,723	15,560,669
Cost of Sales	18,207,029	18,050,176	17,924,809	14,209,372	13,601,581
Gross Margin	2,482,777	2,473,049	2,565,371	2,050,351	1,959,088
Officers Comp	165,518	147,767	147,529	113,818	101,144
Salary- Wages	1,024,145	1,003,586	1,026,558	825,994	788,926
Rent	171,725	172,395	186,461	147,963	149,382
Taxes Paid	169,656	168,290	170,068	143,086	135,378
Advertising	229,657	231,912	217,196	172,353	163,387
Benefits- Pensions	101,380	100,564	98,353	78,047	74,691
Repairs	37,242	36,942	36,882	29,268	28,009
Bad Debt	10,345	12,314	12,294	8,130	10,892
Other SG&A Exp.	527,590	519,238	542,990	416,249	415,470
EBITDA	45,519	80,041	127,040	115,443	91,809
Amort- Deprec- Depl	101,380	106,721	79,912	65,039	63,799
Operating Expenses	2,538,638	2,499,729	2,518,243	1,999,947	1,931,078
Operating Income	-55,861	-26,680	47,128	50,404	28,010
Interest Income	55,862	47,203	36,882	4,878	18,673
Interest Expense	111,725	98,511	133,186	138,208	132,266
Other Income	405,520	383,784	391,362	63,413	317,438
Pre- Tax Net Profit	293,796	305,796	342,186	-19,513	231,855
Income Tax	97,830	102,510	116,343	0	73,673
After Tax Net Profit	195,966	203,286	225,843	-16,586	158,182

Dollar- based sales and other dollar- based data in this report reflect averages for sales of the industry segment, not total industry- wide averages. As a result, sales levels may vary from year to year, depending on the mix of firms that fall within the selected segment.

Bizminer Auto Dealerships Report

Income and Expense- Profit and Loss %					
	2005	2006	2007	2008	2009
Business Revenue	100.0%	100.0%	100.0%	100.0%	100.0%
Cost of Sales	88.00%	87.95%	87.48%	87.39%	87.41%
Gross Margin	12.00%	12.05%	12.52%	12.61%	12.59%
Officers Comp	0.80%	0.72%	0.72%	0.70%	0.65%
Salary- Wages	4.95%	4.89%	5.01%	5.08%	5.07%
Rent	0.83%	0.84%	0.91%	0.91%	0.96%
Taxes Paid	0.82%	0.82%	0.83%	0.88%	0.87%
Advertising	1.11%	1.13%	1.06%	1.06%	1.05%
Benefits- Pensions	0.49%	0.49%	0.48%	0.48%	0.48%
Repairs	0.18%	0.18%	0.18%	0.18%	0.18%
Bad Debt	0.05%	0.06%	0.06%	0.05%	0.07%
Other SG&A Exp.	2.55%	2.53%	2.65%	2.56%	2.67%
EBITDA	0.24%	0.38%	0.64%	0.72%	0.59%
Amort- Deprec- Depl	0.49%	0.52%	0.39%	0.40%	0.41%
Operating Expenses	12.27%	12.18%	12.29%	12.30%	12.41%
Operating Income	-0.27%	-0.13%	0.23%	0.31%	0.18%
Interest Income	0.27%	0.23%	0.18%	0.03%	0.12%
Interest Expense	0.54%	0.48%	0.65%	0.85%	0.85%
Other Income	1.96%	1.87%	1.91%	0.39%	2.04%
Pre- Tax Net Profit	1.42%	1.49%	1.67%	-0.12%	1.49%
Income Tax	0.47%	0.50%	0.57%	0.00%	0.47%
After Tax Net Profit	0.95%	0.99%	1.10%	-0.10%	1.02%

Business Revenue includes receipts from core business operations. Interest Income and Other income (such as rents and royalties) are generally detailed separately below Operating Income. While Business Revenue is separated from Interest Income for most classifications, Business Revenue includes interest income from the private sector where it is central to financial industry operations, including Depository Institutions (60xx); Non- Depository Credit Institutions (61xx); Holding and Other Investment Offices (67xx except 6794).

Cost of Sales includes materials and labor involved in the direct delivery of a product or service. Other costs are included in the cost of sales to the extent that they are involved in bringing goods to their location and condition ready to be sold. Non- production overheads such as development costs may be attributable to the cost of goods sold. The costs of services provided will consist primarily of personnel directly engaged in providing the service, including supervisory personnel and attributable overhead.

Gross Margin represents direct operating expenses plus net profit. In addition to the labor portion of Cost of Sales, wage costs are reflected in the **Officers Compensation** and **Wages- Salary** line items. In many cases, **SG&A** (Sales, General and Administrative) costs also include some overhead, administrative and supervisory wages.

Bizminer Auto Dealerships Report

Rent covers the rental cost of any business property, including land, buildings and equipment.

The **Taxes paid** line item includes payroll other paid-in tax items, but not business income taxes due for the period. Although it can be calculated in many ways and is a controversial measure, the **EBITDA** line item (Earnings before **Interest Expense**, income tax due, **Depreciation and Amortization**) adds back interest payments, depreciation, amortization and depletion allowances, and excludes income taxes due to reduce the effect of accounting decisions on the bottom line of the Profit and Loss Statement. Since some firms utilize EBITDA to "add back" non-cash and flexible expenses which may be altered through credits and accounting procedures (such as income tax), paid-in income taxes from the Taxes Paid line item are not added back in the EBITDA calculation.

Pre-Tax Net Profit represents net profit before income tax due. **Income Tax** calculates the federal corporate tax rate before credits, leaving **After-Tax Profit** at the bottom line.

Advertising includes advertising, promotion and publicity for the reporting business, but not on behalf of others.

Benefits-Pension includes, but is not limited to, employee health care and retirement costs.

In addition to varying proportions of overhead, administrative and supervisory wages, some generally more minor expenses are aggregated under **SG&A** (Sales, General and Administrative).

Operating Expenses sums the individual expense line items above, yielding the Operating Income or net of core business operations, when subtracted from the Gross Margin.

Bizminer Auto Dealerships Report

Balance Sheet - dollar- based	2005	2006	2007	2008	2009
Assets					
Cash	521,101	520,757	545,822	445,474	598,496
Receivables	638,140	557,556	574,083	472,486	434,494
Inventory	3,145,558	3,105,030	3,010,054	2,337,187	2,256,041
Other Current Assets	213,457	217,447	221,099	181,112	175,685
Total Current Assets	4,518,256	4,400,790	4,351,058	3,436,259	3,464,716
Gross Fixed Assets	1,224,858	1,252,899	1,314,047	1,100,433	1,188,179
Accumulated Depreciation- Amortization- Depletion	449,631	439,328	466,275	385,866	406,482
Net Fixed Assets	775,243	813,474	847,825	714,706	781,819
Other Non- Current Assets	279,778	361,298	342,454	277,203	246,676
Total Assets	5,573,277	5,575,562	5,541,337	4,428,168	4,493,211
Liabilities					
Accounts Payable	332,725	242,537	252,131	206,795	190,512
Loans/ Notes Payable	2,861,878	2,790,011	2,641,555	2,039,614	1,502,080
Other Current Liabilities	327,151	346,800	364,620	288,717	303,292
Total Current Liabilities	3,521,754	3,379,348	3,258,306	2,535,126	1,995,884
Total Long Term Liabilities	751,835	784,482	841,729	747,032	869,436
Total Liabilities	4,273,589	4,163,830	4,100,035	3,282,158	2,865,320
Net Worth	1,299,688	1,411,732	1,441,302	1,146,010	1,627,891
Total Liabilities & Net Worth	5,573,277	5,575,562	5,541,337	4,428,168	4,493,211

Cash: Money on hand in checking, savings or redeemable certificate accounts.

Receivables: A short- term asset (to be collected within one year) in the form of accounts or notes receivable, and usually representing a credit for a completed sale or loan.

Inventory: The stockpile of unsold products.

Current Assets: The sum of a firm's cash, accounts and notes receivable, inventory, prepaid expenses and marketable securities which can be converted to cash within a single operating cycle.

Fixed Assets: Long- term assets such as building and machinery, net of accumulated amortization- depreciation- depletion.

Total Assets: The sum of current assets and fixed assets such as plant and equipment.

Accounts Payable: Invoices due to suppliers within the current business cycle.

Loans/ Notes Payable: Loan amounts due to suppliers within the current business cycle.

Current Liabilities: Measurable debt owed within one year, including accounts, loans and notes payable, accrued liabilities and taxes due.

Long Term Liabilities: Debt which is due in more than one year, including the portion of loans and mortgages that become due after the current business cycle.

Total Liabilities: Current Liabilities plus Long Term Liabilities such as notes and mortgages due over more than one year.

Net Worth: Current assets plus fixed assets minus current and long- term liabilities.

Bizminer Auto Dealerships Report

Balance Sheet - percentage- based					
Assets	2005	2006	2007	2008	2009
Cash	9.35%	9.34%	9.85%	10.06%	13.32%
Receivables	11.45%	10.00%	10.36%	10.67%	9.67%
Inventory	56.44%	55.69%	54.32%	52.78%	50.21%
Other Current Assets	3.83%	3.90%	3.99%	4.09%	3.91%
Total Current Assets	81.07%	78.93%	78.52%	77.60%	77.11%
Gross Fixed Assets	21.98%	22.47%	23.71%	24.85%	26.44%
Accumulated Depreciation- Amortization- Depletion	8.07%	7.88%	8.41%	8.71%	9.05%
Net Fixed Assets	13.91%	14.59%	15.30%	16.14%	17.40%
Other Non- Current Assets	5.02%	6.48%	6.18%	6.26%	5.49%
Total Assets	100.00%	100.00%	100.00%	100.00%	100.00%
Liabilities					
Accounts Payable	5.97%	4.35%	4.55%	4.67%	4.24%
Loans/ Notes Payable	51.35%	50.04%	47.66%	46.05%	33.43%
Other Current Liabilities	5.87%	6.22%	6.58%	6.52%	6.75%
Total Current Liabilities	63.19%	60.61%	58.79%	57.24%	44.42%
Total Long Term Liabilities	13.49%	14.07%	15.19%	16.87%	19.35%
Total Liabilities	76.68%	74.68%	73.98%	74.11%	63.77%
Net Worth	23.32%	25.32%	26.02%	25.89%	36.23%
Total Liabilities & Net Worth	100.00%	100.00%	100.00%	100.00%	100.00%

The Balance Sheet reflects average balance sheet percentages and dollars for the industry segment analyzed. Liabilities, net worth and ratios are calculated for each industry segment and class, while asset line items are blended with the closest four digit industry segment.

Cash Flow Analysis				
	2006	2007	2008	2009
Operating Cash Flow				
After Tax Net Income	203,286	225,843	-16,586	158,182
Adjustments				
Amort- Deprec- Depl	106,721	79,912	65,039	63,799
Change In Receivables	80,584	-16,527	101,597	37,992
Change In Inventory	40,528	94,976	672,867	81,146
Change In Accounts Payable	-90,188	9,594	-45,336	-16,283
Change In Other Operating Activities	15,659	13,610	-35,916	20,002
Total Adjustments	153,304	181,565	758,251	186,656
Cash from Operating Activities	356,590	407,408	741,665	344,838
Investing Activities				
Change in Fixed Assets	-38,231	-34,351	133,119	-67,113
Change in Other Long Term Assets	-81,520	18,844	65,251	30,527
Cash from Investing Activities	-119,751	-15,507	198,370	-36,586
Financing Activities				
Change in Short Term Debt	-71,867	-149,571	-601,941	-537,534
Change in Long Term Debt	32,647	56,690	-94,697	122,404
Change in Net Worth	112,044	31,800	-295,292	481,881
Cash from Financing Activities	72,824	-61,081	-991,930	66,751

Cash Flow Analysis: Cash flow analysis is a measure of cash inflows and cash outflows, providing a basis for cash flow management. The Cash Flow Analysis includes three sections: Operating Cash Flow, including net profit and changes in various balance sheet line items from the prior year; Investing Activities, measured by the change in long term assets from the prior year; and Financing Activities, measured by the change from the prior year in debt items and net worth.

Bizminer Auto Dealerships Report

Financial Ratios: Cash Flow- Solvency					
	2005	2006	2007	2008	2009
Accounts Payable: Business Revenue (%)	0.02	0.01	0.01	0.01	0.01
Current Liabilities: Inventory (%)	1.12	1.09	1.08	1.08	0.88
Current Liabilities: Net Worth (%)	2.71	2.39	2.26	2.21	1.23
Current Ratio (%)	1.28	1.30	1.34	1.36	1.74
Days Payable (%)	6.67	4.90	5.13	5.31	5.11
Quick Ratio (%)	0.33	0.32	0.34	0.36	0.52
Total Liabilities: Net Worth (%)	3.29	2.95	2.84	2.86	1.76

Accounts Payable: Business Revenue: Accounts Payable divided by Annual Business Revenue, measuring the speed with which a company pays vendors relative to business revenue. Numbers higher than typical industry ratios suggest that the company may be using suppliers to float operations.

Current Liabilities: Inventory: Current Liabilities divided by Inventory: A high ratio, relative to industry norms, suggests over- reliance on unsold goods to finance operations.

Current Liabilities: Net Worth: Current Liabilities divided by Net Worth, reflecting a level of security for creditors. The larger the ratio relative to industry norms, the less security there is for creditors.

Current Ratio: This is the same as Current Assets divided by Current Liabilities, measuring current assets available to cover current liabilities, a test of near- term solvency. The ratio indicates to what extent cash on hand and disposable assets are enough to pay off near term liabilities. The Quick Ratio is applied as a more stringent test.

Days Payables: 365/ (Cost of Sales: Accounts Payable ratio): Reflects the average number of days for each payable before payment is made.

Quick Ratio: Cash plus Accounts Receivable, divided by Current Liabilities, indicating liquid assets available to cover current debt. Also known as the Acid Ratio. This is a harsher version of the Current Ratio, which balances short- term liabilities against cash and liquid instruments.

Total Liabilities: Net Worth: Total liabilities divided by Net Worth. This ratio helps to clarify the impact of long- term debt, which can be seen by comparing this ratio with Current Liabilities: Net Worth. Creditors are concerned to the extent that total liability levels exceed Net Worth.

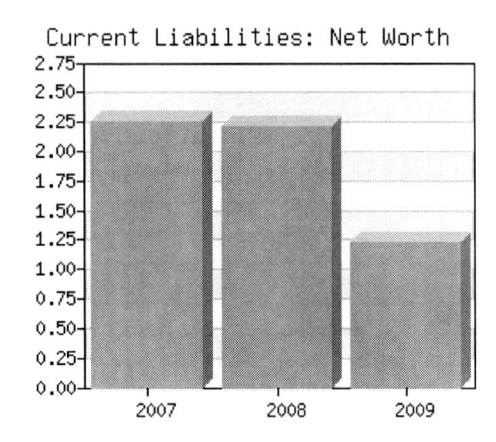

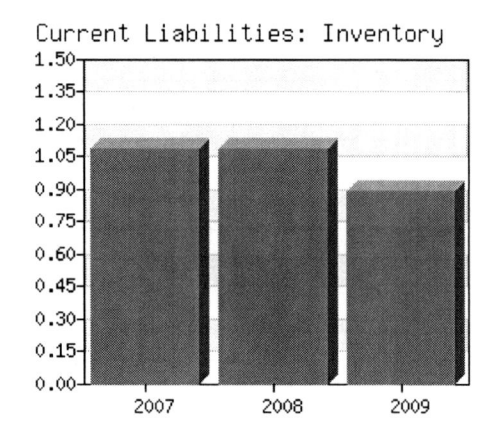

Bizminer Auto Dealerships Report

Cash Flow- Solvency Ratios:

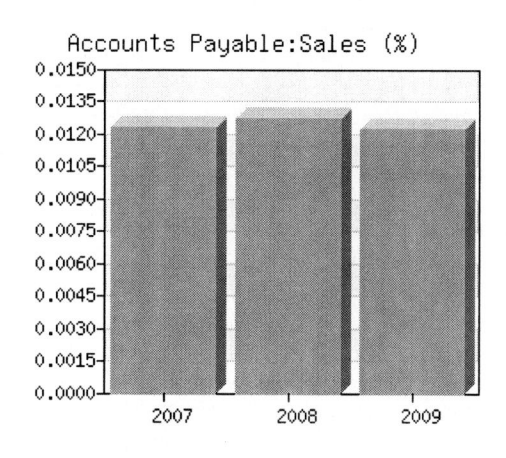

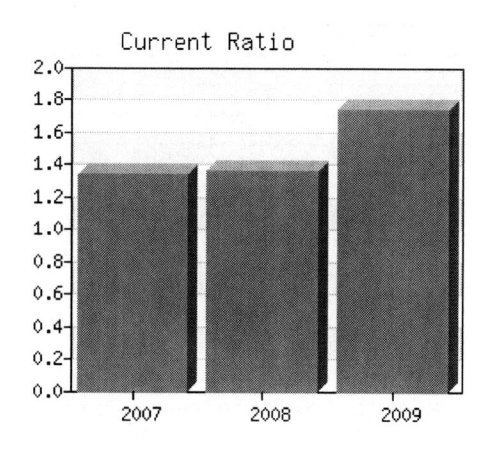

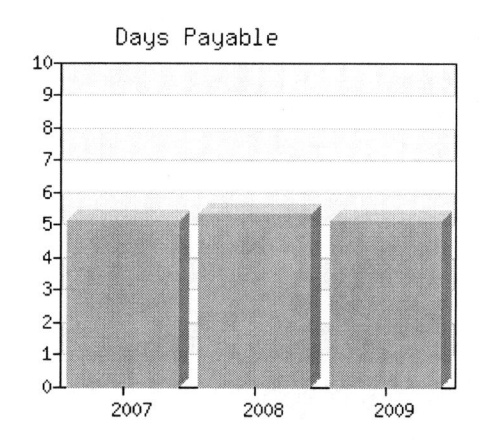

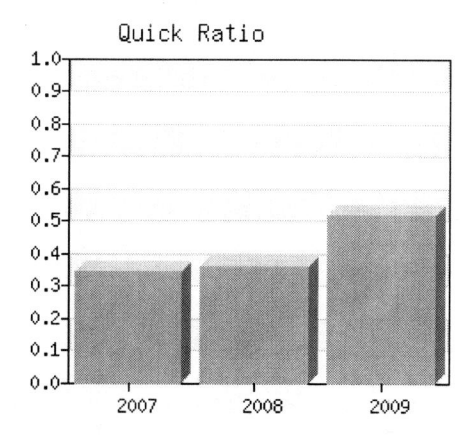

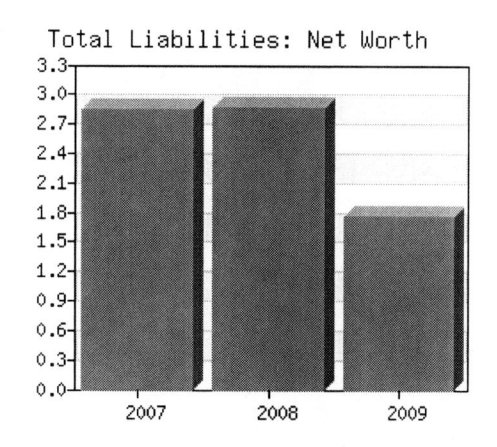

Financial Ratios: Profitability					
	2005	2006	2007	2008	2009
EBITDA: Business Revenue (%)	0.22	0.39	0.62	0.71	0.59
Pre- Tax Return On Assets (%)	5.27	5.48	6.18	-0.44	5.16
Pre- Tax Return on Net Worth (%)	22.61	21.66	23.73	-1.70	14.24
Pre- Tax Return on Business Revenue (%)	1.42	1.49	1.67	-0.12	1.49
After Tax Return on Assets (%)	3.53	3.64	4.07	-0.37	3.53
After Tax Return on Net Worth (%)	15.12	14.39	15.63	-1.42	9.75
After Tax Return on Business Revenue (%)	0.95	0.99	1.10	-0.10	1.02

EBITDA: EBITDA: Business Revenue: Earnings Before Interest, (income) Taxes due, Depreciation and Amortization divided by Business Revenue. EBITDA: Business Revenue is a relatively controversial (and often criticized) metric designed to eliminate the effect of finance and accounting decisions when comparing companies and industry benchmarks. Tax credits and deferral procedures and non- cash expenditures (Amortization and Depreciation) are not deducted from the profit equation, as are interest expenditures.

Return on Assets: Pre- Tax or After Tax Net Profit divided by Total Assets, a critical indicator of profitability. Companies which use their assets efficiently will tend to show a ratio higher than the industry norm. The ratio may appear higher for small businesses due to owner compensation draws accounted as net profit.

Return on Net Worth: Pre- Tax or After Tax Net Profit divided by Net Worth. This is the 'final measure' of profitability to evaluate overall return. This ratio measures return relative to investment, how well a company leverages the investment in it. May appear higher for small businesses due to owner compensation draws accounted as net profit.

Return on Business Revenue: Pre- Tax or After Tax Net Profit Net Profit divided by Annual Business Revenue, indicating the level of profit from each dollar of business revenue. This ratio can be used as a predictor of the company's ability to withstand changes in prices or market conditions. May appear higher for small businesses due to owner compensation draws accounted as net profit.

Bizminer Auto Dealerships Report

Profitability Ratios

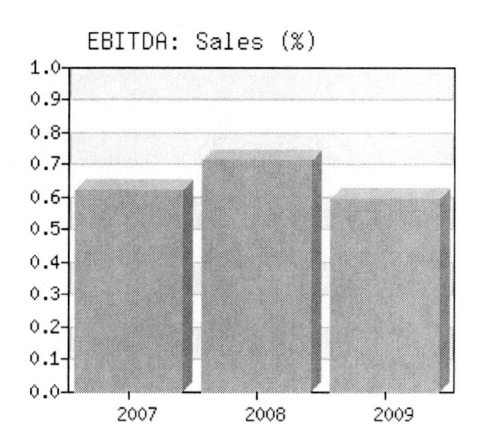

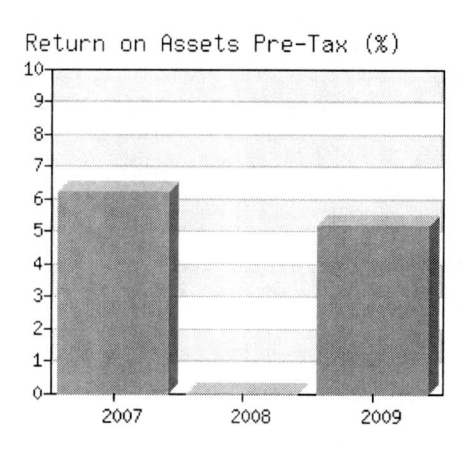

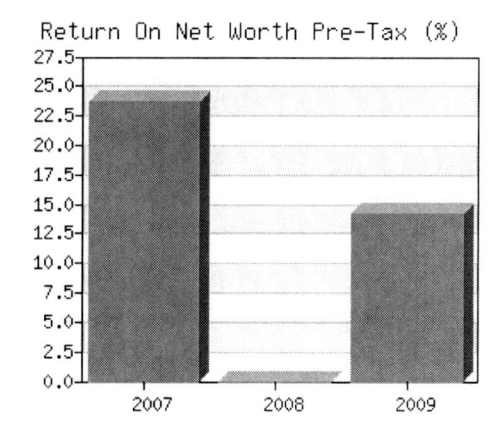

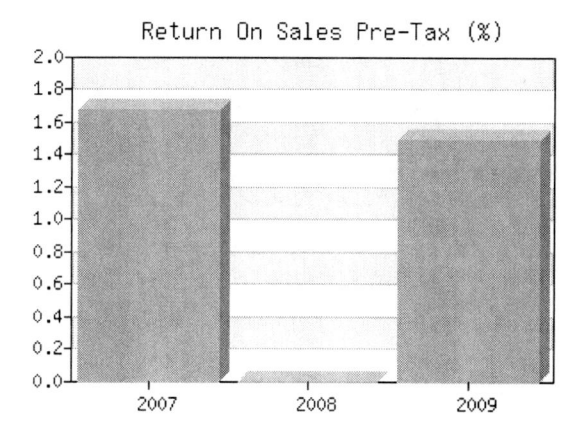

EBITDA: Sales (%)
- 2007: ~0.62
- 2008: ~0.72
- 2009: ~0.58

Return on Assets Pre-Tax (%)
- 2007: ~6.1
- 2008: ~0.2
- 2009: ~5.1

Return On Net Worth Pre-Tax (%)
- 2007: ~24.0
- 2008: ~0.5
- 2009: ~14.5

Return On Sales Pre-Tax (%)
- 2007: ~1.7
- 2008: ~0.05
- 2009: ~1.45

Industry Transaction & Profile Annual Report: Auto Dealerships—2010 Edition

Bizminer Auto Dealerships Report

Financial Ratios: Efficiency- Debt- Risk:					
	2005	2006	2007	2008	2009
Assets: Business Revenue	0.27	0.27	0.27	0.27	0.29
Cost of Sales: Accounts Payable	54.72	74.42	71.09	68.71	71.39
Cost of Sales: Inventory	5.79	5.81	5.95	6.08	6.03
Days Inventory	63.06	62.79	61.29	60.04	60.54
Days Receivables	11.26	9.92	10.23	10.61	10.19
Days Working Capital	17.58	18.17	19.48	20.24	34.45
EBITDA: Interest Expense	0.41	0.81	0.95	0.84	0.69
Fixed Assets: Net Worth	0.60	0.58	0.59	0.62	0.48
Gross Margin: Business Revenue	0.12	0.12	0.13	0.13	0.13
Net Working Capital: Business Revenue	0.05	0.05	0.05	0.06	0.09

Assets: Business Revenue: Total Assets divided by Net Business Revenue, indicating whether a company is handling too high a volume of business revenue in relation to investment. Very low percentages relative to industry norms might indicate overly conservative sales efforts or poor sales management.

Cost of Sales:Accounts Payable: Measures the number of times payables turn over in the course of the year. High measures may indicate cash flow concerns.

Cost of Sales: Inventory: Reflects the number of times inventory is turned over during the course of the year. High levels can mean good liquidity or business revenue, or shortages requiring better management. Low levels may indicate poor cash flow or overstocking.

Days Inventory: 365/ (Cost of Sales: Inventory): The average number of days of items in inventory.

Days Receivables: 365/ (Receivables Turnover): Reflects the number of days that receivables are outstanding. Target average or lower.

Days Working Capital: 365/ (Working Capital Turnover): Expresses the coverage in number of days of available working capital.

EBITDA: interest expense: Earnings before Interest, (income) Taxes due, Depreciation and Amortization divided by Interest expense. Assesses financial stability by examining whether a company is at least profitable enough to pay interest expense. A ratio >1.00 indicates it is. See cautions in the listing for EBITDA.

Fixed Assets: Net Worth: Fixed Assets divided by Net Worth. High ratios relative to the industry can indicate low working capital or high levels of debt.

Gross Margin: Business Revenue: Pre- tax profits divided by Annual Business Revenue. This is the profit ratio before product and business revenue costs, as well as taxes. This ratio can indicate the "play" in other expenses which could be adjusted to increase the Net Profit margin.

Net Working Capital: Business Revenue: Net Working Capital divided by Business Revenue. Indicates if a company is maintaining a reasonable level of liquidity relative to its business revenue volume. A high ratio indicate an overly conservative reliance on liquid assets, while low ratios suggests the opposite.

Bizminer Auto Dealerships Report

Efficiency- Debt- Risk Ratios

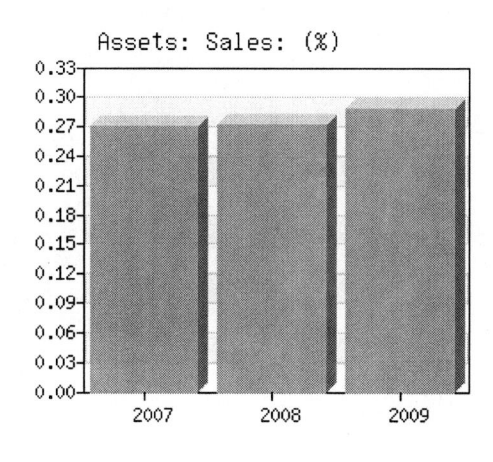

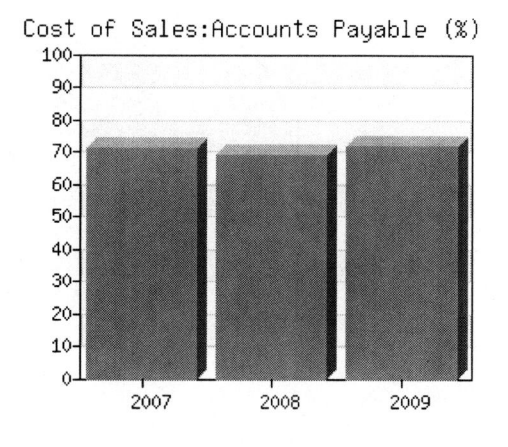

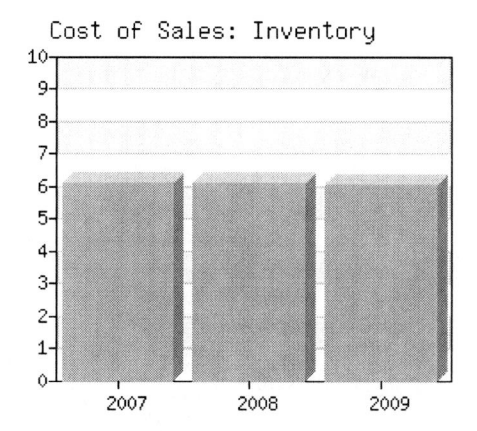

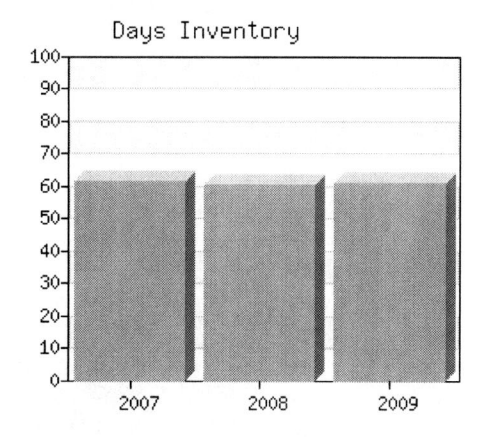

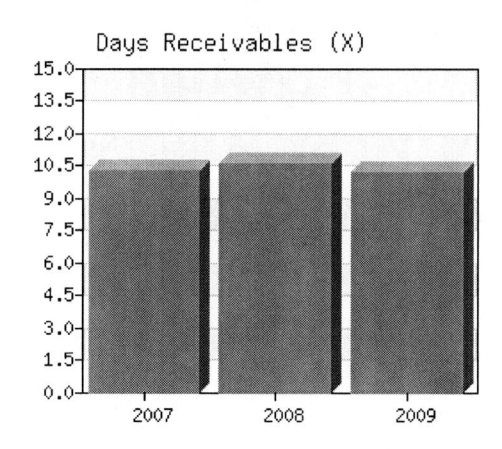

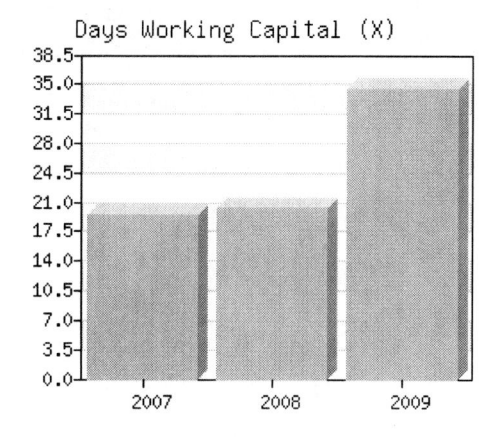

Bizminer Auto Dealerships Report

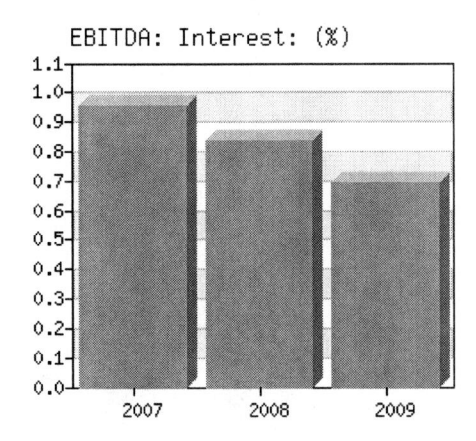

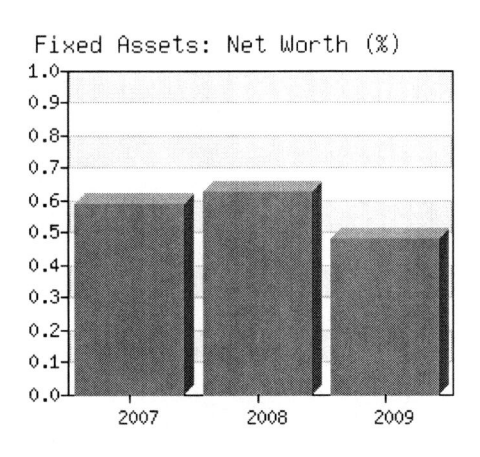

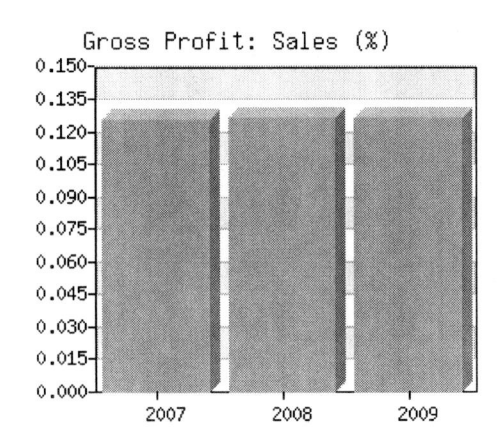

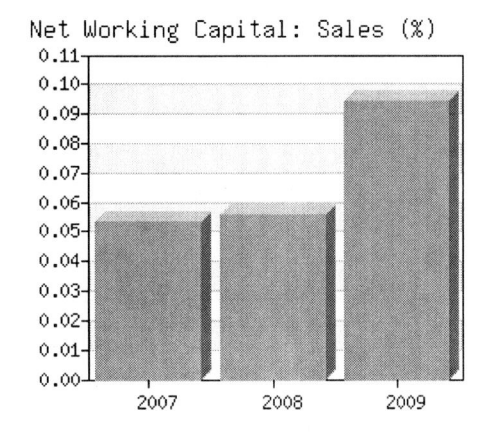

Bizminer Auto Dealerships Report

Financial Ratios: Turnover:	2005	2006	2007	2008	2009
Cash Turnover (X)	39.70	39.41	37.54	36.50	26.00
Current Asset Turnover	4.58	4.66	4.71	4.73	4.49
Fixed Asset Turnover	26.69	25.23	24.17	22.75	19.90
Inventory Turnover (X)	6.58	6.61	6.81	6.96	6.90
Receivables Turnover (X)	32.42	36.81	35.69	34.41	35.81
Total Asset Turnover (X)	3.71	3.68	3.70	3.67	3.46
Working Capital Turnover (X)	20.76	20.09	18.74	18.03	10.59

Cash Turnover: Business Revenue divided by Cash. Indicates efficiency in the use of cash to develop business revenue. A more stringent ratio than Working Capital Turnover (below). Target at or slightly below industry level.

Current Asset Turnover: Business Revenue divided by Current Assets. A general indicator of the efficiency of asset use. Target at or slightly below industry level.

Fixed Asset Turnover: Business Revenue divided by Fixed Assets. An indicator of the efficiency of investment in fixed asset such as plant and equipment. Target at or slightly below industry level.

Inventory Turnover: Business Revenue divided by Inventory. This ratio gives a picture of how quickly inventory turns over. Ratios below the industry norm suggest high levels of inventory. High ratios could indicate product levels insufficient to satisfy demand in a timely manner. Target: at or slightly above industry level.

Receivables Turnover: Business Revenue divided by Receivables. An indicator of how efficiently invoiced sales are collected. Target at or slightly above industry level.

Total Asset Turnover: Business Revenue divided by Total Assets. Target: at or slightly below industry level.

Working Capital Turnover: Business Revenue divided by Net Working Capital (current assets minus current liabilities). Ratios higher than industry norms may indicate a strain on available liquid assets, while low ratios may suggest too much liquidity. Target: at or above industry level.

Bizminer Auto Dealerships Report

Turnover Ratios

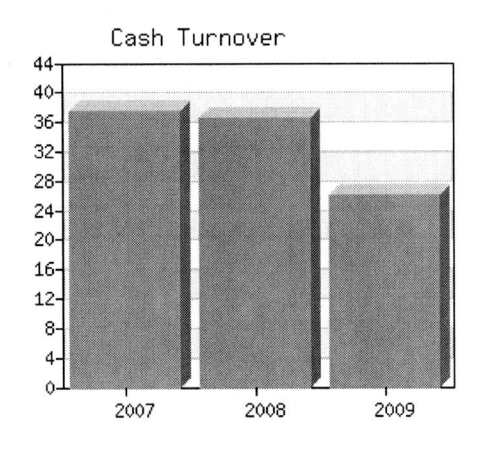

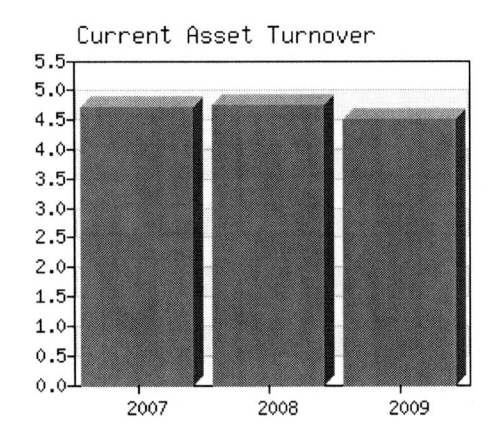

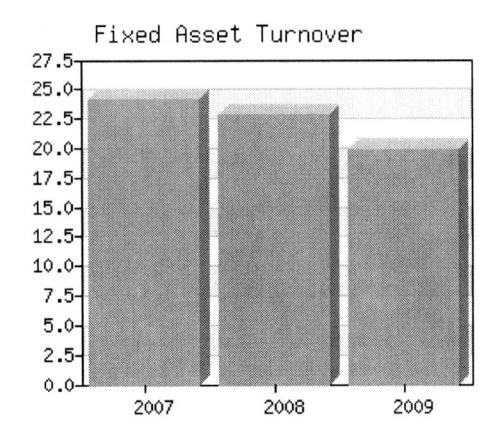

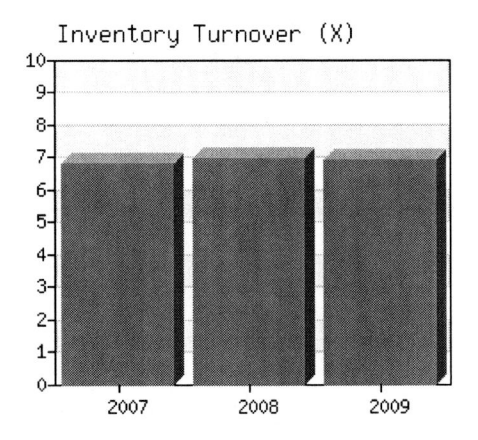

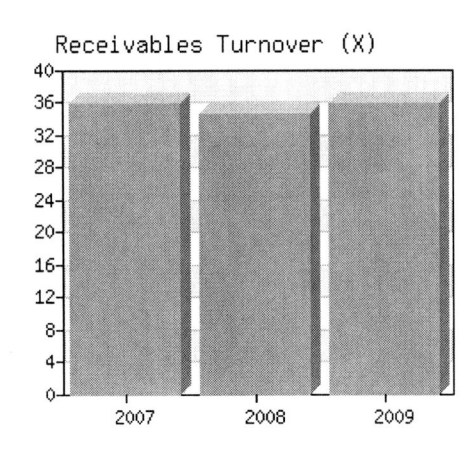

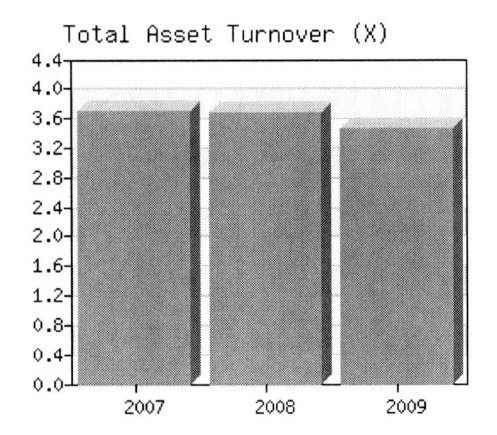

Cash Turnover
Year	Value
2007	~37
2008	~36
2009	~26

Current Asset Turnover
Year	Value
2007	~4.7
2008	~4.7
2009	~4.5

Fixed Asset Turnover
Year	Value
2007	~24
2008	~23
2009	~20

Inventory Turnover (X)
Year	Value
2007	~7
2008	~7
2009	~7

Receivables Turnover (X)
Year	Value
2007	~36
2008	~34
2009	~35

Total Asset Turnover (X)
Year	Value
2007	~3.7
2008	~3.7
2009	~3.5

Bizminer Auto Dealerships Report

About the Data

Raw data analyzed for BizMiner reports is sourced from an array of the nation's government and private statistical sources. None of these raw data sources creates the final measures reflected in BizMiner industry profiles. In total, BizMiner accesses over a billion sourced data points from eighteen million business operations for each of its twice annual updates covering a 3-5 year time series. Historical data and BizMiner algorithms are used to inform and test projections for non- reporting firms. Data elements are sourced specifically from:

- IRS SOI Corporation Income Tax Returns
- IRS SOI Corporation Tax Book
- IRS SOI 1040 Schedule C Income Tax Returns
- IRS SOI Statistics of Income- Individual Tax Statistics
- US Economic Census of Manufactures
- US Census Economy Overview
- US Census Annual Survey of Manufactures
- US Census Annual Retail Trade Survey
- US Census Annual Wholesale Trade Survey
- US Census Quarterly Financial Reports
- US Census County Business Patterns
- Bureau of Labor Statistics Monthly Employment Reports
- Bureau of Labor Statistics Monthly Unemployment Reports
- US Census Wholesale Trade Report
- US Census Quarterly (New Housing) Sales by Price and Financing
- US Census Total Construction Spending
- US Census Retail Trade Report
- US Census Quarterly Services Survey
- Commercial Real Estate Survey
- Credit Reporting Agencies
- Business Directories

While 100% firm coverage is desirable for analysis purposes, the greatest value of BizMiner reports rests in discerning patterns of activity, which are reflected in the large samples used to develop our reports. The overall current coverage of the databases surpasses 13 million active business operations at any point in time.

As is the case with any databases this large, some errors are inevitable. Some firms are missed and specific information on others is lacking from the database. Not all information received is uniform or complete, resulting in the need to develop projection algorithms for specific industry segments and metrics in some report series. No representation is made as to the accuracy of the databases utilized or the results of subsequent analyses. Neither the Brandow Company nor its resellers has undertaken independent primary research to confirm the accuracy of the data utilized in the Profile analyses. Neither the Brandow Company nor its resellers are responsible for conclusions drawn or decisions made based upon this data or analysis. In no event will the Brandow Company or its resellers be liable for any damages, direct, indirect, incidental or consequential resulting from the use of the information contained in BizMiner reports.

BizMiner
2601 Market Street
Camp Hill, PA 17011
717-909-6000
fax: 717-763-1232
© 1998-2010 The Brandow Company. All rights reserved.
www.bizminer.com
services@bizminer.com

Build Time: 1283537928.21 seconds.

Section 4
Business Reference Guide
Rules of Thumb and General Information

Copyright 2010, by Business Brokerage Press. Reprinted with permission

Business Reference Guide Rules of Thumb and General Information

Business Reference Guide 2011 Auto Dealers--New

Industry Name	Auto Dealers--New
See	
Book Only	
Franchise	
	Approx. Total Investment Estimated Annual Sales/Unit
SIC	5511-02
NAICS 1	441110
NAICS 2	
Number of Businesses/Units	18,500
# of Businesses/Units Notes	

Rules of Thumb

0 to 10 percent of annual sales plus inventory

0 to 6 times SDE plus inventory

0 to 5 times EBIT

0 to 5 times EBITDA

Depending on the franchise, makes three to six times EBITDA plus real estate and hard assets

Blue Sky—two to four times EBIT Earnings

Total transaction value in the industry currently ranges from two to four times pretax earnings

Blue Sky—two to three times net profit or new unit sales (most recent year) times average

Industry Transaction & Profile Annual Report: Auto Dealerships—2010 Edition 4-1

Business Reference Guide Rules of Thumb and General Information

front-end gross profit per unit

Hard assets at cost—new parts, FF&E– Book + 50 percent depreciation,

Blue Sky—3 times recast earnings

The goodwill component of the sale price of an auto dealership (franchised only) normally falls within the range of two to six percent of gross revenues. Where added to the assets or book value of the business, this is a reliable method of determining price.

Goodwill = 1 to 3 times pretax earnings (recast)
Parts = current returnable parts
FF&E = book value + one-half depreciation
New Vehicles = net dealer cost
Used Cars = as agreed

Pricing Tips

"Adjust rent to fair market"

"At least 5% to 10% profit, EBIT and location are still the key."

"Earnings multiple, new car PV multiple, new unit sales multiple."

"Real estate is critical for any purchase."

"The two most important characteristics are brands sold and location within a market. Competing outlets affect value. Market analysis, including measuring consumer demand in the area, is critical. Facility age is also a factor."

"Blue sky is not as important as real estate and brand.

"The brand is the key factor when buying or selling a dealership; Toyota and Honda are about the most difficult to buy and make the highest profits."

"New auto dealerships usually have 4 profit centers, parts, used cars, F&I, and service. New car sales typically have very little margin. Ask the dealer about their absorption ratio (an industry term that indicates how much of their back-end is absorbing their overhead). Any new buyer would have to be approved by the manufacturer (Ford, GM, Toyota, etc.) Key people: used car manager, parts manager, service manager."

"Depends on franchise and area of the country. Generally requires 400 per vehicle and up."

"The health of the brand is vital."

"Blue sky is a key factor in pricing. Real estate is very important or a long term lease with options for renewal is a must."

"Watch for phantom profits in both car sales and warranty sales. Some dealers miss proper submission of warranty and rebate claims. Profits can be overstated as a result."

"The current value is two to four times net profit of the most recent year. However, the new car franchises that are bringing up to five times net profit are Honda, Toyota and Mercedes Benz."

"The two most important characteristics are brands sold, and location within a market. Competing outlets also affect value. Market analysis, including measuring consumer demand in the area, is critical. Facility age is also a factor."

"Adjusted book value + blue sky is calculated as a multiple of adjusted pre-tax earnings. These multiples vary with the popularity of franchise, consolidated acquisition trends, vehicle market location, historical performance, etc."

"FF&E—Priced at book price + one-half accumulated depreciation. Parts inventory = as inventoried—current returnable parts. Used cars—take or leave. New Vehicles—dealer net less holdback."

"Other pricing methods include: (1) application of industry averages for gross profit as percentage of sales to the total revenues of the dealership being evaluated; (2) assessing financial data and applying appropriate multiples to recast net profit; (3) projection of potential based on industry average penetration statistics times appropriate multiples."

"The goodwill of an auto dealership can generally be valued at one year's pretax profit plus the dealer's salary and benefits, plus any adjustments from normalizing the financial statement against standard industry operating data."

Expert Ratings

Competition	2.2
Amount of Risk	2.4

Business Reference Guide Rules of Thumb and General Information

Historical Profit Trend	1.8
Location & Facilities	2.4
Marketability	2.2
Industry Trend	1.2
Ease of Replication	2

Expert Comments

"Current economy shows how this industry is changing and more difficult to make a profit."

"Further consolidations or brand eliminations by OEMs will have significant impact on dealers. Brand risk is high."

"Difficult to enter, and profits have been declining over the past 3 years; many dealers are in the red."

Benchmarks

"Used cars must be at least twice the sales of new cars to be profitable."

For 2009, the average sales of a dealership in the U.S. was $26,379,000 and average number of employees per dealership (estimated) was 49.

"The number of new car dealerships for 2010 was 18,460 compared to 10,010 for 2009."

Source: 2010 National Auto Dealers Association (NADA) Data

Statistics	
Number of Enterprises	14,437
Average Wages per Employee	$47,192
Average Profit Margin	1.5%
Average Revenue of Enterprise	$30,397,790

Source: IBISWorld, July 2010

Product/Services	Share
New Vehicle Sales	57.2%
Used Vehicle Sales	28.6%

Service & Parts   14.2%

Source: IBISWorld, February 2010

Cost Structure

Item	Cost
Purchases	73.9%
Wages	9.7%
Rent	4.6%
Utilities	0.5%
Other	10.8%
Profit	1.5%

Source: IBISWorld, July 2010

"The top 2 players account for 4.6% of industry revenue:

- AutoNation, Inc.
- Penske Automotive Group, Inc."

Source: IBISWorld, July 2010

Profile of dealerships' service and parts operations, 2009

Total service and parts sales	$4,128,580
Total gross profit as percent of service and parts sales	46.24%
Total net profit as percent of service and parts sales	8.38%
Total number of repair orders written	13,884
Total service and parts sales per customer repair order	$217
Total service and parts sales per warranty repair order	$273
Number of technicians (including body)	14
Number of service bays (excluding body)	17
Total parts inventory	$260,448
Average customer mechanical labor rate	$91

Source: NADA Industry Analysis Division, 2010

"A sales manager should be generating $45,000 or more per month in gross profit."

"% net profit to gross profit"

"Some on the list sell just 35 vehicles a year, he said. Before the recessionary collapse last year, dealerships were averaging more than 650 new-vehicle sales a year, according to the dealers' main trade group, the National Automobile Dealers Association...."
"Dealerships able to manage that might fare well, according to Sageworks, which collects and analyzes data from accounting firms. Its data show that used-car dealerships have a much higher profit margin than new-car dealerships: 3.19% to 5.67% the past four years, vs. 0.41% to 0.66% for new-car dealerships in the same period."

"Number of new units sold, and number of units in operation, are important metrics."

"The key benchmark is new car sales per population in the primary market area."

"Profit is around 2.75 to 3.25 percent of sales. Payroll should not exceed 41 percent of gross profit."

"Each sales manager should be creating $55,000 to $70,000 per month in gross profit on his or her sales efforts. Everything else being at normal levels, the store will make a good profit, whether a large or small store. This is a very good benchmark."

"Cost of Goods + Payroll/Labor Costs—88 percent"

"Occupancy Cost—Total rent factor should not exceed 1 percent of gross sales."

"Occupancy Cost—$300 to $400 per new car sold per year."

"Profit (estimated)—3 percent of sales"

"Number of new units sold, and number of units in operation, are important metrics."

Average Dealership Profile - 2009

Total Dealership Sales	$26,378,752
Total Dealership Gross	$4,020,028
Total Dealership Expense	$3,621,961
Net Profit before Taxes	$398,067
Average Net worth	$2,213,007

Net profit as % of net worth   18%

Source: 2010 National Auto Dealers Association (NADA) Data

Major expenses for the average dealership in 2009

Payroll	$2,354,000
Advertising	$292,010
Rent and equivalent	$398,456

Source: 2010 National Auto Dealers Association (NADA) Data

Share of total dealership sales dollars in 2009

New Vehicle	52.3%
Used Vehicle	32.0%
Service and Parts	15.7%

Source: 2010 National Auto Dealers Association (NADA) Data

Expenses as a percentage of annual sales

Cost Of Goods	80%
Payroll/Labor Costs	8% to 10% of gross profit
Occupancy Costs	10% of gross profit
Profit (estimated pre-tax)	1.5% to 3%

General Info

"Very select buyers for dealerships"

"Location and product are very important for your success."

"It takes experience to profit in this industry."

"Location and dealer reputation are important, but brand is the number one consideration."

"Requires about $2000 x the new car annual planning volume in working capital, plus any blue sky paid, plus the real estate."

"If you can get a hold of the dealership's claims history for the last 4 years, this can be very telling of how the dealership has been run. If there are frequent claims of customer complaints, theft, slips and falls, these areas will have to be addressed. Find out what the dealership's CSI scores have been. This is the customer satisfaction index. Location and visibility are very important for used cars. Toyota/Mercedes/ Jaguar/BMW and to some extent VW dealerships have the advantage of being destination dealerships. People will travel to buy from these dealerships."

"The franchise system here is very deeply entrenched; however, there are cracks starting to appear, such as DCX's decision to use United Auto Group, rather than their own dealer network, to distribute Smart cars in the U.S."

"Type of product selling, location and reputation of the existing dealer. Growth population in your area and type of growth, commercial or residential."

Number of New-Car Dealerships

Year	Number
1998	22,600
1999	22,400
2000	22,250
2001	22,150
2002	21,800
2003	21,725
2004	21,650
2005	21,640
2006	21,495
2007	20,770
2009	18,460

Note: All of the above was excerpted from information found at The National Automobile Dealers Association Web site, http://www.nada.org/.

The largest number of dealerships was in 1982 when there were 25,700.

Business Reference Guide Rules of Thumb and General Information

Advantages

- "Dynamic industry once understood"
- "Transportation is a must for everyone whether it is new or used vehicles."
- "Very dynamic opportunity to make or lose a lot of money"
- "Still a good business if run right"
- "Excellent profits when sales are good; excellent 'fringe benefits' if you like cars"
- "Excellent training by the manufacturers. Good business model."
- "Always a demand for the product, and profits are good"
- "The risk is low and the rewards are high. The value of the dealership will never fall to a distressed price because there are only so many available."

Disadvantages

- "Competitive, high capital requirements"
- "Profit margins have declined and the competition is tougher than before."
- "High risk, including brand and business risk. Manufacturer pressure to make expenditures, which sometimes are unnecessary."
- "Very dynamic opportunity to make or lose a lot of money"
- "Large investment with small return"
- "You are captive to the product of the manufacturer; there is overcapacity especially among Ford and GM dealers. The ability to price new cars profitably has been sharply reduced, given the widespread availability of pricing information on the Internet. The manufacturers are often jamming 'customer satisfaction' initiatives on dealers, many of whom do an excellent job. Sometimes, the lack of satisfaction is from the product, not the dealer."
- "People are your key, and the new generation is demanding more time off and more money for the same job."
- "Need to keep tight controls. It can be very cutthroat on new vehicles; remember that service, used cars, and finance and insurance are the profit centers. I would never recommend buying the stock of the company; there could be undisclosed liabilities."
- "High personnel turnover, and cost of land and facilities is rising"

Industry Trend

"Some growth"

"Better sales over the next 3 years as the economy improves."

Seller Financing

- "3 years—very small percentage of selling price is carried."
- "Seller financing occurs in less than 30 percent of our transactions and does not normally extend beyond a five-year term."
- "5 years—only goodwill is seller-financed."

Questions

"New car planning volume"

"Employee retention figures. Years at this location, age of equipment."

"Are you ready to sell for market value?"

"Is financing in place for new and used sales? Do you have a floor plan? Does the factory have any future plans for your facility—new or larger?"

"Employee retention is key at this time with the downturn in the economy and sales."

"Manufacturers' planning and future products. Market penetration figures and where do you stand with the manufacturer. Total registrations for your area."

"Age of key personnel? What is the absorption ratio? Can I see your claims history? Who finances the new and used inventory? If this is a multiple-franchise operation under one roof, discover if the manufacturers are pushing for the dealership to split the franchise out into separate facilities."

"Sales trends; consumer satisfaction survey results; recent market studies commissioned by manufacturer; facility standards adopted by manufacturer"

"How many family members on the payroll? What dollar amount of personal items is being deducted from the financial statement?"

Notes

Online Only

Resources

Websites	
Trade Publication	AutomotiveNews: www.crain.com
	Guide to Dealerships: www.ppc.thomson.com
Associations	National Automobile Dealers Association: www.nada.org
	American International Automobile Dealers: www.aiada.org

Business Reference Guide Rules of Thumb and General Information

Business Reference Guide 2011 Auto Dealers--Used

Industry Name	Auto Dealers--Used
SIC	5511-03
NAICS 1	441120
NAICS 2	
Number of Businesses/Units	97,000

Rules of Thumb

Wholesale book value of cars; no goodwill; add parts, fixtures & equipment

Benchmarks

Statistics

Number of Enterprises	97,089
Average Wages per Employee	$30,000
Average Profit Margin	2.5%
Average Revenue of Enterprise	$686,858

Source: IBISWorld, March 2010

Item	Cost
Purchases	61.1%
Bad Debts	19.9%
Wages	5.6%
Reconditioning Costs	4.1%
Rent	3.2%
Advertising	2.5%
Depreciation	0.8%
Utilities	0.3%
Other	0.0%
Profit	2.5%

Source: IBISWorld, March 2010

Annual Retail Sales 2009

Business Reference Guide Rules of Thumb and General Information

0-100 vehicles	10.8%
101-250 vehicles	39.0%
251-400 vehicles	20.1%
401-550 vehicles	12.9%
551-700 vehicles	2.2%
701-850 vehicles	5.5%
851-1000 vehicles	3.3%
1,000 + vehicles	6.2%

Source:

Market Share Breakdown

Independent Dealers 2009	33.0%
Franchise Dealers	36.1%
Casual Sales	30.9%

Source: 2010 National Independent Automobile Dealers Association data. www.niada.com. Based on research provided by CNW Marketing Research

Used Car Industry Data

Average price of used vehicles sold by independent dealers in 2009 -- $8,459

Average Independent Dealers 2009

Asking Price	$8,903
Transaction Price	$8,314

Advertising Expenses -- $267 per vehicle

Rent and Equivalent -- $346 per vehicle

Floor Plan Interest -- $127 per vehicle

Gross Profit 2009

Sales	100%
Cost of Vehicle Sales	(59%)
Subtotal	41%
Financing Income	16%
Bad Debts	(20%)
Gross Profit	37%

Business Reference Guide Rules of Thumb and General Information

Source: National Independent Automobile Dealers Association (ADA): www.niada.com. Based on research provided by CNW Marketing Research

General Info

"New-car dealers sold nearly 15 million used vehicles during 2009. Of these, 9.1 million were retailed and 5.8 million wholesaled. The average selling price of a used unit retailed was $14,976, down slightly from the $15,201 of 2008.. New-car dealers acquired 50 percent of the used units from trade-ins and the remaining 50 percent from auctions, street purchases, or other sources. Auctions have jumped from less than 10 percent as the source of the dealer's inventory in the early 1980s to 34 percent in 2009."
    Source: National Automobile Dealers Association (NADA), 2010 NADA Data

Questions

General Questions
What types of sales transactions did you have for the year under examination?
a. Any sales at auctions? If yes, which?
b. Any sales to wholesalers? If yes, which?
c. Any sales to other dealers? If yes, which?
d. Any consignment sales? If yes, describe.
e. Any scrap sales? If yes, describe.
f. Any in-house dealer financing sales?
g. Any third-party financing sales?
h. Did you have any other types of sales transactions?
i. Did you have any sales that resulted in a loss on the sale? If yes, describe the nature of these sales.
j. What sales did you have to relatives or family friends during the year? Identify.

The above is excerpted from an IRS Audit Technique Guide (Market Segment Specialization Program—MSSAP). This is an excellent source of information and is available at

www.irs.gov/businesses/small/article/0,,id=108149,00.html#P

(Search under IRS—IRS Audit Technique Guides.)

Resources

Associations	National Independent Automobile Dealers Association (ADA): www.niada.com

Section 5
Pratt's Stats® Auto Dealership Report

Pratt's Stats® Auto Dealership Report

Pratt's Stats Transaction Data- Auto Dealerships

Pratt's Stats® is used by a wide variety of merger and acquisition professionals including, business appraisers, business brokers, investment bankers and venture capitalists. Primarily, the data found in **Pratt's Stats®** is used to conduct the market approach to valuing a business in an effort to determine a business' fair market value or to perform financial research on the pricing of similar companies. Additionally, **Pratt's Stats®** data is used in price discovery by entrepreneurs, investors, advisors and business owners that are considering a business purchase or sale.

Below is the transaction summary of **Pratt's Stats®** deals as of September 2010. Following that is a detailed report of each transaction.

Transaction Summary for Auto dealerships- New and Used

Statistic	Count	Range	Mean	Median	Coefficient of Variation
Sale Date	75	8/15/1995 - 1/2/2010	N/A	N/A	N/A
Net Sales	75	$199,000 - $617,912,072	$104,658,495	$65,793,000	N/A
Market Value of Invested Capital (MVIC)	75	$30,000 - $100,000,000	$20,129,258	$12,000,000	N/A
EBITDA	64	($3,253,000) - $13,283,000	$2,620,430	$2,036,609	N/A
EBIT	75	($3,829,000) - $12,745,000	$2,057,586	$1,129,000	N/A
Net Income	75	($1,611,800) - $11,933,000	$1,601,912	$565,000	N/A
Gross Profit Margin	75	0.05 - 1.00	0.20	0.14	N/A
Operating Profit Margin	68	-0.06 - 0.30	0.04	0.02	N/A
Net Profit Margin	75	-0.06 - 0.30	0.03	0.02	N/A
MVIC/Net Sales	75	0.01 - 0.66	0.22	0.18	0.66
MVIC/Gross Profit	75	0.03 - 3.91	1.32	1.30	0.54
MVIC/EBIT	65	0.30 - 174.74	11.93	7.63	1.90
MVIC/EBITDA	57	0.71 - 52.35	8.74	6.89	0.85
MVIC/DiscEarnings	14	0.58 - 30.61	5.57	3.60	1.39
MVIC/Book Value of Invested Capital	48	0.28 - 15.17	4.48	3.09	0.80

Pratt's Stats® Auto Dealership Report

Pratt's Stats® Transaction Report
Prepared: 8/20/2010 2:09:43 PM (PST)

Seller Details
Target Name:	Lynn Hickey Dodge, Inc.
Business Description:	New and Used Auto Sales, Dodge
SIC:	5511 Motor Vehicle Dealers (New and Used)
NAICS:	441110 New Car Dealers
Sale Location:	Oklahoma City, OK, United States
Years in Business:	N/A
Number Employees:	N/A

Source Data
Public Buyer Name:	CROSS COUNTRY AUTO RETAILERS INC
8-K Date:	N/A
8-K/A Date:	N/A
Other Filing Type:	S-1/A
Other Filing Date:	7/10/1996
CIK Code:	0001016919

Income Data
Data is "Latest Full Year" Reported	Yes
Data is Restated (see Notes for any explanation)	No
Income Statement Date	12/31/1995
Net Sales	$122,221,000
COGS	$106,826,000
Gross Profit	$15,395,000
Yearly Rent	N/A
Owner's Compensation	N/A
Other Operating Expenses	N/A
Noncash Charges	$346,000
Total Operating Expenses	$13,495,000
Operating Profit	$1,900,000
Interest Expenses	$1,737,000
EBT	$565,000
Taxes	$0
Net Income	$565,000

Asset Data
Data is Latest Reported	Yes
Data is "Purchase Price Allocation agreed upon by Buyer and Seller"	No
Balance Sheet Date	3/31/1996
Cash Equivalents	$7,149,000
Trade Receivables	$4,106,000
Inventory	$17,765,000
Other Current Assets	$228,000
Total Current Assets	$29,248,000
Fixed Assets	$1,918,000
Real Estate	N/A
Intangibles	N/A
Other Noncurrent Assets	N/A
Total Assets	$31,166,000
Long-term Liabilities	$5,797,000
Total Liabilities	$27,655,000
Stockholder's Equity	$3,511,000

Transaction Data
Date Sale Initiated:	N/A
Date of Sale:	6/17/1996
Days to Sell:	N/A
Asking Price:	N/A
Market Value of Invested Capital*:	$13,850,000
Debt Assumed:	N/A
Employment Agreement Value:	N/A
Noncompete Value:	N/A
Amount of Down Payment:	$13,850,000
Stock or Asset Sale:	Asset
Company Type:	S Corporation
Was there an Employment/Consulting Agreement?	No
Was there an Assumed Lease in the sale?	No
Was there a Renewal Option with the Lease?	No

*Includes noncompete value and interest-bearing debt; excludes real estate, employment/consulting agreement values, and all contingent payments.

Additional Transaction Information
Was there a Note in the consideration paid? No
Terms:
Assumed Lease (Months): N/A
Noncompete Length (Months): N/A
Employment/Consulting Agreement Description:
Additional Notes:
EBT includes $402,000 Interest Income. Inventory stated using FIFO.

Was there a personal guarantee on the Note? No
Terms of Lease: N/A
Noncompete Description: N/A

Valuation Multiples
MVIC/Net Sales	0.11
MVIC/Gross Profit	0.90
MVIC/EBITDA	6.17
MVIC/EBIT	7.29
MVIC/Discretionary Earnings	N/A
MVIC/Book Value of Invested Capital	1.49

Profitability Ratios
Net Profit Margin	0.00
Operating Profit Margin	0.02
Gross Profit Margin	0.13
Return on Assets	0.02
Return on Equity	0.16

Leverage Ratios
Fixed Charge Coverage	1.33
Long-Term Debt to Assets	0.19
Long-Term Debt to Equity	1.65

Earnings
EBITDA	$2,246,000
Discretionary Earnings	N/A

Liquidity Ratios
Current Ratio	1.34
Quick Ratio	0.53

Activity Ratios
Total Asset Turnover	3.92
Fixed Asset Turnover	63.72
Inventory Turnover	6.88

Copyright © 2010 Business Valuation Resources, LLC. All rights reserved. www.BVResources.com℠
(888) BUS-VALU, (503) 291-7963

Pratt's Stats® Auto Dealership Report

Pratt's Stats® Transaction Report
Prepared: 8/20/2010 2:09:43 PM (PST)

Seller Details
Target Name:	Jim Clover Dodge, Inc.
Business Description:	New and Used Auto Sales, Dodge
SIC:	5511 Motor Vehicle Dealers (New and Used)
NAICS:	441110 New Car Dealers
Sale Location:	Oklahoma City, OK, United States
Years in Business:	N/A Number Employees: N/A

Source Data
Public Buyer Name:	CROSS COUNTRY AUTO RETAILERS INC
8-K Date:	N/A
8-K/A Date:	N/A
Other Filing Type:	S-1/A
Other Filing Date:	7/10/1996
CIK Code:	0001016919

Income Data
Data is "Latest Full Year" Reported	Yes
Data is Restated (see Notes for any explanation)	No
Income Statement Date	11/30/1995
Net Sales	$63,917,000
COGS	$55,370,000
Gross Profit	$8,547,000
Yearly Rent	$236,000
Owner's Compensation	N/A
Other Operating Expenses	N/A
Noncash Charges	$24,000
Total Operating Expenses	$7,268,000
Operating Profit	$1,279,000
Interest Expenses	$367,000
EBT	$912,000
Taxes	$0
Net Income	$912,000

Asset Data
Data is Latest Reported	Yes
Data is "Purchase Price Allocation agreed upon by Buyer and Seller"	No
Balance Sheet Date	11/30/1995
Cash Equivalents	$632,000
Trade Receivables	$2,267,000
Inventory	$7,475,000
Other Current Assets	N/A
Total Current Assets	$10,374,000
Fixed Assets	$130,000
Real Estate	N/A
Intangibles	N/A
Other Noncurrent Assets	N/A
Total Assets	$10,504,000
Long-term Liabilities	$0
Total Liabilities	$7,532,000
Stockholder's Equity	$2,972,000

Transaction Data
Date Sale Initiated:	N/A
Date of Sale:	12/4/1995
Days to Sell:	N/A
Asking Price:	N/A
Market Value of Invested Capital*:	$5,852,000
Debt Assumed:	N/A
Employment Agreement Value:	N/A
Noncompete Value:	N/A
Amount of Down Payment:	$5,852,000
Stock or Asset Sale:	Asset
Company Type:	S Corporation
Was there an Employment/Consulting Agreement?	No
Was there an Assumed Lease in the sale?	No
Was there a Renewal Option with the Lease?	No

*Includes noncompete value and interest-bearing debt; excludes real estate, employment/consulting agreement values, and all contingent payments.

Additional Transaction Information
Was there a Note in the consideration paid? No
Terms:
Assumed Lease (Months): N/A
Noncompete Length (Months): N/A
Employment/Consulting Agreement Description:
Additional Notes:
Inventory stated using FIFO.

Was there a personal guarantee on the Note? No

Terms of Lease: N/A
Noncompete Description: N/A

Valuation Multiples
MVIC/Net Sales	0.09
MVIC/Gross Profit	0.68
MVIC/EBITDA	4.49
MVIC/EBIT	4.58
MVIC/Discretionary Earnings	N/A
MVIC/Book Value of Invested Capital	1.97

Profitability Ratios
Net Profit Margin	0.01
Operating Profit Margin	0.02
Gross Profit Margin	0.13
Return on Assets	0.09
Return on Equity	0.31

Leverage Ratios
Fixed Charge Coverage	3.49
Long-Term Debt to Assets	0.00
Long-Term Debt to Equity	0.00

Earnings
EBITDA	$1,303,000
Discretionary Earnings	N/A

Liquidity Ratios
Current Ratio	1.38
Quick Ratio	0.38

Activity Ratios
Total Asset Turnover	6.09
Fixed Asset Turnover	491.67
Inventory Turnover	8.55

Copyright © 2010 Business Valuation Resources, LLC. All rights reserved. www.BVResources.com^{SM}
(888) BUS-VALU, (503) 291-7963

Pratt's Stats® Auto Dealership Report

Pratt's Stats® Transaction Report
Prepared: 8/20/2010 2:09:43 PM (PST)

Seller Details

Target Name:	SUN VALLEY FORD, Inc.
Business Description:	New Auto Sales, Ford, Hyundai, Volkswagen
SIC:	5511 Motor Vehicle Dealers (New and Used)
NAICS:	441110 New Car Dealers
Sale Location:	Concord, CA, United States
Years in Business:	N/A
Number Employees:	N/A

Source Data

Public Buyer Name:	LITHIA MOTORS INC
8-K Date:	8/21/1997
8-K/A Date:	10/14/1997
Other Filing Type:	N/A
Other Filing Date:	N/A
CIK Code:	0001023128

Income Data

Data is "Latest Full Year" Reported	Yes
Data is Restated (see Notes for any explanation)	No
Income Statement Date	12/31/1996
Net Sales	$72,401,000
COGS	$63,374,600
Gross Profit	$9,026,400
Yearly Rent	$651,100
Owner's Compensation	N/A
Other Operating Expenses	N/A
Noncash Charges	$304,800
Total Operating Expenses	$8,564,900
Operating Profit	$461,500
Interest Expenses	$116,000
EBT	$430,100
Taxes	$8,900
Net Income	$421,200

Asset Data

Data is Latest Reported	Yes
Data is "Purchase Price Allocation agreed upon by Buyer and Seller"	No
Balance Sheet Date	6/30/1997
Cash Equivalents	$16,500
Trade Receivables	$4,390,500
Inventory	$10,587,100
Other Current Assets	$499,900
Total Current Assets	$15,494,000
Fixed Assets	$970,300
Real Estate	N/A
Intangibles	N/A
Other Noncurrent Assets	$45,700
Total Assets	$16,510,000
Long-term Liabilities	$189,900
Total Liabilities	$15,405,600
Stockholder's Equity	$1,104,400

Transaction Data

Date Sale Initiated:	N/A
Date of Sale:	8/8/1997
Days to Sell:	N/A
Asking Price:	N/A
Market Value of Invested Capital*:	$17,000,000
Debt Assumed:	N/A
Employment Agreement Value:	N/A
Noncompete Value:	N/A
Amount of Down Payment:	$12,600,000
Stock or Asset Sale:	Asset
Company Type:	S Corporation
Was there an Employment/Consulting Agreement?	No
Was there an Assumed Lease in the sale?	Yes
Was there a Renewal Option with the Lease?	Yes

*Includes noncompete value and interest-bearing debt; excludes real estate, employment/consulting agreement values, and all contingent payments.

Additional Transaction Information

Was there a Note in the consideration paid? Yes   Was there a personal guarantee on the Note? No

Terms:
Consideration paid: $2,800,000 cash, $9,800,000 financed through company flooring line of credit, $4,400,000 note payable.

Assumed Lease (Months): 120   Terms of Lease: $28,200 per month, adjusted annually by Consumer Price Index

Noncompete Length (Months): N/A   Noncompete Description: N/A

Employment/Consulting Agreement Description:

Additional Notes:
EBT includes $25,600 Interest Income, $59,000 Miscellaneous Income. New auto inventory stated using LIFO, parts inventory stated using FIFO, used auto inventory stated using specific identification method.

Valuation Multiples

MVIC/Net Sales	0.23
MVIC/Gross Profit	1.88
MVIC/EBITDA	22.18
MVIC/EBIT	36.84
MVIC/Discretionary Earnings	N/A
MVIC/Book Value of Invested Capital	13.13

Profitability Ratios

Net Profit Margin	0.01
Operating Profit Margin	0.01
Gross Profit Margin	0.12
Return on Assets	0.03
Return on Equity	0.38

Leverage Ratios

Fixed Charge Coverage	4.71
Long-Term Debt to Assets	0.01
Long-Term Debt to Equity	0.17

Earnings

EBITDA	$766,300
Discretionary Earnings	N/A

Liquidity Ratios

Current Ratio	1.02
Quick Ratio	0.32

Activity Ratios

Total Asset Turnover	4.39
Fixed Asset Turnover	74.62
Inventory Turnover	6.84

Copyright © 2010 Business Valuation Resources, LLC. All rights reserved. www.BVResources.com[SM]
(888) BUS-VALU, (503) 291-7963

Pratt's Stats® Auto Dealership Report

Pratt's Stats® Transaction Report
Prepared: 8/20/2010 2:09:43 PM (PST)

Seller Details
Target Name:	Shannon Automotive Ltd.
Business Description:	Auto Dealers
SIC:	5511 Motor Vehicle Dealers (New and Used)
NAICS:	441110 New Car Dealers
Sale Location:	Houston, TX, United States
Years in Business:	N/A Number Employees: N/A

Source Data
Public Buyer Name:	UNITED AUTO GROUP INC
8-K Date:	3/21/1997
8-K/A Date:	4/30/1997
Other Filing Type:	N/A
Other Filing Date:	N/A
CIK Code:	0001019849

Income Data
Data is "Latest Full Year" Reported	Yes
Data is Restated (see Notes for any explanation)	No
Income Statement Date	12/31/1996
Net Sales	$96,962,172
COGS	$83,290,350
Gross Profit	$13,671,822
Yearly Rent	$839,000
Owner's Compensation	N/A
Other Operating Expenses	N/A
Noncash Charges	$104,597
Total Operating Expenses	$10,549,140
Operating Profit	$3,122,682
Interest Expenses	$0
EBT	$3,122,682
Taxes	$0
Net Income	$3,122,682

Asset Data
Data is Latest Reported	Yes
Data is "Purchase Price Allocation agreed upon by Buyer and Seller"	No
Balance Sheet Date	12/31/1996
Cash Equivalents	$2,279,337
Trade Receivables	$376,536
Inventory	$8,335,102
Other Current Assets	$1,818,462
Total Current Assets	$12,809,437
Fixed Assets	$285,209
Real Estate	N/A
Intangibles	N/A
Other Noncurrent Assets	$238,392
Total Assets	$13,333,038
Long-term Liabilities	$250,651
Total Liabilities	$9,212,186
Stockholder's Equity	$4,120,852

Transaction Data
Date Sale Initiated:	N/A
Date of Sale:	3/6/1997
Days to Sell:	N/A
Asking Price:	N/A
Market Value of Invested Capital*:	$14,000,000
Debt Assumed:	N/A
Employment Agreement Value:	N/A
Noncompete Value:	N/A
Amount of Down Payment:	$14,000,000
Stock or Asset Sale:	Asset
Company Type:	Partnership
Was there an Employment/Consulting Agreement?	No
Was there an Assumed Lease in the sale?	No
Was there a Renewal Option with the Lease?	No

*Includes noncompete value and interest-bearing debt; excludes real estate, employment/consulting agreement values, and all contingent payments.

Additional Transaction Information
Was there a Note in the consideration paid? No   Was there a personal guarantee on the Note? No

Terms:
Consideration: $1,400,000 cash, buyer's public company common stock valued at $7,000,000 and the repayment of the sellers' indebtedness in the amount of $5.6 million.

Assumed Lease (Months): N/A

Noncompete Length (Months): N/A

Terms of Lease: Future minimum rental payments of $4,295,935 through 2001.

Noncompete Description: N/A

Employment/Consulting Agreement Description:
Additional Notes:
Seller consists of Crown Dodge and Crown Jeep-Eagle Chrysler-Plymouth. Inventory stated using LIFO.

Valuation Multiples
MVIC/Net Sales	0.14
MVIC/Gross Profit	1.02
MVIC/EBITDA	4.34
MVIC/EBIT	4.48
MVIC/Discretionary Earnings	N/A
MVIC/Book Value of Invested Capital	3.20

Profitability Ratios
Net Profit Margin	0.03
Operating Profit Margin	0.03
Gross Profit Margin	0.14
Return on Assets	0.23
Return on Equity	0.76

Leverage Ratios
Fixed Charge Coverage	N/A
Long-Term Debt to Assets	0.02
Long-Term Debt to Equity	0.06

Earnings
EBITDA	$3,227,279
Discretionary Earnings	N/A

Liquidity Ratios
Current Ratio	1.43
Quick Ratio	0.50

Activity Ratios
Total Asset Turnover	7.27
Fixed Asset Turnover	339.97
Inventory Turnover	11.63

Copyright © 2010 Business Valuation Resources, LLC. All rights reserved.   www.BVResources.com℠
(888) BUS-VALU, (503) 291-7963

Pratt's Stats® Auto Dealership Report

Pratt's Stats® Transaction Report
Prepared: 8/20/2010 2:09:43 PM (PST)

Seller Details

Target Name:	Ed Mullinax, Inc.
Business Description:	Operates Automobile Dealerships
SIC:	5511 Motor Vehicle Dealers (New and Used)
NAICS:	441110 New Car Dealers
Sale Location:	Amherst, OH, United States
Years in Business:	10
Number Employees:	N/A

Source Data

Public Buyer Name:	REPUBLIC INDUSTRIES INC
8-K Date:	1/17/1997
8-K/A Date:	N/A
Other Filing Type:	N/A
Other Filing Date:	N/A
CIK Code:	0000350698

Income Data

Data is "Latest Full Year" Reported	Yes
Data is Restated (see Notes for any explanation)	No
Income Statement Date	4/30/1996
Net Sales	$617,912,072
COGS	$553,042,632
Gross Profit	$64,869,440
Yearly Rent	$934,176
Owner's Compensation	N/A
Other Operating Expenses	N/A
Noncash Charges	$1,045,083
Total Operating Expenses	$56,180,332
Operating Profit	$8,689,108
Interest Expenses	$2,727,688
EBT	$5,961,420
Taxes	$2,323,750
Net Income	$3,637,670

Asset Data

Data is Latest Reported	Yes
Data is "Purchase Price Allocation agreed upon by Buyer and Seller"	No
Balance Sheet Date	10/31/1996
Cash Equivalents	$3,752,256
Trade Receivables	$16,541,183
Inventory	$84,890,774
Other Current Assets	$2,454,658
Total Current Assets	$107,638,871
Fixed Assets	$15,120,363
Real Estate	N/A
Intangibles	$14,500
Other Noncurrent Assets	$157,056
Total Assets	$122,930,790
Long-term Liabilities	$10,051,270
Total Liabilities	$100,060,462
Stockholder's Equity	$22,870,328

Transaction Data

Date Sale Initiated:	N/A
Date of Sale:	1/3/1997
Days to Sell:	N/A
Asking Price:	N/A
Market Value of Invested Capital*:	$100,000,000
Debt Assumed:	N/A
Employment Agreement Value:	N/A
Noncompete Value:	N/A
Amount of Down Payment:	$100,000,000
Stock or Asset Sale:	Asset
Company Type:	C Corporation
Was there an Employment/Consulting Agreement?	No
Was there an Assumed Lease in the sale?	Yes
Was there a Renewal Option with the Lease?	Yes

*Includes noncompete value and interest-bearing debt; excludes real estate, employment/consulting agreement values, and all contingent payments.

Additional Transaction Information

Was there a Note in the consideration paid? No
Was there a personal guarantee on the Note? No
Terms:
Consideration paid as follows: 3,600,000 shares of buyer's public company common stock valued at $100,000,000.
Assumed Lease (Months): 69
Terms of Lease: Future Minimum Lease Payments: $2,298,690
Noncompete Length (Months): N/A
Noncompete Description: N/A
Employment/Consulting Agreement Description:
Additional Notes:
Inventory stated at lower of cost (LIFO) or market. Total current assets include other receivables: $12,392,330 finance contracts in transit, $480,366 due from finance companies, $1,929,098 factory claims, $106,012 employee and officers, and $569,311 affiliated companies. Company operates Ford dealerships in Amherst, Wickliffe, North Canton, Ohio, Margate, Florida, and a Lincoln-Mercury dealership in Brunswick, Ohio.

Valuation Multiples

MVIC/Net Sales	0.16
MVIC/Gross Profit	1.54
MVIC/EBITDA	10.27
MVIC/EBIT	11.51
MVIC/Discretionary Earnings	N/A
MVIC/Book Value of Invested Capital	3.04

Profitability Ratios

Net Profit Margin	0.01
Operating Profit Margin	0.01
Gross Profit Margin	0.10
Return on Assets	0.03
Return on Equity	0.16

Leverage Ratios

Fixed Charge Coverage	3.19
Long-Term Debt to Assets	0.08
Long-Term Debt to Equity	0.44

Earnings

EBITDA	$9,734,191
Discretionary Earnings	N/A

Liquidity Ratios

Current Ratio	1.20
Quick Ratio	0.25

Activity Ratios

Total Asset Turnover	5.03
Fixed Asset Turnover	40.87
Inventory Turnover	7.28

Copyright © 2010 Business Valuation Resources, LLC. All rights reserved. www.BVResources.com[SM]
(888) BUS-VALU, (503) 291-7963

Pratt's Stats® Auto Dealership Report

Pratt's Stats® Transaction Report
Prepared: 8/20/2010 2:09:43 PM (PST)

Seller Details
Target Name:	Melody Vacaville, Inc.
Business Description:	New and Used Auto Sales, Toyota, Kia
SIC:	5511 Motor Vehicle Dealers (New and Used)
NAICS:	441110 New Car Dealers
Sale Location:	Vacaville, CA, United States
Years in Business:	N/A
Number Employees:	N/A

Source Data
Public Buyer Name:	LITHIA MOTORS INC
8-K Date:	N/A
8-K/A Date:	N/A
Other Filing Type:	S-1/A
Other Filing Date:	11/1/1996
CIK Code:	0001023128

Income Data
Data is "Latest Full Year" Reported	Yes
Data is Restated (see Notes for any explanation)	No
Income Statement Date	12/31/1995
Net Sales	$27,810,400
COGS	$24,858,100
Gross Profit	$2,952,300
Yearly Rent	$470,000
Owner's Compensation	N/A
Other Operating Expenses	N/A
Noncash Charges	$109,900
Total Operating Expenses	$4,254,400
Operating Profit	($1,302,100)
Interest Expenses	$474,700
EBT	($1,611,800)
Taxes	$0
Net Income	($1,611,800)

Asset Data
Data is Latest Reported	Yes
Data is "Purchase Price Allocation agreed upon by Buyer and Seller"	No
Balance Sheet Date	6/30/1996
Cash Equivalents	$2,201,800
Trade Receivables	$888,000
Inventory	$4,223,000
Other Current Assets	$129,100
Total Current Assets	$7,441,900
Fixed Assets	$230,500
Real Estate	N/A
Intangibles	N/A
Other Noncurrent Assets	N/A
Total Assets	$7,672,400
Long-term Liabilities	$586,000
Total Liabilities	$8,637,800
Stockholder's Equity	($965,400)

Transaction Data
Date Sale Initiated:	N/A
Date of Sale:	11/15/1996
Days to Sell:	N/A
Asking Price:	N/A
Market Value of Invested Capital*:	$6,630,000
Debt Assumed:	N/A
Employment Agreement Value:	N/A
Noncompete Value:	N/A
Amount of Down Payment:	$6,630,000
Stock or Asset Sale:	Asset
Company Type:	S Corporation
Was there an Employment/Consulting Agreement?	No
Was there an Assumed Lease in the sale?	Yes
Was there a Renewal Option with the Lease?	Yes

*Includes noncompete value and interest-bearing debt; excludes real estate, employment/consulting agreement values, and all contingent payments.

Additional Transaction Information
Was there a Note in the consideration paid? No
Terms:
Consideration paid: Cash.
Assumed Lease (Months): 60
Noncompete Length (Months): N/A
Employment/Consulting Agreement Description:
Additional Notes:
EBT includes $165,000 Other Income. Seller is doing business as Melody Toyota, Kia. Inventory stated using FIFO.

Was there a personal guarantee on the Note? No

Terms of Lease: N/A
Noncompete Description: N/A

Valuation Multiples
MVIC/Net Sales	0.24
MVIC/Gross Profit	2.25
MVIC/EBITDA	N/A
MVIC/EBIT	N/A
MVIC/Discretionary Earnings	N/A
MVIC/Book Value of Invested Capital	N/A

Profitability Ratios
Net Profit Margin	-0.06
Operating Profit Margin	-0.04
Gross Profit Margin	0.11
Return on Assets	-0.21
Return on Equity	N/A

Leverage Ratios
Fixed Charge Coverage	-2.40
Long-Term Debt to Assets	0.08
Long-Term Debt to Equity	N/A

Earnings
EBITDA	($1,192,200)
Discretionary Earnings	N/A

Liquidity Ratios
Current Ratio	0.92
Quick Ratio	0.40

Activity Ratios
Total Asset Turnover	3.62
Fixed Asset Turnover	120.65
Inventory Turnover	6.59

Copyright © 2010 Business Valuation Resources, LLC. All rights reserved. www.BVResources.com^SM
(888) BUS-VALU, (503) 291-7963

Pratt's Stats® Auto Dealership Report

Pratt's Stats® Transaction Report
Prepared: 8/20/2010 2:09:43 PM (PST)

Seller Details
Target Name:	Young Automotive Group
Business Description:	Operates 18 Automobile Franchises
SIC:	5511 Motor Vehicle Dealers (New and Used)
NAICS:	441110 New Car Dealers
Sale Location:	N/A
Years in Business:	N/A
Number Employees:	N/A

Source Data
Public Buyer Name:	UNITED AUTO GROUP INC
8-K Date:	2/20/1998
8-K/A Date:	4/22/1998
Other Filing Type:	N/A
Other Filing Date:	N/A
CIK Code:	0001019849

Income Data
Data is "Latest Full Year" Reported	Yes
Data is Restated (see Notes for any explanation)	No
Income Statement Date	12/31/1997
Net Sales	$410,298,000
COGS	$359,496,000
Gross Profit	$50,802,000
Yearly Rent	$2,730,000
Owner's Compensation	N/A
Other Operating Expenses	$35,149,000
Noncash Charges	$538,000
Total Operating Expenses	$38,057,000
Operating Profit	$12,745,000
Interest Expenses	$1,000,000
EBT	$11,933,000
Taxes	$0
Net Income	$11,933,000

Asset Data
Data is Latest Reported	Yes
Data is "Purchase Price Allocation agreed upon by Buyer and Seller"	No
Balance Sheet Date	12/31/1997
Cash Equivalents	$3,184,000
Trade Receivables	$11,647,000
Inventory	$53,879,000
Other Current Assets	$409,000
Total Current Assets	$69,119,000
Fixed Assets	$6,506,000
Real Estate	N/A
Intangibles	$7,575,000
Other Noncurrent Assets	$1,107,000
Total Assets	$84,307,000
Long-term Liabilities	$8,036,000
Total Liabilities	$72,782,000
Stockholder's Equity	$11,525,000

Transaction Data
Date Sale Initiated:	N/A
Date of Sale:	2/6/1998
Days to Sell:	N/A
Asking Price:	N/A
Market Value of Invested Capital*:	$68,600,000
Debt Assumed:	N/A
Employment Agreement Value:	N/A
Noncompete Value:	N/A
Amount of Down Payment:	$61,600,000
Stock or Asset Sale:	Stock
Company Type:	S Corporation
Was there an Employment/Consulting Agreement?	No
Was there an Assumed Lease in the sale?	Yes
Was there a Renewal Option with the Lease?	No

*Includes noncompete value and interest-bearing debt; excludes real estate, employment/consulting agreement values, and all contingent payments.

Additional Transaction Information
Was there a Note in the consideration paid? Yes
Was there a personal guarantee on the Note? No
Terms:
Consideration paid: $50,000,000 in cash, $7,000,000 Note Payable, terms and interest not disclosed, 1,040,039 shares of buyers stock valued at $11,600.000
Assumed Lease (Months): N/A
Terms of Lease: N/A
Noncompete Length (Months): N/A
Noncompete Description: N/A
Employment/Consulting Agreement Description:
Additional Notes:
Earnings Before Tax includes $100,000 interest income, and $88,000 in other income. Operates 18 Automobile Franchises consisting mainly of GM autos -- they also sell Toyota and BMW. Inventory stated using LIFO.

Valuation Multiples
MVIC/Net Sales	0.17
MVIC/Gross Profit	1.35
MVIC/EBITDA	5.16
MVIC/EBIT	5.38
MVIC/Discretionary Earnings	N/A
MVIC/Book Value of Invested Capital	3.51

Profitability Ratios
Net Profit Margin	0.03
Operating Profit Margin	0.03
Gross Profit Margin	0.12
Return on Assets	0.14
Return on Equity	1.04

Leverage Ratios
Fixed Charge Coverage	12.93
Long-Term Debt to Assets	0.10
Long-Term Debt to Equity	0.70

Earnings
EBITDA	$13,283,000
Discretionary Earnings	N/A

Liquidity Ratios
Current Ratio	1.07
Quick Ratio	0.24

Activity Ratios
Total Asset Turnover	4.87
Fixed Asset Turnover	63.06
Inventory Turnover	7.62

Copyright © 2010 Business Valuation Resources, LLC. All rights reserved. www.BVResources.com℠
(888) BUS-VALU, (503) 291-7963

Pratt's Stats® Auto Dealership Report

Pratt's Stats® Transaction Report
Prepared: 8/20/2010 2:09:43 PM (PST)

Seller Details

Target Name:	United Nissan (formerly Steve Rayman Nissan, Inc.)
Business Description:	New and Used Auto Sales, Nissan
SIC:	5511 Motor Vehicle Dealers (New and Used)
NAICS:	441110 New Car Dealers
Sale Location:	Morrow, GA, United States
Years in Business:	N/A
Number Employees:	N/A

Source Data

Public Buyer Name:	UNITED AUTO GROUP INC
8-K Date:	N/A
8-K/A Date:	N/A
Other Filing Type:	S-1
Other Filing Date:	8/2/1996
CIK Code:	0001019849

Income Data

Data is "Latest Full Year" Reported	Yes
Data is Restated (see Notes for any explanation)	No
Income Statement Date	12/31/1995
Net Sales	$60,268,000
COGS	$50,166,000
Gross Profit	$10,102,000
Yearly Rent	$226,000
Owner's Compensation	N/A
Other Operating Expenses	N/A
Noncash Charges	$183,000
Total Operating Expenses	$8,989,000
Operating Profit	$1,113,000
Interest Expenses	N/A
EBT	$1,114,000
Taxes	$0
Net Income	$1,114,000

Asset Data

Data is Latest Reported	Yes
Data is "Purchase Price Allocation agreed upon by Buyer and Seller"	No
Balance Sheet Date	3/31/1996
Cash Equivalents	$267,000
Trade Receivables	$2,153,000
Inventory	$7,467,000
Other Current Assets	$104,000
Total Current Assets	$9,991,000
Fixed Assets	$188,000
Real Estate	N/A
Intangibles	$525,000
Other Noncurrent Assets	N/A
Total Assets	$10,704,000
Long-term Liabilities	$616,000
Total Liabilities	$8,583,000
Stockholder's Equity	$2,121,000

Transaction Data

Date Sale Initiated:	N/A
Date of Sale:	5/1/1996
Days to Sell:	N/A
Asking Price:	N/A
Market Value of Invested Capital*:	$11,500,000
Debt Assumed:	N/A
Employment Agreement Value:	N/A
Noncompete Value:	N/A
Amount of Down Payment:	$11,500,000
Stock or Asset Sale:	Stock
Company Type:	S Corporation
Was there an Employment/Consulting Agreement?	No
Was there an Assumed Lease in the sale?	No
Was there a Renewal Option with the Lease?	No

*Includes noncompete value and interest-bearing debt; excludes real estate, employment/consulting agreement values, and all contingent payments.

Additional Transaction Information

Was there a Note in the consideration paid? No
Terms:
Considerations paid in cash.
Assumed Lease (Months): 60
Noncompete Length (Months): N/A
Employment/Consulting Agreement Description:
Additional Notes:
EBT includes $1,000 Other Income. Inventory stated using LIFO.

Was there a personal guarantee on the Note? No

Terms of Lease: Present Value of Future Minimum Payments: $2,332,000
Noncompete Description: N/A

Valuation Multiples

MVIC/Net Sales	0.19
MVIC/Gross Profit	1.14
MVIC/EBITDA	8.87
MVIC/EBIT	10.33
MVIC/Discretionary Earnings	N/A
MVIC/Book Value of Invested Capital	4.20

Profitability Ratios

Net Profit Margin	0.02
Operating Profit Margin	N/A
Gross Profit Margin	0.17
Return on Assets	0.10
Return on Equity	0.53

Leverage Ratios

Fixed Charge Coverage	N/A
Long-Term Debt to Assets	0.06
Long-Term Debt to Equity	0.29

Earnings

EBITDA	$1,296,000
Discretionary Earnings	N/A

Liquidity Ratios

Current Ratio	1.25
Quick Ratio	0.32

Activity Ratios

Total Asset Turnover	5.63
Fixed Asset Turnover	320.57
Inventory Turnover	8.07

Copyright © 2010 Business Valuation Resources, LLC. All rights reserved. www.BVResources.com^SM
(888) BUS-VALU, (503) 291-7963

Pratt's Stats® Auto Dealership Report

Pratt's Stats® Transaction Report
Prepared: 8/20/2010 2:09:43 PM (PST)

Seller Details

Target Name:	Dick Donnelly Automotive Enterprises, Inc. dba Dick Donnelly Lincoln-Mercury, Audi, Suz
Business Description:	Lincoln-Mercury, Audi, Suzuki, Isuzu
SIC:	5511 Motor Vehicle Dealers (New and Used)
NAICS:	441110 New Car Dealers
Sale Location:	Reno, NV, United States
Years in Business:	N/A
Number Employees:	N/A

Source Data

Public Buyer Name:	LITHIA MOTORS INC
8-K Date:	10/14/1997
8-K/A Date:	12/12/1997
Other Filing Type:	N/A
Other Filing Date:	N/A
CIK Code:	0001023128

Income Data

Data is "Latest Full Year" Reported	Yes
Data is Restated (see Notes for any explanation)	No
Income Statement Date	12/31/1996
Net Sales	$80,588,000
COGS	$73,350,700
Gross Profit	$7,237,300
Yearly Rent	$1,025,700
Owner's Compensation	N/A
Other Operating Expenses	N/A
Noncash Charges	$112,800
Total Operating Expenses	$6,723,200
Operating Profit	$514,100
Interest Expenses	$301,800
EBT	$303,900
Taxes	$0
Net Income	$303,900

Asset Data

Data is Latest Reported	Yes
Data is "Purchase Price Allocation agreed upon by Buyer and Seller"	No
Balance Sheet Date	9/30/1997
Cash Equivalents	$90,700
Trade Receivables	$2,147,500
Inventory	$6,660,000
Other Current Assets	$63,900
Total Current Assets	$8,962,100
Fixed Assets	$535,400
Real Estate	N/A
Intangibles	N/A
Other Noncurrent Assets	$117,300
Total Assets	$9,614,800
Long-term Liabilities	$188,400
Total Liabilities	$5,897,400
Stockholder's Equity	$3,717,400

Transaction Data

Date Sale Initiated:	N/A
Date of Sale:	10/1/1997
Days to Sell:	N/A
Asking Price:	N/A
Market Value of Invested Capital*:	$12,800,000
Debt Assumed:	N/A
Employment Agreement Value:	N/A
Noncompete Value:	N/A
Amount of Down Payment:	$12,200,000
Stock or Asset Sale:	Asset
Company Type:	S Corporation
Was there an Employment/Consulting Agreement?	No
Was there an Assumed Lease in the sale?	Yes
Was there a Renewal Option with the Lease?	Yes

*Includes noncompete value and interest-bearing debt; excludes real estate, employment/consulting agreement values, and all contingent payments.

Additional Transaction Information

Was there a Note in the consideration paid? Yes
Was there a personal guarantee on the Note? No
Terms:
Consideration paid: $6,000,000 cash, $6,200,000 financed from company's flooring line of credit, $600,000 note payable.
Assumed Lease (Months): 24
Terms of Lease: $30,000 per month
Noncompete Length (Months): N/A
Noncompete Description: N/A
Employment/Consulting Agreement Description:
Additional Notes:
EBT includes $91,600 Other Income. New and used car inventory stated using the lower of cost or market, parts inventory stated using FIFO.

Valuation Multiples

MVIC/Net Sales	0.16
MVIC/Gross Profit	1.77
MVIC/EBITDA	20.42
MVIC/EBIT	24.90
MVIC/Discretionary Earnings	N/A
MVIC/Book Value of Invested Capital	3.28

Profitability Ratios

Net Profit Margin	0.00
Operating Profit Margin	0.01
Gross Profit Margin	0.09
Return on Assets	0.03
Return on Equity	0.08

Leverage Ratios

Fixed Charge Coverage	2.01
Long-Term Debt to Assets	0.02
Long-Term Debt to Equity	0.05

Earnings

EBITDA	$626,900
Discretionary Earnings	N/A

Liquidity Ratios

Current Ratio	1.57
Quick Ratio	0.40

Activity Ratios

Total Asset Turnover	8.38
Fixed Asset Turnover	150.52
Inventory Turnover	12.10

Copyright © 2010 Business Valuation Resources, LLC. All rights reserved. www.BVResources.com[SM]
(888) BUS-VALU, (503) 291-7963

Pratt's Stats® Auto Dealership Report

Pratt's Stats® Transaction Report
Prepared: 8/20/2010 2:09:43 PM (PST)

Seller Details
Target Name:	Landers Auto Sales, Inc.
Business Description:	New and Used Auto Sales, Chrysler-Plymouth, Dodge, GMC Truck, Jeep-Eagle, Oldsmobile.
SIC:	5511 Motor Vehicle Dealers (New and Used)
NAICS:	441110 New Car Dealers
Sale Location:	Benton, AR, United States
Years in Business:	N/A
Number Employees:	N/A

Source Data
Public Buyer Name:	UNITED AUTO GROUP INC
8-K Date:	N/A
8-K/A Date:	N/A
Other Filing Type:	S-1
Other Filing Date:	8/2/1996
CIK Code:	0001019849

Income Data
Data is "Latest Full Year" Reported	Yes
Data is Restated (see Notes for any explanation)	No
Income Statement Date	12/31/1994
Net Sales	$228,912,000
COGS	$208,932,000
Gross Profit	$19,980,000
Yearly Rent	$429,000
Owner's Compensation	N/A
Other Operating Expenses	N/A
Noncash Charges	$317,000
Total Operating Expenses	$15,445,000
Operating Profit	$4,535,000
Interest Expenses	N/A
EBT	$4,744,000
Taxes	$1,810,000
Net Income	$2,934,000

Asset Data
Data is Latest Reported	Yes
Data is "Purchase Price Allocation agreed upon by Buyer and Seller"	No
Balance Sheet Date	7/31/1995
Cash Equivalents	$2,278,000
Trade Receivables	$6,593,000
Inventory	$22,433,000
Other Current Assets	$29,000
Total Current Assets	$31,333,000
Fixed Assets	$927,000
Real Estate	N/A
Intangibles	$49,000
Other Noncurrent Assets	N/A
Total Assets	$32,309,000
Long-term Liabilities	$239,000
Total Liabilities	$28,315,000
Stockholder's Equity	$3,994,000

Transaction Data
Date Sale Initiated:	N/A
Date of Sale:	8/15/1995
Days to Sell:	N/A
Asking Price:	N/A
Market Value of Invested Capital*:	$24,000,000
Debt Assumed:	N/A
Employment Agreement Value:	N/A
Noncompete Value:	N/A
Amount of Down Payment:	$20,000,000
Stock or Asset Sale:	Stock
Company Type:	C Corporation
Was there an Employment/Consulting Agreement?	No
Was there an Assumed Lease in the sale?	No
Was there a Renewal Option with the Lease?	No

*Includes noncompete value and interest-bearing debt; excludes real estate, employment/consulting agreement values, and all contingent payments.

Additional Transaction Information
Was there a Note in the consideration paid? No
Was there a personal guarantee on the Note? No
Terms:
Consideration: $20,000,000 in cash and $4,000,000 in promissory notes. The acquisition agreement provides for additional contingent purchase price payments to the sellers based on the future profitability of the acquired dealerships.
Assumed Lease (Months): 60
Terms of Lease: Present Value of Future Minimum Payments: $10,800,000
Noncompete Length (Months): N/A
Noncompete Description: N/A
Employment/Consulting Agreement Description:
Additional Notes:
EBT includes $209,000 Other Income. Sale was an 80% interest. As of December 22, 1994, Landers Oldsmobile-GMC, Inc. and Landers Jeep-Eagle, Inc. were merged into Landers Auto Sales, Inc. and operates as divisions of Landers Auto Sales, Inc. under the trade names of Landers Oldsmobile-GMC Trust and Landers Jeep-Eagle/Chrysler-Plymouth-Dodge, respectively. All material divisional accounts and transactions have been eliminated. Inventory stated using LIFO.

Valuation Multiples
MVIC/Net Sales	0.10
MVIC/Gross Profit	1.20
MVIC/EBITDA	4.95
MVIC/EBIT	5.29
MVIC/Discretionary Earnings	N/A
MVIC/Book Value of Invested Capital	5.67

Profitability Ratios
Net Profit Margin	0.01
Operating Profit Margin	N/A
Gross Profit Margin	0.09
Return on Assets	0.09
Return on Equity	0.73

Leverage Ratios
Fixed Charge Coverage	N/A
Long-Term Debt to Assets	0.01
Long-Term Debt to Equity	0.06

Earnings
EBITDA	$4,852,000
Discretionary Earnings	N/A

Liquidity Ratios
Current Ratio	1.12
Quick Ratio	0.32

Activity Ratios
Total Asset Turnover	7.09
Fixed Asset Turnover	246.94
Inventory Turnover	10.20

Copyright © 2010 Business Valuation Resources, LLC. All rights reserved. www.BVResources.com℠
(888) BUS-VALU, (503) 291-7963

Pratt's Stats® Auto Dealership Report

Pratt's Stats® Transaction Report
Prepared: 8/20/2010 2:09:43 PM (PST)

Seller Details
Target Name:	Standefer Motor Sales, Inc.
Business Description:	New and Used Auto Sales, Nissan
SIC:	5511 Motor Vehicle Dealers (New and Used)
NAICS:	441110 New Car Dealers
Sale Location:	Chattanooga, TN, United States
Years in Business:	N/A
Number Employees:	N/A

Source Data
Public Buyer Name:	UNITED AUTO GROUP INC
8-K Date:	N/A
8-K/A Date:	N/A
Other Filing Type:	S-1/A
Other Filing Date:	9/13/1996
CIK Code:	0001019849

Income Data
Data is "Latest Full Year" Reported	Yes
Data is Restated (see Notes for any explanation)	No
Income Statement Date	12/31/1995
Net Sales	$65,793,000
COGS	$58,284,000
Gross Profit	$7,509,000
Yearly Rent	$282,000
Owner's Compensation	N/A
Other Operating Expenses	N/A
Noncash Charges	N/A
Total Operating Expenses	$5,192,000
Operating Profit	$2,317,000
Interest Expenses	N/A
EBT	$2,500,000
Taxes	$147,000
Net Income	$2,353,000

Asset Data
Data is Latest Reported	Yes
Data is "Purchase Price Allocation agreed upon by Buyer and Seller"	No
Balance Sheet Date	6/30/1996
Cash Equivalents	$232,000
Trade Receivables	$1,431,000
Inventory	$8,430,000
Other Current Assets	N/A
Total Current Assets	$10,093,000
Fixed Assets	$226,000
Real Estate	N/A
Intangibles	N/A
Other Noncurrent Assets	$150,000
Total Assets	$10,469,000
Long-term Liabilities	$0
Total Liabilities	$3,865,000
Stockholder's Equity	$6,604,000

Transaction Data
Date Sale Initiated:	N/A
Date of Sale:	9/5/1996
Days to Sell:	N/A
Asking Price:	N/A
Market Value of Invested Capital*:	$18,200,000
Debt Assumed:	N/A
Employment Agreement Value:	N/A
Noncompete Value:	N/A
Amount of Down Payment:	$18,200,000
Stock or Asset Sale:	Stock
Company Type:	S Corporation
Was there an Employment/Consulting Agreement?	No
Was there an Assumed Lease in the sale?	No
Was there a Renewal Option with the Lease?	No

*Includes noncompete value and interest-bearing debt; excludes real estate, employment/consulting agreement values, and all contingent payments.

Additional Transaction Information
Was there a Note in the consideration paid? No
Terms:
Considerations paid in cash.
Assumed Lease (Months): N/A
Noncompete Length (Months): N/A
Employment/Consulting Agreement Description:
Additional Notes:
EBT includes $183,000 Other Income. Seller is a Nissan franchise. Inventory stated using LIFO.

Was there a personal guarantee on the Note? No

Terms of Lease: N/A
Noncompete Description: N/A

Valuation Multiples
MVIC/Net Sales	0.28
MVIC/Gross Profit	2.42
MVIC/EBITDA	N/A
MVIC/EBIT	7.85
MVIC/Discretionary Earnings	N/A
MVIC/Book Value of Invested Capital	2.76

Profitability Ratios
Net Profit Margin	0.04
Operating Profit Margin	N/A
Gross Profit Margin	0.11
Return on Assets	0.22
Return on Equity	0.36

Leverage Ratios
Fixed Charge Coverage	N/A
Long-Term Debt to Assets	0.00
Long-Term Debt to Equity	0.00

Earnings
EBITDA	N/A
Discretionary Earnings	N/A

Liquidity Ratios
Current Ratio	2.61
Quick Ratio	0.43

Activity Ratios
Total Asset Turnover	6.28
Fixed Asset Turnover	291.12
Inventory Turnover	7.80

Copyright © 2010 Business Valuation Resources, LLC. All rights reserved. www.BVResources.com[SM]
(888) BUS-VALU, (503) 291-7963

… Pratt's Stats® Auto Dealership Report

Pratt's Stats® Transaction Report
Prepared: 8/20/2010 2:09:43 PM (PST)

Seller Details
Target Name:	GARY HANNA NISSAN INC.
Business Description:	Auto Dealer
SIC:	5511 Motor Vehicle Dealers (New and Used)
NAICS:	441110 New Car Dealers
Sale Location:	Las Vegas, NV, United States
Years in Business:	N/A
Number Employees:	N/A

Source Data
Public Buyer Name:	UNITED AUTO GROUP INC
8-K Date:	10/31/1997
8-K/A Date:	N/A
Other Filing Type:	N/A
Other Filing Date:	N/A
CIK Code:	0001019849

Income Data
Data is "Latest Full Year" Reported	Yes
Data is Restated (see Notes for any explanation)	No
Income Statement Date	12/31/1996
Net Sales	$67,504,000
COGS	$58,082,000
Gross Profit	$9,422,000
Yearly Rent	$600,000
Owner's Compensation	N/A
Other Operating Expenses	N/A
Noncash Charges	$53,000
Total Operating Expenses	$6,463,000
Operating Profit	$2,959,000
Interest Expenses	$0
EBT	$2,959,000
Taxes	$0
Net Income	$2,959,000

Asset Data
Data is Latest Reported	Yes
Data is "Purchase Price Allocation agreed upon by Buyer and Seller"	No
Balance Sheet Date	12/31/1996
Cash Equivalents	$0
Trade Receivables	$2,565,000
Inventory	$4,716,000
Other Current Assets	$21,000
Total Current Assets	$7,302,000
Fixed Assets	$157,000
Real Estate	N/A
Intangibles	N/A
Other Noncurrent Assets	$82,000
Total Assets	$7,541,000
Long-term Liabilities	$0
Total Liabilities	$6,406,000
Stockholder's Equity	$1,135,000

Transaction Data
Date Sale Initiated:	N/A
Date of Sale:	4/22/1997
Days to Sell:	N/A
Asking Price:	N/A
Market Value of Invested Capital*:	$13,700,000
Debt Assumed:	N/A
Employment Agreement Value:	N/A
Noncompete Value:	N/A
Amount of Down Payment:	$13,700,000
Stock or Asset Sale:	Stock
Company Type:	S Corporation
Was there an Employment/Consulting Agreement?	No
Was there an Assumed Lease in the sale?	No
Was there a Renewal Option with the Lease?	No

*Includes noncompete value and interest-bearing debt; excludes real estate, employment/consulting agreement values, and all contingent payments.

Additional Transaction Information
Was there a Note in the consideration paid? No
Terms:
Assumed Lease (Months): N/A
Noncompete Length (Months): N/A
Employment/Consulting Agreement Description:
Additional Notes:
Seller is the largest Nissan dealer in NV. Net sales consist of 89% vehicle sales, 7% service and parts and 4% financing and insurance.

Was there a personal guarantee on the Note? No
Terms of Lease: N/A
Noncompete Description: N/A

Valuation Multiples
MVIC/Net Sales	0.20
MVIC/Gross Profit	1.45
MVIC/EBITDA	4.55
MVIC/EBIT	4.63
MVIC/Discretionary Earnings	N/A
MVIC/Book Value of Invested Capital	12.07

Profitability Ratios
Net Profit Margin	0.04
Operating Profit Margin	0.04
Gross Profit Margin	0.14
Return on Assets	0.39
Return on Equity	2.61

Leverage Ratios
Fixed Charge Coverage	N/A
Long-Term Debt to Assets	0.00
Long-Term Debt to Equity	0.00

Earnings
EBITDA	$3,012,000
Discretionary Earnings	N/A

Liquidity Ratios
Current Ratio	1.14
Quick Ratio	0.40

Activity Ratios
Total Asset Turnover	8.95
Fixed Asset Turnover	429.96
Inventory Turnover	14.31

Copyright © 2010 Business Valuation Resources, LLC. All rights reserved. www.BVResources.com[SM]
(888) BUS-VALU, (503) 291-7963

Pratt's Stats® Auto Dealership Report

Pratt's Stats® Transaction Report
Prepared: 8/20/2010 2:09:43 PM (PST)

Seller Details
Target Name:	Champion Automotive Group
Business Description:	New and Used Auto Sales, Ford, Lincoln-Mercury, Isuzu
SIC:	5511 Motor Vehicle Dealers (New and Used)
NAICS:	441110 New Car Dealers
Sale Location:	Houston, TX, United States
Years in Business:	N/A
Number Employees:	N/A

Source Data
Public Buyer Name:	REPUBLIC INDUSTRIES INC
8-K Date:	2/20/1998
8-K/A Date:	N/A
Other Filing Type:	N/A
Other Filing Date:	N/A
CIK Code:	0000350698

Income Data
Data is "Latest Full Year" Reported	Yes
Data is Restated (see Notes for any explanation)	No
Income Statement Date	10/31/1997
Net Sales	$298,730,000
COGS	$273,181,000
Gross Profit	$25,549,000
Yearly Rent	$524,000
Owner's Compensation	N/A
Other Operating Expenses	N/A
Noncash Charges	$1,169,000
Total Operating Expenses	$17,739,000
Operating Profit	$7,810,000
Interest Expenses	$168,000
EBT	$7,868,000
Taxes	$3,074,000
Net Income	$4,526,000

Asset Data
Data is Latest Reported	Yes
Data is "Purchase Price Allocation agreed upon by Buyer and Seller"	No
Balance Sheet Date	10/31/1997
Cash Equivalents	$7,599,000
Trade Receivables	$12,055,000
Inventory	$52,125,000
Other Current Assets	$994,000
Total Current Assets	$72,773,000
Fixed Assets	$8,979,000
Real Estate	N/A
Intangibles	N/A
Other Noncurrent Assets	$1,181,000
Total Assets	$82,933,000
Long-term Liabilities	$2,598,000
Total Liabilities	$75,142,000
Stockholder's Equity	$7,791,000

Transaction Data
Date Sale Initiated:	N/A
Date of Sale:	11/1/1997
Days to Sell:	N/A
Asking Price:	N/A
Market Value of Invested Capital*:	$67,000,000
Debt Assumed:	N/A
Employment Agreement Value:	N/A
Noncompete Value:	N/A
Amount of Down Payment:	$67,000,000
Stock or Asset Sale:	Asset
Company Type:	C Corporation
Was there an Employment/Consulting Agreement?	No
Was there an Assumed Lease in the sale?	Yes
Was there a Renewal Option with the Lease?	Yes

*Includes noncompete value and interest-bearing debt; excludes real estate, employment/consulting agreement values, and all contingent payments.

Additional Transaction Information
Was there a Note in the consideration paid? No
Terms:
Consideration paid: $67,000,000 in cash.
Assumed Lease (Months): N/A
Noncompete Length (Months): N/A
Employment/Consulting Agreement Description:

Was there a personal guarantee on the Note? No

Terms of Lease: N/A
Noncompete Description: N/A

Additional Notes:
Income Data is for 10 months ended 10/31/97. EBT includes $226,000 Miscellaneous Income. Net Income includes $268,000 Loss from Financing Operations. Auto inventory stated using LIFO, parts inventory stated using FIFO.

Valuation Multiples
MVIC/Net Sales	0.22
MVIC/Gross Profit	2.62
MVIC/EBITDA	7.46
MVIC/EBIT	8.58
MVIC/Discretionary Earnings	N/A
MVIC/Book Value of Invested Capital	6.45

Profitability Ratios
Net Profit Margin	0.02
Operating Profit Margin	0.03
Gross Profit Margin	0.09
Return on Assets	0.05
Return on Equity	0.58

Leverage Ratios
Fixed Charge Coverage	46.24
Long-Term Debt to Assets	0.03
Long-Term Debt to Equity	0.33

Earnings
EBITDA	$8,979,000
Discretionary Earnings	N/A

Liquidity Ratios
Current Ratio	1.00
Quick Ratio	0.28

Activity Ratios
Total Asset Turnover	3.60
Fixed Asset Turnover	33.27
Inventory Turnover	5.73

Copyright © 2010 Business Valuation Resources, LLC. All rights reserved. www.BVResources.com(SM)
(888) BUS-VALU, (503) 291-7963

Pratt's Stats® Auto Dealership Report

Pratt's Stats® Transaction Report
Prepared: 8/20/2010 2:09:43 PM (PST)

Seller Details

Target Name:	225 North Military Corporation d/b/a Miracle Mile Motors
Business Description:	Sales and Financing of New and Used Automobiles
SIC:	5511 Motor Vehicle Dealers (New and Used)
NAICS:	441110 New Car Dealers
Sale Location:	West palm Beach, FL, United States
Years in Business:	N/A
Number Employees:	N/A

Source Data

Public Buyer Name:	SMART CHOICE AUTOMOTIVE GROUP INC
8-K Date:	N/A
8-K/A Date:	N/A
Other Filing Type:	S-1
Other Filing Date:	7/17/1998
CIK Code:	0000949091

Income Data

Data is "Latest Full Year" Reported	Yes
Data is Restated (see Notes for any explanation)	No
Income Statement Date	12/31/1996
Net Sales	$11,998,847
COGS	$8,446,683
Gross Profit	$3,552,164
Yearly Rent	$144,000
Owner's Compensation	N/A
Other Operating Expenses	N/A
Noncash Charges	$1,748
Total Operating Expenses	$2,989,802
Operating Profit	$562,362
Interest Expenses	$22,593
EBT	$539,769
Taxes	$0
Net Income	$539,769

Asset Data

Data is Latest Reported	Yes
Data is "Purchase Price Allocation agreed upon by Buyer and Seller"	No
Balance Sheet Date	12/31/1996
Cash Equivalents	$192,999
Trade Receivables	$4,057,682
Inventory	$799,358
Other Current Assets	N/A
Total Current Assets	$5,050,039
Fixed Assets	$10,086
Real Estate	N/A
Intangibles	N/A
Other Noncurrent Assets	$48,275
Total Assets	$5,108,400
Long-term Liabilities	$0
Total Liabilities	$649,093
Stockholder's Equity	$4,459,307

Transaction Data

Date Sale Initiated:	N/A
Date of Sale:	2/14/1997
Days to Sell:	N/A
Asking Price:	N/A
Market Value of Invested Capital*:	$5,487,460
Debt Assumed:	N/A
Employment Agreement Value:	N/A
Noncompete Value:	N/A
Amount of Down Payment:	$4,014,285
Stock or Asset Sale:	Stock
Company Type:	S Corporation
Was there an Employment/Consulting Agreement?	No
Was there an Assumed Lease in the sale?	Yes
Was there a Renewal Option with the Lease?	Yes

*Includes noncompete value and interest-bearing debt; excludes real estate, employment/consulting agreement values, and all contingent payments.

Additional Transaction Information

Was there a Note in the consideration paid? Yes
Was there a personal guarantee on the Note? No
Terms:
Consideration Paid: $3,050,000 in Cash, 285,714 shares of buyers public company common stock valued at $964,285, and a $1,473,175 Note payable
Assumed Lease (Months): 34
Terms of Lease: $12,000 per month from a selling shareholder
Noncompete Length (Months): N/A
Noncompete Description: N/A
Employment/Consulting Agreement Description:
Additional Notes:
Vehicle inventory stated at the lower of cost (specific identification) or market

Valuation Multiples

MVIC/Net Sales	0.46
MVIC/Gross Profit	1.54
MVIC/EBITDA	9.73
MVIC/EBIT	9.76
MVIC/Discretionary Earnings	N/A
MVIC/Book Value of Invested Capital	1.23

Profitability Ratios

Net Profit Margin	0.04
Operating Profit Margin	0.05
Gross Profit Margin	0.30
Return on Assets	0.11
Return on Equity	0.12

Leverage Ratios

Fixed Charge Coverage	24.89
Long-Term Debt to Assets	0.00
Long-Term Debt to Equity	0.00

Earnings

EBITDA	$564,110
Discretionary Earnings	N/A

Liquidity Ratios

Current Ratio	7.78
Quick Ratio	6.55

Activity Ratios

Total Asset Turnover	2.35
Fixed Asset Turnover	1,189.65
Inventory Turnover	15.01

Copyright © 2010 Business Valuation Resources, LLC. All rights reserved. www.BVResources.com^{SM}
(888) BUS-VALU, (503) 291-7963

Pratt's Stats® Auto Dealership Report

Pratt's Stats® Transaction Report
Prepared: 8/20/2010 2:09:43 PM (PST)

Seller Details
Target Name:	Dyer & Dyer, Inc.
Business Description:	Owns and Operates Automobile Dealership
SIC:	5511 Motor Vehicle Dealers (New and Used)
NAICS:	441110 New Car Dealers
Sale Location:	Atlanta, GA, United States
Years in Business:	20
Number Employees:	N/A

Source Data
Broker Name:	N/A
Broker Firm Name:	N/A

Income Data
Data is "Latest Full Year" Reported	Yes
Data is Restated (see Notes for any explanation)	No
Income Statement Date	12/31/1996
Net Sales	$72,576,623
COGS	$62,547,497
Gross Profit	$10,029,126
Yearly Rent	$715,000
Owner's Compensation	N/A
Other Operating Expenses	N/A
Noncash Charges	$202,214
Total Operating Expenses	$7,123,642
Operating Profit	$2,905,484
Interest Expenses	$372,590
EBT	$2,984,957
Taxes	$954,846
Net Income	$2,030,111

Asset Data
Data is Latest Reported	Yes
Data is "Purchase Price Allocation agreed upon by Buyer and Seller"	No
Balance Sheet Date	6/30/1997
Cash Equivalents	$172,937
Trade Receivables	$2,535,230
Inventory	$11,128,333
Other Current Assets	$32,267
Total Current Assets	$13,868,767
Fixed Assets	$1,156,207
Real Estate	N/A
Intangibles	N/A
Other Noncurrent Assets	$297,424
Total Assets	$15,322,398
Long-term Liabilities	N/A
Total Liabilities	N/A
Stockholder's Equity	N/A

Transaction Data
Date Sale Initiated:	N/A
Date of Sale:	8/1/1997
Days to Sell:	N/A
Asking Price:	N/A
Market Value of Invested Capital*:	$18,000,000
Debt Assumed:	N/A
Employment Agreement Value:	N/A
Noncompete Value:	N/A
Amount of Down Payment:	$18,000,000
Stock or Asset Sale:	Asset
Company Type:	S Corporation
Was there an Employment/Consulting Agreement?	No
Was there an Assumed Lease in the sale?	Yes
Was there a Renewal Option with the Lease?	No

*Includes noncompete value and interest-bearing debt; excludes real estate, employment/consulting agreement values, and all contingent payments.

Additional Transaction Information
Was there a Note in the consideration paid? No
Terms:
Consideration paid as follows: Cash.
Assumed Lease (Months): N/A
Noncompete Length (Months): N/A
Employment/Consulting Agreement Description:
Additional Notes:
EBT includes $452,063 in other income, inventory stated at lower of cost (LIFO) or market. Company owns a Volvo dealership in Atlanta, Georgia.

Was there a personal guarantee on the Note? No

Terms of Lease: Future Minimum Lease Payments: $9,351,110
Noncompete Description: N/A

Valuation Multiples
MVIC/Net Sales	0.25
MVIC/Gross Profit	1.79
MVIC/EBITDA	5.79
MVIC/EBIT	6.20
MVIC/Discretionary Earnings	N/A
MVIC/Book Value of Invested Capital	N/A

Profitability Ratios
Net Profit Margin	0.03
Operating Profit Margin	0.05
Gross Profit Margin	0.14
Return on Assets	0.13
Return on Equity	N/A

Leverage Ratios
Fixed Charge Coverage	9.01
Long-Term Debt to Assets	N/A
Long-Term Debt to Equity	N/A

Earnings
EBITDA	$3,107,698
Discretionary Earnings	N/A

Liquidity Ratios
Current Ratio	N/A
Quick Ratio	N/A

Activity Ratios
Total Asset Turnover	4.74
Fixed Asset Turnover	62.77
Inventory Turnover	6.52

Copyright © 2010 Business Valuation Resources, LLC. All rights reserved. www.BVResources.com[SM]
(888) BUS-VALU, (503) 291-7963

Pratt's Stats® Auto Dealership Report

Pratt's Stats® Transaction Report
Prepared: 8/20/2010 2:09:43 PM (PST)

Seller Details
Target Name:	Sam Linder Inc.
Business Description:	New and Used Auto Sales, Cadillac, Honda, Oldsmobile
SIC:	5511 Motor Vehicle Dealers (New and Used)
NAICS:	441110 New Car Dealers
Sale Location:	Salinas, CA, United States
Years in Business:	N/A Number Employees: N/A

Source Data
Public Buyer Name:	LITHIA MOTORS INC
8-K Date:	N/A
8-K/A Date:	N/A
Other Filing Type:	S-1/A
Other Filing Date:	11/1/1996
CIK Code:	0001023128

Income Data
Data is "Latest Full Year" Reported	Yes
Data is Restated (see Notes for any explanation)	No
Income Statement Date	12/31/1995
Net Sales	$26,857,400
COGS	$22,646,000
Gross Profit	$4,211,400
Yearly Rent	$285,000
Owner's Compensation	N/A
Other Operating Expenses	$3,550,500
Noncash Charges	$92,500
Total Operating Expenses	$3,928,000
Operating Profit	$283,400
Interest Expenses	$346,700
EBT	($64,100)
Taxes	$0
Net Income	($64,100)

Asset Data
Data is Latest Reported	Yes
Data is "Purchase Price Allocation agreed upon by Buyer and Seller"	No
Balance Sheet Date	6/30/1996
Cash Equivalents	$537,200
Trade Receivables	$471,600
Inventory	$2,931,100
Other Current Assets	$189,800
Total Current Assets	$4,129,700
Fixed Assets	$354,400
Real Estate	N/A
Intangibles	N/A
Other Noncurrent Assets	$32,000
Total Assets	$4,516,100
Long-term Liabilities	$104,200
Total Liabilities	$4,393,300
Stockholder's Equity	$122,800

Transaction Data
Date Sale Initiated:	N/A
Date of Sale:	1/15/1997
Days to Sell:	N/A
Asking Price:	N/A
Market Value of Invested Capital*:	$3,250,000
Debt Assumed:	N/A
Employment Agreement Value:	N/A
Noncompete Value:	N/A
Amount of Down Payment:	$3,250,000
Stock or Asset Sale:	Asset
Company Type:	S Corporation
Was there an Employment/Consulting Agreement?	No
Was there an Assumed Lease in the sale?	Yes
Was there a Renewal Option with the Lease?	Yes

*Includes noncompete value and interest-bearing debt; excludes real estate, employment/consulting agreement values, and all contingent payments.

Additional Transaction Information
Was there a Note in the consideration paid? No
Terms:
Consideration paid: Cash.
Assumed Lease (Months): 36
Noncompete Length (Months): N/A
Employment/Consulting Agreement Description:
Additional Notes:
EBT includes $800 Other Expenses. Selling Price includes $2,100,000 for new and used car and parts inventory. Seller is doing business as Sam Linder Cadillac, Honda, Oldsmobile. Inventory stated using LIFO.

Was there a personal guarantee on the Note? No
Terms of Lease: N/A
Noncompete Description: N/A

Valuation Multiples
MVIC/Net Sales	0.12
MVIC/Gross Profit	0.77
MVIC/EBITDA	8.65
MVIC/EBIT	11.47
MVIC/Discretionary Earnings	N/A
MVIC/Book Value of Invested Capital	14.32

Profitability Ratios
Net Profit Margin	-0.00
Operating Profit Margin	0.01
Gross Profit Margin	0.16
Return on Assets	-0.01
Return on Equity	-0.52

Leverage Ratios
Fixed Charge Coverage	0.82
Long-Term Debt to Assets	0.02
Long-Term Debt to Equity	0.85

Earnings
EBITDA	$375,900
Discretionary Earnings	N/A

Liquidity Ratios
Current Ratio	0.96
Quick Ratio	0.28

Activity Ratios
Total Asset Turnover	5.95
Fixed Asset Turnover	75.78
Inventory Turnover	9.16

Copyright © 2010 Business Valuation Resources, LLC. All rights reserved. www.BVResources.com℠
(888) BUS-VALU, (503) 291-7963

Pratt's Stats® Auto Dealership Report

Pratt's Stats® Transaction Report
Prepared: 8/20/2010 2:09:43 PM (PST)

Seller Details
Target Name:	Roberts Dodge, Inc.
Business Description:	New and Used Auto Sales
SIC:	5511 Motor Vehicle Dealers (New and Used)
NAICS:	441110 New Car Dealers
Sale Location:	Eugene, OR, United States
Years in Business:	N/A
Number Employees:	N/A

Source Data
Public Buyer Name:	LITHIA MOTORS INC
8-K Date:	N/A
8-K/A Date:	N/A
Other Filing Type:	S-1/A
Other Filing Date:	11/1/1996
CIK Code:	0001023128

Income Data
Data is "Latest Full Year" Reported	Yes
Data is Restated (see Notes for any explanation)	No
Income Statement Date	12/31/1995
Net Sales	$31,894,000
COGS	$27,270,000
Gross Profit	$4,624,000
Yearly Rent	N/A
Owner's Compensation	N/A
Other Operating Expenses	N/A
Noncash Charges	$125,000
Total Operating Expenses	$3,828,000
Operating Profit	$796,000
Interest Expenses	$602,000
EBT	$269,000
Taxes	$0
Net Income	$269,000

Asset Data
Data is Latest Reported	Yes
Data is "Purchase Price Allocation agreed upon by Buyer and Seller"	No
Balance Sheet Date	6/30/1996
Cash Equivalents	$1,202,000
Trade Receivables	$785,000
Inventory	$4,766,000
Other Current Assets	$42,000
Total Current Assets	$6,795,000
Fixed Assets	$1,452,000
Real Estate	N/A
Intangibles	$20,000
Other Noncurrent Assets	$352,000
Total Assets	$8,619,000
Long-term Liabilities	$1,056,000
Total Liabilities	$7,553,000
Stockholder's Equity	$1,066,000

Transaction Data
Date Sale Initiated:	N/A
Date of Sale:	11/1/1996
Days to Sell:	N/A
Asking Price:	N/A
Market Value of Invested Capital*:	$5,350,000
Debt Assumed:	N/A
Employment Agreement Value:	N/A
Noncompete Value:	N/A
Amount of Down Payment:	$4,850,000
Stock or Asset Sale:	Asset
Company Type:	S Corporation
Was there an Employment/Consulting Agreement?	No
Was there an Assumed Lease in the sale?	No
Was there a Renewal Option with the Lease?	No

*Includes noncompete value and interest-bearing debt; excludes real estate, employment/consulting agreement values, and all contingent payments.

Additional Transaction Information
Was there a Note in the consideration paid? Yes
Terms:
Consideration paid: $4,850,000 cash, $500,000 note payable monthly for 5 years at 8.5%.
Assumed Lease (Months): N/A
Noncompete Length (Months): N/A
Employment/Consulting Agreement Description:
Additional Notes:
EBT includes $101,000 Interest Income, $26,000 Other Expenses. Selling Price allocated as follows: $1,900,000 for new cars and parts, $1,100,000 used cars, $2,350,000 other. Inventory stated using LIFO.

Was there a personal guarantee on the Note? No
Terms of Lease: N/A
Noncompete Description: N/A

Valuation Multiples
MVIC/Net Sales	0.17
MVIC/Gross Profit	1.16
MVIC/EBITDA	5.81
MVIC/EBIT	6.72
MVIC/Discretionary Earnings	N/A
MVIC/Book Value of Invested Capital	2.52

Profitability Ratios
Net Profit Margin	0.01
Operating Profit Margin	0.03
Gross Profit Margin	0.14
Return on Assets	0.03
Return on Equity	0.25

Leverage Ratios
Fixed Charge Coverage	1.45
Long-Term Debt to Assets	0.12
Long-Term Debt to Equity	0.99

Earnings
EBITDA	$921,000
Discretionary Earnings	N/A

Liquidity Ratios
Current Ratio	1.05
Quick Ratio	0.31

Activity Ratios
Total Asset Turnover	3.70
Fixed Asset Turnover	21.97
Inventory Turnover	6.69

Copyright © 2010 Business Valuation Resources, LLC. All rights reserved. www.BVResources.com[SM]
(888) BUS-VALU, (503) 291-7963

Pratt's Stats® Auto Dealership Report

Pratt's Stats® Transaction Report
Prepared: 8/20/2010 2:09:43 PM (PST)

Seller Details

Target Name:	Kendall Automotive Group
Business Description:	New and Used Automobiles, Toyota, Kia, Lexus
SIC:	5511 Motor Vehicle Dealers (New and Used)
NAICS:	441110 New Car Dealers
Sale Location:	South Florida, FL, United States
Years in Business:	N/A
Number Employees:	N/A

Source Data

Public Buyer Name:	REPUBLIC INDUSTRIES INC
8-K Date:	3/14/1997
8-K/A Date:	N/A
Other Filing Type:	N/A
Other Filing Date:	N/A
CIK Code:	0000350698

Income Data

Data is "Latest Full Year" Reported	Yes
Data is Restated (see Notes for any explanation)	No
Income Statement Date	10/31/1996
Net Sales	$340,642,210
COGS	$307,494,140
Gross Profit	$33,148,070
Yearly Rent	$257,821
Owner's Compensation	N/A
Other Operating Expenses	$28,428,762
Noncash Charges	$723,650
Total Operating Expenses	$29,410,233
Operating Profit	$3,737,837
Interest Expenses	$1,113,820
EBT	$3,163,757
Taxes	$0
Net Income	$3,163,757

Asset Data

Data is Latest Reported	Yes
Data is "Purchase Price Allocation agreed upon by Buyer and Seller"	No
Balance Sheet Date	10/31/1996
Cash Equivalents	$6,876,561
Trade Receivables	$14,634,782
Inventory	$23,066,290
Other Current Assets	$5,129,665
Total Current Assets	$49,707,298
Fixed Assets	$21,586,597
Real Estate	N/A
Intangibles	N/A
Other Noncurrent Assets	$2,913,824
Total Assets	$74,207,719
Long-term Liabilities	$19,654,433
Total Liabilities	$71,799,291
Stockholder's Equity	$2,408,428

Transaction Data

Date Sale Initiated:	N/A
Date of Sale:	2/28/1997
Days to Sell:	N/A
Asking Price:	N/A
Market Value of Invested Capital*:	$66,000,000
Debt Assumed:	N/A
Employment Agreement Value:	N/A
Noncompete Value:	N/A
Amount of Down Payment:	$66,000,000
Stock or Asset Sale:	Stock
Company Type:	S Corporation
Was there an Employment/Consulting Agreement?	No
Was there an Assumed Lease in the sale?	Yes
Was there a Renewal Option with the Lease?	No

*Includes noncompete value and interest-bearing debt; excludes real estate, employment/consulting agreement values, and all contingent payments.

Additional Transaction Information

Was there a Note in the consideration paid? No
Terms:
Consideration paid: Buyers stock valued at $66,000,000.
Assumed Lease (Months): N/A
Noncompete Length (Months): 60
Employment/Consulting Agreement Description:
Additional Notes:
EBT includes $539,740 Other Income, Income Data for 10 months ended 10/31/96. Inventory stated using LIFO.

Was there a personal guarantee on the Note? No

Terms of Lease: N/A
Noncompete Description: United States

Valuation Multiples

MVIC/Net Sales	0.19
MVIC/Gross Profit	1.99
MVIC/EBITDA	14.79
MVIC/EBIT	17.66
MVIC/Discretionary Earnings	N/A
MVIC/Book Value of Invested Capital	2.99

Profitability Ratios

Net Profit Margin	0.01
Operating Profit Margin	0.01
Gross Profit Margin	0.10
Return on Assets	0.04
Return on Equity	1.31

Leverage Ratios

Fixed Charge Coverage	3.84
Long-Term Debt to Assets	0.26
Long-Term Debt to Equity	8.16

Earnings

EBITDA	$4,461,487
Discretionary Earnings	N/A

Liquidity Ratios

Current Ratio	0.95
Quick Ratio	0.51

Activity Ratios

Total Asset Turnover	4.59
Fixed Asset Turnover	15.78
Inventory Turnover	14.77

Copyright © 2010 Business Valuation Resources, LLC. All rights reserved. www.BVResources.com^SM
(888) BUS-VALU, (503) 291-7963

Pratt's Stats® Auto Dealership Report

Pratt's Stats® Transaction Report
Prepared: 8/20/2010 2:09:43 PM (PST)

Seller Details
Target Name:	Atlanta Toyota, Inc.
Business Description:	New and Used Auto Sales, Toyota
SIC:	5511 Motor Vehicle Dealers (New and Used)
NAICS:	441110 New Car Dealers
Sale Location:	Duluth, GA, United States
Years in Business:	N/A Number Employees: N/A

Source Data
Public Buyer Name:	UNITED AUTO GROUP INC
8-K Date:	N/A
8-K/A Date:	N/A
Other Filing Type:	S-1
Other Filing Date:	8/2/1996
CIK Code:	0001019849

Income Data
Data is "Latest Full Year" Reported	Yes
Data is Restated (see Notes for any explanation)	No
Income Statement Date	12/31/1995
Net Sales	$112,162,000
COGS	$98,969,000
Gross Profit	$13,193,000
Yearly Rent	$1,085,000
Owner's Compensation	N/A
Other Operating Expenses	N/A
Noncash Charges	$215,000
Total Operating Expenses	$11,182,000
Operating Profit	$2,011,000
Interest Expenses	N/A
EBT	$2,028,000
Taxes	$0
Net Income	$2,028,000

Asset Data
Data is Latest Reported	Yes
Data is "Purchase Price Allocation agreed upon by Buyer and Seller"	No
Balance Sheet Date	12/31/1995
Cash Equivalents	$555,000
Trade Receivables	$1,714,000
Inventory	$8,123,000
Other Current Assets	$843,000
Total Current Assets	$11,235,000
Fixed Assets	$1,150,000
Real Estate	N/A
Intangibles	$30,000
Other Noncurrent Assets	$858,000
Total Assets	$13,273,000
Long-term Liabilities	$0
Total Liabilities	$14,439,000
Stockholder's Equity	($1,166,000)

Transaction Data
Date Sale Initiated:	N/A
Date of Sale:	1/16/1996
Days to Sell:	N/A
Asking Price:	N/A
Market Value of Invested Capital*:	$11,500,000
Debt Assumed:	N/A
Employment Agreement Value:	N/A
Noncompete Value:	N/A
Amount of Down Payment:	$9,100,000
Stock or Asset Sale:	Stock
Company Type:	S Corporation
Was there an Employment/Consulting Agreement?	No
Was there an Assumed Lease in the sale?	No
Was there a Renewal Option with the Lease?	No

*Includes noncompete value and interest-bearing debt; excludes real estate, employment/consulting agreement values, and all contingent payments.

Additional Transaction Information
Was there a Note in the consideration paid? No
Terms:
Consideration paid as follows; $9,100,000 cash, $2,400,000 in notes.
Assumed Lease (Months): N/A
Noncompete Length (Months): N/A
Employment/Consulting Agreement Description:
Additional Notes:
EBT includes $17,000 Other Income. Seller sells and services new Toyota and Buick vehicles and used vehicles. Seller is largest Toyota dealer in the Atlanta Metropolitan area and seventh largest in the United States. Inventory stated using LIFO.

Was there a personal guarantee on the Note? No

Terms of Lease: N/A
Noncompete Description: N/A

Valuation Multiples
MVIC/Net Sales	0.10
MVIC/Gross Profit	0.87
MVIC/EBITDA	5.17
MVIC/EBIT	5.72
MVIC/Discretionary Earnings	N/A
MVIC/Book Value of Invested Capital	N/A

Profitability Ratios
Net Profit Margin	0.02
Operating Profit Margin	N/A
Gross Profit Margin	0.12
Return on Assets	0.15
Return on Equity	N/A

Leverage Ratios
Fixed Charge Coverage	N/A
Long-Term Debt to Assets	0.00
Long-Term Debt to Equity	N/A

Earnings
EBITDA	$2,226,000
Discretionary Earnings	N/A

Liquidity Ratios
Current Ratio	0.78
Quick Ratio	0.22

Activity Ratios
Total Asset Turnover	8.45
Fixed Asset Turnover	97.53
Inventory Turnover	13.81

Copyright © 2010 Business Valuation Resources, LLC. All rights reserved. www.BVResources.com℠
(888) BUS-VALU, (503) 291-7963

Pratt's Stats® Auto Dealership Report

Pratt's Stats® Transaction Report
Prepared: 8/20/2010 2:09:43 PM (PST)

Seller Details
Target Name:	Sun Automotive Group
Business Description:	New and Used Auto Sales, Acura, Audi, Aston Martin, BMW, Jaguar, Land Rover, Lexus, Porsche
SIC:	5511 Motor Vehicle Dealers (New and Used)
NAICS:	441110 New Car Dealers
Sale Location:	Phoenix, AZ, United States
Years in Business:	N/A
Number Employees:	N/A

Source Data
Public Buyer Name:	UNITED AUTO GROUP INC
8-K Date:	N/A
8-K/A Date:	N/A
Other Filing Type:	S-1
Other Filing Date:	8/2/1996
CIK Code:	0001019849

Income Data
Data is "Latest Full Year" Reported	Yes
Data is Restated (see Notes for any explanation)	No
Income Statement Date	12/31/1995
Net Sales	$154,502,000
COGS	$133,980,000
Gross Profit	$20,522,000
Yearly Rent	$1,183,000
Owner's Compensation	N/A
Other Operating Expenses	N/A
Noncash Charges	$726,000
Total Operating Expenses	$18,469,000
Operating Profit	$2,053,000
Interest Expenses	N/A
EBT	$2,022,000
Taxes	$0
Net Income	$2,022,000

Asset Data
Data is Latest Reported	Yes
Data is "Purchase Price Allocation agreed upon by Buyer and Seller"	No
Balance Sheet Date	3/31/1996
Cash Equivalents	N/A
Trade Receivables	$7,815,000
Inventory	$18,765,000
Other Current Assets	$29,000
Total Current Assets	$26,609,000
Fixed Assets	$11,335,000
Real Estate	N/A
Intangibles	$1,147,000
Other Noncurrent Assets	$765,000
Total Assets	$39,856,000
Long-term Liabilities	$13,443,000
Total Liabilities	$36,890,000
Stockholder's Equity	$2,966,000

Transaction Data
Date Sale Initiated:	N/A
Date of Sale:	10/28/1996
Days to Sell:	N/A
Asking Price:	N/A
Market Value of Invested Capital*:	$24,666,000
Debt Assumed:	N/A
Employment Agreement Value:	N/A
Noncompete Value:	N/A
Amount of Down Payment:	$24,666,000
Stock or Asset Sale:	Stock
Company Type:	S Corporation
Was there an Employment/Consulting Agreement?	No
Was there an Assumed Lease in the sale?	No
Was there a Renewal Option with the Lease?	No

*Includes noncompete value and interest-bearing debt; excludes real estate, employment/consulting agreement values, and all contingent payments.

Additional Transaction Information
Was there a Note in the consideration paid? No
Was there a personal guarantee on the Note? No
Terms:
Consideration: $24,666,000 in cash. If seller achieves certain levels of pre-tax earnings for the two-year period from 11/1/96 - 10/31/98, purchaser will be obligated for an additional purchase price.
Assumed Lease (Months): 60
Terms of Lease: Present Value of Future Minimum Payments: $10,158,000
Noncompete Length (Months): N/A
Noncompete Description: N/A
Employment/Consulting Agreement Description:
Additional Notes:
EBT includes $(31,000) Other Expenses. Seller operates in the state of Arizona and is engaged in the sale of new and used vehicles, as well as finance, insurance and service contracts thereon. Seller operates dealerships which hold franchise agreements with a number of automotive manufacturers. In accordance with the individual franchise agreement, each dealership is subject to certain rights and restrictions typical of the industry. Inventory stated using LIFO.

Valuation Multiples
MVIC/Net Sales	0.16
MVIC/Gross Profit	1.20
MVIC/EBITDA	8.88
MVIC/EBIT	12.01
MVIC/Discretionary Earnings	N/A
MVIC/Book Value of Invested Capital	1.50

Profitability Ratios
Net Profit Margin	0.01
Operating Profit Margin	N/A
Gross Profit Margin	0.13
Return on Assets	0.05
Return on Equity	0.68

Leverage Ratios
Fixed Charge Coverage	N/A
Long-Term Debt to Assets	0.34
Long-Term Debt to Equity	4.53

Earnings
EBITDA	$2,779,000
Discretionary Earnings	N/A

Liquidity Ratios
Current Ratio	1.13
Quick Ratio	0.33

Activity Ratios
Total Asset Turnover	3.88
Fixed Asset Turnover	13.63
Inventory Turnover	8.23

Copyright © 2010 Business Valuation Resources, LLC. All rights reserved. www.BVResources.com℠
(888) BUS-VALU, (503) 291-7963

Pratt's Stats® Auto Dealership Report

Pratt's Stats® Transaction Report
Prepared: 8/20/2010 2:09:44 PM (PST)

Seller Details
Target Name:	Carlisle Motors, Inc.
Business Description:	Owns and Operates New and Used Automobile Dealerships
SIC:	5511 Motor Vehicle Dealers (New and Used)
NAICS:	441110 New Car Dealers
Sale Location:	FL, United States
Years in Business:	49
Number Employees:	N/A

Source Data
Public Buyer Name:	REPUBLIC INDUSTRIES INC
8-K Date:	1/28/1997
8-K/A Date:	N/A
Other Filing Type:	N/A
Other Filing Date:	N/A
CIK Code:	0000350698

Income Data
Data is "Latest Full Year" Reported	Yes
Data is Restated (see Notes for any explanation)	No
Income Statement Date	11/30/1996
Net Sales	$239,092,799
COGS	$210,021,622
Gross Profit	$29,071,177
Yearly Rent	N/A
Owner's Compensation	N/A
Other Operating Expenses	N/A
Noncash Charges	$1,038,342
Total Operating Expenses	$26,611,245
Operating Profit	$2,459,932
Interest Expenses	$1,714,670
EBT	($370,679)
Taxes	$0
Net Income	($370,679)

Asset Data
Data is Latest Reported	Yes
Data is "Purchase Price Allocation agreed upon by Buyer and Seller"	No
Balance Sheet Date	11/30/1996
Cash Equivalents	$2,892,810
Trade Receivables	$6,027,634
Inventory	$28,434,025
Other Current Assets	$704,671
Total Current Assets	$38,059,140
Fixed Assets	$15,694,494
Real Estate	N/A
Intangibles	$562,376
Other Noncurrent Assets	$1,183,283
Total Assets	$55,499,293
Long-term Liabilities	$11,764,773
Total Liabilities	$55,137,988
Stockholder's Equity	$361,305

Transaction Data
Date Sale Initiated:	N/A
Date of Sale:	1/21/1997
Days to Sell:	N/A
Asking Price:	N/A
Market Value of Invested Capital*:	$35,000,000
Debt Assumed:	N/A
Employment Agreement Value:	N/A
Noncompete Value:	N/A
Amount of Down Payment:	$35,000,000
Stock or Asset Sale:	Asset
Company Type:	S Corporation
Was there an Employment/Consulting Agreement?	No
Was there an Assumed Lease in the sale?	Yes
Was there a Renewal Option with the Lease?	Yes

*Includes noncompete value and interest-bearing debt; excludes real estate, employment/consulting agreement values, and all contingent payments.

Additional Transaction Information
Was there a Note in the consideration paid? No
Terms:
Consideration paid as follows: Cash.
Assumed Lease (Months): 24
Noncompete Length (Months): N/A
Employment/Consulting Agreement Description:

Was there a personal guarantee on the Note? No

Terms of Lease: Future Minimum Lease Payments: $460,052
Noncompete Description: N/A

Additional Notes:
EBT includes $1,336,810 of other income, $238,227 in other expense, $726,000 in management fees, and $1,488,524 in bonus expense. Inventory stated at lower of cost (FIFO) or market. Company owns Ford, Lincoln-Mercury and Hyundai dealerships in St. Petersburg and Clearwater, Florida.

Valuation Multiples
MVIC/Net Sales	0.15
MVIC/Gross Profit	1.20
MVIC/EBITDA	10.00
MVIC/EBIT	14.23
MVIC/Discretionary Earnings	N/A
MVIC/Book Value of Invested Capital	2.89

Profitability Ratios
Net Profit Margin	-0.00
Operating Profit Margin	0.01
Gross Profit Margin	0.12
Return on Assets	-0.01
Return on Equity	-1.03

Leverage Ratios
Fixed Charge Coverage	0.78
Long-Term Debt to Assets	0.21
Long-Term Debt to Equity	32.56

Earnings
EBITDA	$3,498,274
Discretionary Earnings	N/A

Liquidity Ratios
Current Ratio	0.88
Quick Ratio	0.22

Activity Ratios
Total Asset Turnover	4.31
Fixed Asset Turnover	15.23
Inventory Turnover	8.41

Copyright © 2010 Business Valuation Resources, LLC. All rights reserved. www.BVResources.com[SM]
(888) BUS-VALU, (503) 291-7963

Pratt's Stats® Auto Dealership Report

Pratt's Stats® Transaction Report
Prepared: 8/20/2010 2:09:44 PM (PST)

Seller Details
Target Name:	B & B Enterprises Inc.
Business Description:	Auto Dealer, Retail
SIC:	5511 Motor Vehicle Dealers (New and Used)
NAICS:	441110 New Car Dealers
Sale Location:	Stuart, FL, United States
Years in Business:	N/A
Number Employees:	N/A

Source Data
Public Buyer Name:	SMART CHOICE AUTOMOTIVE GROUP INC
8-K Date:	9/15/1997
8-K/A Date:	11/14/1997
Other Filing Type:	N/A
Other Filing Date:	N/A
CIK Code:	0000949091

Income Data
Data is "Latest Full Year" Reported	Yes
Data is Restated (see Notes for any explanation)	No
Income Statement Date	12/31/1996
Net Sales	$24,473,010
COGS	$22,294,117
Gross Profit	$2,178,893
Yearly Rent	N/A
Owner's Compensation	N/A
Other Operating Expenses	N/A
Noncash Charges	$109,465
Total Operating Expenses	$3,278,704
Operating Profit	($942,200)
Interest Expenses	$389,000
EBT	($1,331,200)
Taxes	$0
Net Income	($1,331,200)

Asset Data
Data is Latest Reported	Yes
Data is "Purchase Price Allocation agreed upon by Buyer and Seller"	No
Balance Sheet Date	12/31/1996
Cash Equivalents	$94,628
Trade Receivables	$162,203
Inventory	$2,163,593
Other Current Assets	$11,100
Total Current Assets	$2,431,524
Fixed Assets	$436,641
Real Estate	N/A
Intangibles	N/A
Other Noncurrent Assets	$10,300
Total Assets	$2,878,465
Long-term Liabilities	$50,906
Total Liabilities	$5,407,820
Stockholder's Equity	($2,529,355)

Transaction Data
Date Sale Initiated:	N/A
Date of Sale:	8/29/1997
Days to Sell:	N/A
Asking Price:	N/A
Market Value of Invested Capital*:	$2,977,549
Debt Assumed:	N/A
Employment Agreement Value:	N/A
Noncompete Value:	N/A
Amount of Down Payment:	$2,977,549
Stock or Asset Sale:	Stock
Company Type:	S Corporation
Was there an Employment/Consulting Agreement?	No
Was there an Assumed Lease in the sale?	No
Was there a Renewal Option with the Lease?	No

*Includes noncompete value and interest-bearing debt; excludes real estate, employment/consulting agreement values, and all contingent payments.

Additional Transaction Information
Was there a Note in the consideration paid? No
Terms:
Assumed Lease (Months): N/A
Noncompete Length (Months): N/A
Employment/Consulting Agreement Description:
Additional Notes:
Seller is a Nissan Dealer as well as other consumer vehicles. Operating profit includes $670,147 other income and ($512,536) other expenses.

Was there a personal guarantee on the Note? No
Terms of Lease: N/A
Noncompete Description: N/A

Valuation Multiples
MVIC/Net Sales	0.12
MVIC/Gross Profit	1.37
MVIC/EBITDA	N/A
MVIC/EBIT	N/A
MVIC/Discretionary Earnings	N/A
MVIC/Book Value of Invested Capital	N/A

Profitability Ratios
Net Profit Margin	-0.05
Operating Profit Margin	-0.04
Gross Profit Margin	0.09
Return on Assets	-0.46
Return on Equity	N/A

Leverage Ratios
Fixed Charge Coverage	-2.42
Long-Term Debt to Assets	0.02
Long-Term Debt to Equity	N/A

Earnings
EBITDA	($832,735)
Discretionary Earnings	N/A

Liquidity Ratios
Current Ratio	0.45
Quick Ratio	0.05

Activity Ratios
Total Asset Turnover	8.50
Fixed Asset Turnover	56.05
Inventory Turnover	11.31

Copyright © 2010 Business Valuation Resources, LLC. All rights reserved. www.BVResources.com^{SM}
(888) BUS-VALU, (503) 291-7963

Pratt's Stats® Auto Dealership Report

Pratt's Stats® Transaction Report
Prepared: 8/20/2010 2:09:44 PM (PST)

Seller Details
Target Name:	Spedding Toyota
Business Description:	New and Used Auto Sales, Toyota
SIC:	5511 Motor Vehicle Dealers (New and Used)
NAICS:	441110 New Car Dealers
Sale Location:	United States
Years in Business:	N/A Number Employees: N/A

Source Data
Public Buyer Name:	CROSS CONTINENT AUTO RETAILERS INC M&L
8-K Date:	4/28/1997
8-K/A Date:	6/24/1997
Other Filing Type:	N/A
Other Filing Date:	N/A
CIK Code:	0001016919

Income Data
Data is "Latest Full Year" Reported	Yes
Data is Restated (see Notes for any explanation)	No
Income Statement Date	12/31/1996
Net Sales	$204,983,000
COGS	$169,137,000
Gross Profit	$35,846,000
Yearly Rent	$1,025,262
Owner's Compensation	N/A
Other Operating Expenses	N/A
Noncash Charges	$393,000
Total Operating Expenses	$26,737,000
Operating Profit	$9,109,000
Interest Expenses	$1,849,000
EBT	$7,939,000
Taxes	$0
Net Income	$7,939,000

Asset Data
Data is Latest Reported	Yes
Data is "Purchase Price Allocation agreed upon by Buyer and Seller"	No
Balance Sheet Date	3/31/1997
Cash Equivalents	$7,455,000
Trade Receivables	$7,582,000
Inventory	$18,373,000
Other Current Assets	$156,000
Total Current Assets	$33,566,000
Fixed Assets	$486,000
Real Estate	N/A
Intangibles	N/A
Other Noncurrent Assets	$627,000
Total Assets	$34,679,000
Long-term Liabilities	$3,761,000
Total Liabilities	$31,087,000
Stockholder's Equity	$3,592,000

Transaction Data
Date Sale Initiated:	N/A
Date of Sale:	4/10/1997
Days to Sell:	N/A
Asking Price:	N/A
Market Value of Invested Capital*:	$40,000,000
Debt Assumed:	N/A
Employment Agreement Value:	N/A
Noncompete Value:	N/A
Amount of Down Payment:	$33,000,000
Stock or Asset Sale:	Stock
Company Type:	S Corporation
Was there an Employment/Consulting Agreement?	No
Was there an Assumed Lease in the sale?	No
Was there a Renewal Option with the Lease?	No

*Includes noncompete value and interest-bearing debt; excludes real estate, employment/consulting agreement values, and all contingent payments.

Additional Transaction Information
Was there a Note in the consideration paid? No   Was there a personal guarantee on the Note? No
Terms:
Considerations paid as follows; $28,100,000 cash, 279,720 shares of purchaser's public company common stock and $7,000,000 note payable over 5 years bearing interest at prime.
Assumed Lease (Months): N/A   Terms of Lease: Present Value of Future Minimum Payments: $2,220,000
Noncompete Length (Months): N/A   Noncompete Description: N/A
Employment/Consulting Agreement Description:
Additional Notes:
EBT includes $679,000 Interest Income. Financial statements represent the combined accounts of Douglas Toyota, Inc. and Toyota West Sales and Service, Inc. Seller located in Denver, Colorado and Las Vegas, Nevada. Inventory stated using FIFO.

Valuation Multiples
MVIC/Net Sales	0.20
MVIC/Gross Profit	1.12
MVIC/EBITDA	4.21
MVIC/EBIT	4.39
MVIC/Discretionary Earnings	N/A
MVIC/Book Value of Invested Capital	5.44

Profitability Ratios
Net Profit Margin	0.04
Operating Profit Margin	0.05
Gross Profit Margin	0.17
Return on Assets	0.23
Return on Equity	2.21

Leverage Ratios
Fixed Charge Coverage	5.29
Long-Term Debt to Assets	0.11
Long-Term Debt to Equity	1.05

Earnings
EBITDA	$9,502,000
Discretionary Earnings	N/A

Liquidity Ratios
Current Ratio	1.23
Quick Ratio	0.56

Activity Ratios
Total Asset Turnover	5.91
Fixed Asset Turnover	421.78
Inventory Turnover	11.16

Copyright © 2010 Business Valuation Resources, LLC. All rights reserved. www.BVResources.com^{SM}
(888) BUS-VALU, (503) 291-7963

Pratt's Stats® Auto Dealership Report

Pratt's Stats® Transaction Report
Prepared: 8/20/2010 2:09:44 PM (PST)

Seller Details
Target Name:	Sahara Nissan, Inc.
Business Description:	New and Used Auto Sales, Nissan
SIC:	5511 Motor Vehicle Dealers (New and Used)
NAICS:	441110 New Car Dealers
Sale Location:	Las Vegas, NV, United States
Years in Business:	N/A
Number Employees:	N/A

Source Data
Public Buyer Name:	CROSS CONTINENT AUTO RETAILERS INC M&L
8-K Date:	7/15/1997
8-K/A Date:	8/13/1997
Other Filing Type:	N/A
Other Filing Date:	N/A
CIK Code:	0001016919

Income Data
Data is "Latest Full Year" Reported	Yes
Data is Restated (see Notes for any explanation)	No
Income Statement Date	12/31/1996
Net Sales	$63,736,000
COGS	$53,904,000
Gross Profit	$9,832,000
Yearly Rent	$213,984
Owner's Compensation	N/A
Other Operating Expenses	N/A
Noncash Charges	$151,000
Total Operating Expenses	$6,397,000
Operating Profit	$3,435,000
Interest Expenses	$905,000
EBT	$2,530,000
Taxes	$0
Net Income	$2,530,000

Asset Data
Data is Latest Reported	Yes
Data is "Purchase Price Allocation agreed upon by Buyer and Seller"	No
Balance Sheet Date	3/31/1997
Cash Equivalents	$618,000
Trade Receivables	$2,009,000
Inventory	$9,223,000
Other Current Assets	$11,000
Total Current Assets	$11,861,000
Fixed Assets	$1,615,000
Real Estate	N/A
Intangibles	N/A
Other Noncurrent Assets	$21,000
Total Assets	$13,497,000
Long-term Liabilities	$1,599,000
Total Liabilities	$14,016,000
Stockholder's Equity	($519,000)

Transaction Data
Date Sale Initiated:	N/A
Date of Sale:	7/1/1997
Days to Sell:	N/A
Asking Price:	N/A
Market Value of Invested Capital*:	$12,500,000
Debt Assumed:	N/A
Employment Agreement Value:	N/A
Noncompete Value:	N/A
Amount of Down Payment:	$11,900,000
Stock or Asset Sale:	Stock
Company Type:	S Corporation
Was there an Employment/Consulting Agreement?	No
Was there an Assumed Lease in the sale?	No
Was there a Renewal Option with the Lease?	No

*Includes noncompete value and interest-bearing debt; excludes real estate, employment/consulting agreement values, and all contingent payments.

Additional Transaction Information
Was there a Note in the consideration paid? No
Terms:
Considerations paid as follows: $9,000,000 cash, 125,984 shares of purchaser's public company common stock and $600,000 interest bearing note at prime payable over 5 years.
Assumed Lease (Months): 60
Noncompete Length (Months): N/A
Employment/Consulting Agreement Description:
Additional Notes:
Inventory stated using FIFO.

Was there a personal guarantee on the Note? No

Terms of Lease: Present Value of Future Minimum Payments: $5,064,000
Noncompete Description: N/A

Valuation Multiples
MVIC/Net Sales	0.20
MVIC/Gross Profit	1.27
MVIC/EBITDA	3.49
MVIC/EBIT	3.64
MVIC/Discretionary Earnings	N/A
MVIC/Book Value of Invested Capital	11.57

Profitability Ratios
Net Profit Margin	0.04
Operating Profit Margin	0.05
Gross Profit Margin	0.15
Return on Assets	0.19
Return on Equity	N/A

Leverage Ratios
Fixed Charge Coverage	3.80
Long-Term Debt to Assets	0.12
Long-Term Debt to Equity	N/A

Earnings
EBITDA	$3,586,000
Discretionary Earnings	N/A

Liquidity Ratios
Current Ratio	0.96
Quick Ratio	0.21

Activity Ratios
Total Asset Turnover	4.72
Fixed Asset Turnover	39.47
Inventory Turnover	6.91

Copyright © 2010 Business Valuation Resources, LLC. All rights reserved. www.BVResources.com℠
(888) BUS-VALU, (503) 291-7963

Pratt's Stats® Auto Dealership Report

Pratt's Stats® Transaction Report
Prepared: 8/20/2010 2:09:44 PM (PST)

Seller Details
Target Name:	Ken Marks Ford, Inc.
Business Description:	New and Used Automobile Dealership
SIC:	5511 Motor Vehicle Dealers (New and Used)
NAICS:	441110 New Car Dealers
Sale Location:	Clearwater, FL, United States
Years in Business:	N/A
Number Employees:	N/A

Source Data
Broker Name:	N/A
Broker Firm Name:	N/A

Income Data
Data is "Latest Full Year" Reported	Yes
Data is Restated (see Notes for any explanation)	No
Income Statement Date	4/30/1997
Net Sales	$144,467,067
COGS	$126,870,910
Gross Profit	$17,596,157
Yearly Rent	N/A
Owner's Compensation	N/A
Other Operating Expenses	N/A
Noncash Charges	$100,771
Total Operating Expenses	$15,844,711
Operating Profit	$1,751,446
Interest Expenses	$2,008,408
EBT	$766,327
Taxes	$300,730
Net Income	$465,597

Asset Data
Data is Latest Reported	Yes
Data is "Purchase Price Allocation agreed upon by Buyer and Seller"	No
Balance Sheet Date	4/30/1997
Cash Equivalents	$3,898,793
Trade Receivables	$1,056,650
Inventory	$11,216,499
Other Current Assets	$356,133
Total Current Assets	$16,528,075
Fixed Assets	$470,738
Real Estate	N/A
Intangibles	$14,000
Other Noncurrent Assets	N/A
Total Assets	$17,012,813
Long-term Liabilities	N/A
Total Liabilities	N/A
Stockholder's Equity	N/A

Transaction Data
Date Sale Initiated:	N/A
Date of Sale:	7/1/1997
Days to Sell:	N/A
Asking Price:	N/A
Market Value of Invested Capital*:	$25,500,000
Debt Assumed:	N/A
Employment Agreement Value:	N/A
Noncompete Value:	N/A
Amount of Down Payment:	$25,500,000
Stock or Asset Sale:	Stock
Company Type:	C Corporation
Was there an Employment/Consulting Agreement?	No
Was there an Assumed Lease in the sale?	No
Was there a Renewal Option with the Lease?	No

*Includes noncompete value and interest-bearing debt; excludes real estate, employment/consulting agreement values, and all contingent payments.

Additional Transaction Information
Was there a Note in the consideration paid? No
Terms:
Consideration paid in cash.
Assumed Lease (Months): N/A
Noncompete Length (Months): N/A
Employment/Consulting Agreement Description:
Additional Notes:
EBT includes $1,023,289 in other income. Inventory stated at lower of cost (LIFO) or market. Company operates Ford dealership in Clearwater, Florida.

Was there a personal guarantee on the Note? No

Terms of Lease: N/A
Noncompete Description: N/A

Valuation Multiples
MVIC/Net Sales	0.18
MVIC/Gross Profit	1.45
MVIC/EBITDA	13.77
MVIC/EBIT	14.56
MVIC/Discretionary Earnings	N/A
MVIC/Book Value of Invested Capital	N/A

Profitability Ratios
Net Profit Margin	0.00
Operating Profit Margin	0.02
Gross Profit Margin	0.12
Return on Assets	0.03
Return on Equity	N/A

Leverage Ratios
Fixed Charge Coverage	1.38
Long-Term Debt to Assets	N/A
Long-Term Debt to Equity	N/A

Earnings
EBITDA	$1,852,217
Discretionary Earnings	N/A

Liquidity Ratios
Current Ratio	N/A
Quick Ratio	N/A

Activity Ratios
Total Asset Turnover	8.49
Fixed Asset Turnover	306.89
Inventory Turnover	12.88

Copyright © 2010 Business Valuation Resources, LLC. All rights reserved. www.BVResources.com[SM]
(888) BUS-VALU, (503) 291-7963

Pratt's Stats® Auto Dealership Report

Pratt's Stats® Transaction Report
Prepared: 8/20/2010 2:09:44 PM (PST)

Seller Details
Target Name:	Wallace Automotive Group
Business Description:	New and Used Auto Sales, Ford, Nissan, Dodge, Lincoln-Mercury, Mitsubishi
SIC:	5511 Motor Vehicle Dealers (New and Used)
NAICS:	441110 New Car Dealers
Sale Location:	South Florida, FL, United States
Years in Business:	N/A
Number Employees:	N/A

Source Data
Public Buyer Name:	REPUBLIC INDUSTRIES INC
8-K Date:	3/14/1997
8-K/A Date:	N/A
Other Filing Type:	N/A
Other Filing Date:	N/A
CIK Code:	0000350698

Income Data
Data is "Latest Full Year" Reported	Yes
Data is Restated (see Notes for any explanation)	No
Income Statement Date	12/31/1996
Net Sales	$282,263,000
COGS	$252,810,000
Gross Profit	$29,453,000
Yearly Rent	N/A
Owner's Compensation	N/A
Other Operating Expenses	N/A
Noncash Charges	$1,910,000
Total Operating Expenses	$29,812,000
Operating Profit	$4,390,000
Interest Expenses	$2,467,000
EBT	$3,553,000
Taxes	$110,000
Net Income	$3,443,000

Asset Data
Data is Latest Reported	Yes
Data is "Purchase Price Allocation agreed upon by Buyer and Seller"	No
Balance Sheet Date	12/31/1996
Cash Equivalents	$7,351,000
Trade Receivables	$7,483,000
Inventory	$39,076,000
Other Current Assets	$8,797,000
Total Current Assets	$62,707,000
Fixed Assets	$29,808,000
Real Estate	N/A
Intangibles	$7,806,000
Other Noncurrent Assets	$376,000
Total Assets	$100,697,000
Long-term Liabilities	$28,446,000
Total Liabilities	$92,448,000
Stockholder's Equity	$8,249,000

Transaction Data
Date Sale Initiated:	N/A
Date of Sale:	2/28/1997
Days to Sell:	N/A
Asking Price:	N/A
Market Value of Invested Capital*:	$55,000,000
Debt Assumed:	N/A
Employment Agreement Value:	N/A
Noncompete Value:	N/A
Amount of Down Payment:	$55,000,000
Stock or Asset Sale:	Stock
Company Type:	S Corporation
Was there an Employment/Consulting Agreement?	Yes
Was there an Assumed Lease in the sale?	Yes
Was there a Renewal Option with the Lease?	No

*Includes noncompete value and interest-bearing debt; excludes real estate, employment/consulting agreement values, and all contingent payments.

Additional Transaction Information
Was there a Note in the consideration paid? No
Terms:
Consideration paid: purchaser's stock valued at $55,000,000.
Assumed Lease (Months): N/A
Noncompete Length (Months): 60
Employment/Consulting Agreement Description:
Additional Notes:
Operating Profit includes $4,749,000 in non-selling income. EBT includes $230,000 Investment Income; $739,000 Gain on Sale, $661,000 Other Income. Auto inventory stated using LIFO, parts inventory stated using FIFO.

Was there a personal guarantee on the Note? No
Terms of Lease: N/A
Noncompete Description: United States

Valuation Multiples
MVIC/Net Sales	0.19
MVIC/Gross Profit	1.87
MVIC/EBITDA	8.73
MVIC/EBIT	12.53
MVIC/Discretionary Earnings	N/A
MVIC/Book Value of Invested Capital	1.50

Profitability Ratios
Net Profit Margin	0.01
Operating Profit Margin	0.02
Gross Profit Margin	0.10
Return on Assets	0.03
Return on Equity	0.42

Leverage Ratios
Fixed Charge Coverage	2.44
Long-Term Debt to Assets	0.28
Long-Term Debt to Equity	3.45

Earnings
EBITDA	$6,300,000
Discretionary Earnings	N/A

Liquidity Ratios
Current Ratio	0.98
Quick Ratio	0.37

Activity Ratios
Total Asset Turnover	2.80
Fixed Asset Turnover	9.47
Inventory Turnover	7.22

Copyright © 2010 Business Valuation Resources, LLC. All rights reserved. www.BVResources.com℠
(888) BUS-VALU, (503) 291-7963

Pratt's Stats® Auto Dealership Report

Pratt's Stats® Transaction Report
Prepared: 8/20/2010 2:09:44 PM (PST)

Seller Details
Target Name:	Peachtree Nissan (formerly Hickman Nissan, Inc.)
Business Description:	New and Used Auto Sales, Nissan
SIC:	5511 Motor Vehicle Dealers (New and Used)
NAICS:	441110 New Car Dealers
Sale Location:	Chamblee, GA, United States
Years in Business:	N/A Number Employees: N/A

Source Data
Public Buyer Name:	UNITED AUTO GROUP INC
8-K Date:	N/A
8-K/A Date:	N/A
Other Filing Type:	S-1
Other Filing Date:	8/2/1996
CIK Code:	0001019849

Income Data
Data is "Latest Full Year" Reported	Yes
Data is Restated (see Notes for any explanation)	No
Income Statement Date	12/31/1995
Net Sales	$85,336,000
COGS	$76,588,000
Gross Profit	$8,748,000
Yearly Rent	$408,000
Owner's Compensation	N/A
Other Operating Expenses	N/A
Noncash Charges	$212,000
Total Operating Expenses	$7,619,000
Operating Profit	$1,129,000
Interest Expenses	N/A
EBT	$968,000
Taxes	$0
Net Income	$968,000

Asset Data
Data is Latest Reported	Yes
Data is "Purchase Price Allocation agreed upon by Buyer and Seller"	No
Balance Sheet Date	3/31/1996
Cash Equivalents	$1,683,000
Trade Receivables	$1,984,000
Inventory	$7,818,000
Other Current Assets	$136,000
Total Current Assets	$11,621,000
Fixed Assets	$506,000
Real Estate	N/A
Intangibles	N/A
Other Noncurrent Assets	$61,000
Total Assets	$12,188,000
Long-term Liabilities	$53,000
Total Liabilities	$10,616,000
Stockholder's Equity	$1,572,000

Transaction Data
Date Sale Initiated:	N/A
Date of Sale:	7/12/1996
Days to Sell:	N/A
Asking Price:	N/A
Market Value of Invested Capital*:	$13,000,000
Debt Assumed:	N/A
Employment Agreement Value:	N/A
Noncompete Value:	N/A
Amount of Down Payment:	$11,000,000
Stock or Asset Sale:	Stock
Company Type:	S Corporation
Was there an Employment/Consulting Agreement?	No
Was there an Assumed Lease in the sale?	No
Was there a Renewal Option with the Lease?	No

*Includes noncompete value and interest-bearing debt; excludes real estate, employment/consulting agreement values, and all contingent payments.

Additional Transaction Information
Was there a Note in the consideration paid? No
Terms:
Considerations paid as follows; $11,000,000 cash, $2,000,000 notes
Assumed Lease (Months): 60
Noncompete Length (Months): N/A
Employment/Consulting Agreement Description:
Additional Notes:
EBT includes $(161,000) Other Expenses. Inventory stated using LIFO.

Was there a personal guarantee on the Note? No

Terms of Lease: Present Value of Future Minimum Payments: $8,713,000
Noncompete Description: N/A

Valuation Multiples
MVIC/Net Sales	0.15
MVIC/Gross Profit	1.49
MVIC/EBITDA	9.69
MVIC/EBIT	11.51
MVIC/Discretionary Earnings	N/A
MVIC/Book Value of Invested Capital	8.00

Profitability Ratios
Net Profit Margin	0.01
Operating Profit Margin	N/A
Gross Profit Margin	0.10
Return on Assets	0.08
Return on Equity	0.62

Leverage Ratios
Fixed Charge Coverage	N/A
Long-Term Debt to Assets	0.00
Long-Term Debt to Equity	0.03

Earnings
EBITDA	$1,341,000
Discretionary Earnings	N/A

Liquidity Ratios
Current Ratio	1.10
Quick Ratio	0.36

Activity Ratios
Total Asset Turnover	7.00
Fixed Asset Turnover	168.65
Inventory Turnover	10.92

Copyright © 2010 Business Valuation Resources, LLC. All rights reserved. www.BVResources.com℠
(888) BUS-VALU, (503) 291-7963

Pratt's Stats® Auto Dealership Report

Pratt's Stats® Transaction Report
Prepared: 8/20/2010 2:09:44 PM (PST)

Seller Details
Target Name:	N/A
Business Description:	Retail Automobile Dealership, Chevrolet and Pontiac
SIC:	5511 Motor Vehicle Dealers (New and Used)
NAICS:	441110 New Car Dealers
Sale Location:	Middletown, MD, United States
Years in Business:	87
Number Employees:	15

Source Data
Broker Name:	Gregory, Edmond B.
Broker Firm Name:	Linton, Shater, & Company

Income Data
Data is "Latest Full Year" Reported	Yes
Data is Restated (see Notes for any explanation)	No
Income Statement Date	12/31/1998
Net Sales	$4,024,311
COGS	$3,376,423
Gross Profit	$647,888
Yearly Rent	N/A
Owner's Compensation	$45,000
Other Operating Expenses	$611,474
Noncash Charges	$25,300
Total Operating Expenses	$681,774
Operating Profit	($33,886)
Interest Expenses	$0
EBT	($33,886)
Taxes	$0
Net Income	($33,886)

Asset Data
Data is Latest Reported	Yes
Data is "Purchase Price Allocation agreed upon by Buyer and Seller"	No
Balance Sheet Date	12/31/1998
Cash Equivalents	$196,525
Trade Receivables	$24,353
Inventory	$394,123
Other Current Assets	$24,024
Total Current Assets	$639,025
Fixed Assets	$21,869
Real Estate	$128,377
Intangibles	N/A
Other Noncurrent Assets	N/A
Total Assets	$789,271
Long-term Liabilities	N/A
Total Liabilities	N/A
Stockholder's Equity	N/A

Transaction Data
Date Sale Initiated:	9/15/1998
Date of Sale:	1/15/1999
Days to Sell:	122
Asking Price:	$1,530,000
Market Value of Invested Capital*:	$1,114,506
Debt Assumed:	$0
Employment Agreement Value:	N/A
Noncompete Value:	$337,000
Amount of Down Payment:	$1,114,506
Stock or Asset Sale:	Asset
Company Type:	C Corporation
Was there an Employment/Consulting Agreement?	No
Was there an Assumed Lease in the sale?	No
Was there a Renewal Option with the Lease?	No

*Includes noncompete value and interest-bearing debt; excludes real estate, employment/consulting agreement values, and all contingent payments.

Additional Transaction Information
Was there a Note in the consideration paid? No
Terms:
Consideration: $1,114,506 cash.
Assumed Lease (Months): 36
Noncompete Length (Months): 60
Employment/Consulting Agreement Description:

Was there a personal guarantee on the Note? No

Terms of Lease: Triple Net $5,500 per month, option contract
Noncompete Description: 25 miles

Additional Notes:
Original asking price included real estate and a stock sale. Final Deal was sale of assets only including $412,000 Blue Sky. Seller retained real estate and leased it to the purchaser. Seller retained all liabilities.

Valuation Multiples
MVIC/Net Sales	0.28
MVIC/Gross Profit	1.72
MVIC/EBITDA	N/A
MVIC/EBIT	N/A
MVIC/Discretionary Earnings	30.61
MVIC/Book Value of Invested Capital	N/A

Profitability Ratios
Net Profit Margin	-0.01
Operating Profit Margin	-0.01
Gross Profit Margin	0.16
Return on Assets	-0.04
Return on Equity	N/A

Leverage Ratios
Fixed Charge Coverage	N/A
Long-Term Debt to Assets	N/A
Long-Term Debt to Equity	N/A

Earnings
EBITDA	($8,586)
Discretionary Earnings	$36,414

Liquidity Ratios
Current Ratio	N/A
Quick Ratio	N/A

Activity Ratios
Total Asset Turnover	5.10
Fixed Asset Turnover	184.02
Inventory Turnover	10.21

Copyright © 2010 Business Valuation Resources, LLC. All rights reserved. www.BVResources.com℠
(888) BUS-VALU, (503) 291-7963

Pratt's Stats® Auto Dealership Report

Pratt's Stats® Transaction Report
Prepared: 8/20/2010 2:09:44 PM (PST)

Seller Details
Target Name:	Bowers Dealerships
Business Description:	Owns and Operates Automobile Dealership
SIC:	5511 Motor Vehicle Dealers (New and Used)
NAICS:	441110 New Car Dealers
Sale Location:	Chattanooga, TN, United States
Years in Business:	N/A
Number Employees:	N/A

Source Data
Broker Name:	N/A
Broker Firm Name:	N/A

Income Data
Data is "Latest Full Year" Reported	Yes
Data is Restated (see Notes for any explanation)	No
Income Statement Date	12/31/1996
Net Sales	$127,115,799
COGS	$109,372,977
Gross Profit	$17,742,822
Yearly Rent	$762,725
Owner's Compensation	N/A
Other Operating Expenses	N/A
Noncash Charges	$514,915
Total Operating Expenses	$15,401,526
Operating Profit	$2,341,296
Interest Expenses	$1,668,081
EBT	$830,658
Taxes	$60,850
Net Income	$769,808

Asset Data
Data is Latest Reported	Yes
Data is "Purchase Price Allocation agreed upon by Buyer and Seller"	No
Balance Sheet Date	6/30/1997
Cash Equivalents	$5,797,307
Trade Receivables	$3,398,335
Inventory	$34,070,935
Other Current Assets	$2,452,831
Total Current Assets	$45,719,408
Fixed Assets	$8,744,225
Real Estate	N/A
Intangibles	$8,285,460
Other Noncurrent Assets	$257,465
Total Assets	$63,006,557
Long-term Liabilities	N/A
Total Liabilities	N/A
Stockholder's Equity	N/A

Transaction Data
Date Sale Initiated:	N/A
Date of Sale:	10/1/1997
Days to Sell:	N/A
Asking Price:	N/A
Market Value of Invested Capital*:	$33,500,000
Debt Assumed:	N/A
Employment Agreement Value:	N/A
Noncompete Value:	N/A
Amount of Down Payment:	$33,500,000
Stock or Asset Sale:	Asset
Company Type:	LLP
Was there an Employment/Consulting Agreement?	No
Was there an Assumed Lease in the sale?	Yes
Was there a Renewal Option with the Lease?	No

*Includes noncompete value and interest-bearing debt; excludes real estate, employment/consulting agreement values, and all contingent payments.

Additional Transaction Information
Was there a Note in the consideration paid? Yes
Terms:
Consideration paid as follows: $28,500,000 in cash and $5,000,000 note payable.
Assumed Lease (Months): N/A
Noncompete Length (Months): N/A
Employment/Consulting Agreement Description:
Additional Notes:
EBT includes other income of $157,443. Inventory stated at lower of cost (FIFO) or market. Company operates nine dealerships in Chattanooga and Nashville, TN. Company sells BMW, Chrysler, Ford, Honda, Infiniti, Jaguar, Saturn, Volkswagon, and Dodge.

Was there a personal guarantee on the Note? No

Terms of Lease: Future Minimum Lease Payments: $7,225,684
Noncompete Description: N/A

Valuation Multiples
MVIC/Net Sales	0.26
MVIC/Gross Profit	1.89
MVIC/EBITDA	11.73
MVIC/EBIT	14.31
MVIC/Discretionary Earnings	N/A
MVIC/Book Value of Invested Capital	N/A

Profitability Ratios
Net Profit Margin	0.01
Operating Profit Margin	0.02
Gross Profit Margin	0.14
Return on Assets	0.01
Return on Equity	N/A

Leverage Ratios
Fixed Charge Coverage	1.50
Long-Term Debt to Assets	N/A
Long-Term Debt to Equity	N/A

Earnings
EBITDA	$2,856,211
Discretionary Earnings	N/A

Liquidity Ratios
Current Ratio	N/A
Quick Ratio	N/A

Activity Ratios
Total Asset Turnover	2.02
Fixed Asset Turnover	14.54
Inventory Turnover	3.73

Copyright © 2010 Business Valuation Resources, LLC. All rights reserved. www.BVResources.com[SM]
(888) BUS-VALU, (503) 291-7963

Pratt's Stats® Auto Dealership Report

Pratt's Stats® Transaction Report
Prepared: 8/20/2010 2:09:44 PM (PST)

Seller Details
Target Name:	Emich Automotive Group
Business Description:	Owns and Operates New and Used Auto Dealerships
SIC:	5511 Motor Vehicle Dealers (New and Used)
NAICS:	441110 New Car Dealers
Sale Location:	Denver, CO, United States
Years in Business:	N/A
Number Employees:	N/A

Source Data
Public Buyer Name:	REPUBLIC INDUSTRIES INC
8-K Date:	2/20/1998
8-K/A Date:	N/A
Other Filing Type:	N/A
Other Filing Date:	N/A
CIK Code:	0000350698

Income Data
Data is "Latest Full Year" Reported	Yes
Data is Restated (see Notes for any explanation)	No
Income Statement Date	12/31/1996
Net Sales	$309,933,005
COGS	$269,683,343
Gross Profit	$40,249,662
Yearly Rent	$2,296,245
Owner's Compensation	N/A
Other Operating Expenses	N/A
Noncash Charges	$491,995
Total Operating Expenses	$36,427,172
Operating Profit	$3,822,490
Interest Expenses	$321,250
EBT	$3,501,240
Taxes	$0
Net Income	$3,501,240

Asset Data
Data is Latest Reported	Yes
Data is "Purchase Price Allocation agreed upon by Buyer and Seller"	No
Balance Sheet Date	9/30/1997
Cash Equivalents	$12,156,183
Trade Receivables	$11,848,205
Inventory	$32,120,069
Other Current Assets	$386,671
Total Current Assets	$56,511,128
Fixed Assets	$2,181,607
Real Estate	$82,354
Intangibles	$160,414
Other Noncurrent Assets	$389,877
Total Assets	$59,325,380
Long-term Liabilities	$446,139
Total Liabilities	$40,788,977
Stockholder's Equity	$18,536,403

Transaction Data
Date Sale Initiated:	N/A
Date of Sale:	10/1/1997
Days to Sell:	N/A
Asking Price:	N/A
Market Value of Invested Capital*:	$54,000,000
Debt Assumed:	N/A
Employment Agreement Value:	N/A
Noncompete Value:	N/A
Amount of Down Payment:	$54,000,000
Stock or Asset Sale:	Asset
Company Type:	S Corporation
Was there an Employment/Consulting Agreement?	No
Was there an Assumed Lease in the sale?	Yes
Was there a Renewal Option with the Lease?	Yes

*Includes noncompete value and interest-bearing debt; excludes real estate, employment/consulting agreement values, and all contingent payments.

Additional Transaction Information
Was there a Note in the consideration paid? No
Was there a personal guarantee on the Note? No
Terms:
Consideration paid as follows: Buyer's public company common stock valued at $54,000,000.
Assumed Lease (Months): 36
Terms of Lease: Future Minimum Lease Payments: $2,840,394
Noncompete Length (Months): N/A
Noncompete Description: N/A
Employment/Consulting Agreement Description:
Additional Notes:
Inventory stated at lower of cost (LIFO) or market. Interest expense is net of dealer wholesale account earnings. Company operates Oldsmobile, Jeep, Dodge, Lincoln-Mercury, Subaru, and Chrysler dealership. 8/2003 – Based on public company SEC filing documentation, it can not be determined if the private company seller transferred the listed real estate or its fair market value.

Valuation Multiples
MVIC/Net Sales	0.17
MVIC/Gross Profit	1.34
MVIC/EBITDA	12.52
MVIC/EBIT	14.13
MVIC/Discretionary Earnings	N/A
MVIC/Book Value of Invested Capital	2.84

Profitability Ratios
Net Profit Margin	0.01
Operating Profit Margin	0.01
Gross Profit Margin	0.13
Return on Assets	0.06
Return on Equity	0.19

Leverage Ratios
Fixed Charge Coverage	11.90
Long-Term Debt to Assets	0.01
Long-Term Debt to Equity	0.02

Earnings
EBITDA	$4,314,485
Discretionary Earnings	N/A

Liquidity Ratios
Current Ratio	1.40
Quick Ratio	0.60

Activity Ratios
Total Asset Turnover	5.22
Fixed Asset Turnover	142.07
Inventory Turnover	9.65

Copyright © 2010 Business Valuation Resources, LLC. All rights reserved. www.BVResources.com℠
(888) BUS-VALU, (503) 291-7963

Pratt's Stats® Auto Dealership Report

Pratt's Stats® Transaction Report
Prepared: 8/20/2010 2:09:44 PM (PST)

Seller Details
Target Name:	Gene Reed Automotive Group
Business Description:	Auto Dealers
SIC:	5511 Motor Vehicle Dealers (New and Used)
NAICS:	441110 New Car Dealers
Sale Location:	United States
Years in Business:	N/A
Number Employees:	N/A

Source Data
Public Buyer Name:	UNITED AUTO GROUP INC
8-K Date:	10/31/1997
8-K/A Date:	N/A
Other Filing Type:	N/A
Other Filing Date:	N/A
CIK Code:	0001019849

Income Data
Data is "Latest Full Year" Reported	Yes
Data is Restated (see Notes for any explanation)	No
Income Statement Date	12/31/1996
Net Sales	$138,040,000
COGS	$115,570,000
Gross Profit	$22,470,000
Yearly Rent	$1,224,000
Owner's Compensation	N/A
Other Operating Expenses	N/A
Noncash Charges	$481,000
Total Operating Expenses	$17,284,000
Operating Profit	$5,186,000
Interest Expenses	$455,000
EBT	$4,731,000
Taxes	$0
Net Income	$4,731,000

Asset Data
Data is Latest Reported	Yes
Data is "Purchase Price Allocation agreed upon by Buyer and Seller"	No
Balance Sheet Date	12/31/1996
Cash Equivalents	$7,166,000
Trade Receivables	$3,805,000
Inventory	$14,466,000
Other Current Assets	$350,000
Total Current Assets	$25,787,000
Fixed Assets	$1,140,000
Real Estate	N/A
Intangibles	N/A
Other Noncurrent Assets	$383,000
Total Assets	$27,310,000
Long-term Liabilities	$1,452,000
Total Liabilities	$26,520,000
Stockholder's Equity	$790,000

Transaction Data
Date Sale Initiated:	N/A
Date of Sale:	5/31/1997
Days to Sell:	N/A
Asking Price:	N/A
Market Value of Invested Capital*:	$34,000,000
Debt Assumed:	N/A
Employment Agreement Value:	N/A
Noncompete Value:	N/A
Amount of Down Payment:	$34,000,000
Stock or Asset Sale:	Stock
Company Type:	S Corporation
Was there an Employment/Consulting Agreement?	No
Was there an Assumed Lease in the sale?	No
Was there a Renewal Option with the Lease?	No

*Includes noncompete value and interest-bearing debt; excludes real estate, employment/consulting agreement values, and all contingent payments.

Additional Transaction Information

Was there a Note in the consideration paid? No
Terms:
Assumed Lease (Months): N/A
Noncompete Length (Months): N/A
Employment/Consulting Agreement Description:
Additional Notes:
Seller consists of 3 GM dealerships in NC and SC. Net sales consist of 82% vehicle sales, 12% service and parts and 6% financing and insurance. Inventory stated using LIFO.

Was there a personal guarantee on the Note? No

Terms of Lease: Minimum rental payments of $10,229,000 through 2002 and beyond.
Noncompete Description: N/A

Valuation Multiples
MVIC/Net Sales	0.25
MVIC/Gross Profit	1.51
MVIC/EBITDA	6.00
MVIC/EBIT	6.56
MVIC/Discretionary Earnings	N/A
MVIC/Book Value of Invested Capital	15.17

Profitability Ratios
Net Profit Margin	0.03
Operating Profit Margin	0.04
Gross Profit Margin	0.16
Return on Assets	0.17
Return on Equity	5.99

Leverage Ratios
Fixed Charge Coverage	11.40
Long-Term Debt to Assets	0.05
Long-Term Debt to Equity	1.84

Earnings
EBITDA	$5,667,000
Discretionary Earnings	N/A

Liquidity Ratios
Current Ratio	1.03
Quick Ratio	0.45

Activity Ratios
Total Asset Turnover	5.05
Fixed Asset Turnover	121.09
Inventory Turnover	9.54

Copyright © 2010 Business Valuation Resources, LLC. All rights reserved. www.BVResources.com℠
(888) BUS-VALU, (503) 291-7963

Pratt's Stats® Auto Dealership Report

Pratt's Stats® Transaction Report
Prepared: 8/20/2010 2:09:44 PM (PST)

Seller Details
Target Name:	Staluppi Group
Business Description:	Auto Dealers
SIC:	5511 Motor Vehicle Dealers (New and Used)
NAICS:	441110 New Car Dealers
Sale Location:	United States
Years in Business:	N/A
Number Employees:	N/A

Source Data
Public Buyer Name:	UNITED AUTO GROUP INC
8-K Date:	5/15/1997
8-K/A Date:	7/14/1997
Other Filing Type:	N/A
Other Filing Date:	N/A
CIK Code:	0001019849

Income Data
Data is "Latest Full Year" Reported	Yes
Data is Restated (see Notes for any explanation)	No
Income Statement Date	12/31/1996
Net Sales	$425,621,000
COGS	$377,556,000
Gross Profit	$48,065,000
Yearly Rent	$3,511,000
Owner's Compensation	N/A
Other Operating Expenses	N/A
Noncash Charges	$893,000
Total Operating Expenses	$41,517,000
Operating Profit	$6,548,000
Interest Expenses	$633,000
EBT	$7,049,000
Taxes	$0
Net Income	$7,049,000

Asset Data
Data is Latest Reported	Yes
Data is "Purchase Price Allocation agreed upon by Buyer and Seller"	No
Balance Sheet Date	12/31/1996
Cash Equivalents	$2,206,000
Trade Receivables	$12,991,000
Inventory	$47,489,000
Other Current Assets	$8,927,000
Total Current Assets	$71,613,000
Fixed Assets	$4,367,000
Real Estate	N/A
Intangibles	$3,177,000
Other Noncurrent Assets	$185,000
Total Assets	$79,342,000
Long-term Liabilities	$3,393,000
Total Liabilities	$66,801,000
Stockholder's Equity	$12,541,000

Transaction Data
Date Sale Initiated:	N/A
Date of Sale:	4/30/1997
Days to Sell:	N/A
Asking Price:	N/A
Market Value of Invested Capital*:	$47,000,000
Debt Assumed:	N/A
Employment Agreement Value:	N/A
Noncompete Value:	N/A
Amount of Down Payment:	$47,000,000
Stock or Asset Sale:	Stock
Company Type:	S Corporation
Was there an Employment/Consulting Agreement?	No
Was there an Assumed Lease in the sale?	No
Was there a Renewal Option with the Lease?	No

*Includes noncompete value and interest-bearing debt; excludes real estate, employment/consulting agreement values, and all contingent payments.

Additional Transaction Information

Was there a Note in the consideration paid? No
Was there a personal guarantee on the Note? No

Terms:
Consideration: $25,000,000 in cash, $22,000,000 in the buyer's public company common stock and a $3,000,000 additional contingent payment.

Assumed Lease (Months): N/A
Terms of Lease: Minimum payments of $19,630,000 through 2002 and beyond

Noncompete Length (Months): N/A
Noncompete Description: N/A

Employment/Consulting Agreement Description:

Additional Notes:
Dealerships consist of 2 Nissan Dealers and 2 Toyota Dealers in New York, 1 Chrysler-Plymouth, 1 Infinity, 1 Jeep-Eagle, 1 Nissan, 1 Toyota in West Palm Beach, Florida. Seller consists of 9 dealerships located in West Palm Beach Florida and Long Island New York. Net sales breakdown: 90% vehicle sales, 8% service and parts and 2% financing and insurance. EBT includes $471,000 interest income and $663,000 other income. Seller operates the following dealerships: 3 Toyota, 3 Nissan, 1 Infiniti and 1 Chrysler-Plymouth dealerships. Inventory stated using LIFO.

Valuation Multiples
MVIC/Net Sales	0.11
MVIC/Gross Profit	0.98
MVIC/EBITDA	6.32
MVIC/EBIT	7.18
MVIC/Discretionary Earnings	N/A
MVIC/Book Value of Invested Capital	2.95

Profitability Ratios
Net Profit Margin	0.02
Operating Profit Margin	0.02
Gross Profit Margin	0.11
Return on Assets	0.09
Return on Equity	0.56

Leverage Ratios
Fixed Charge Coverage	12.14
Long-Term Debt to Assets	0.04
Long-Term Debt to Equity	0.27

Earnings
EBITDA	$7,441,000
Discretionary Earnings	N/A

Liquidity Ratios
Current Ratio	1.13
Quick Ratio	0.38

Activity Ratios
Total Asset Turnover	5.36
Fixed Asset Turnover	97.46
Inventory Turnover	8.96

Copyright © 2010 Business Valuation Resources, LLC. All rights reserved. www.BVResources.com℠
(888) BUS-VALU, (503) 291-7963

Pratt's Stats® Auto Dealership Report

Pratt's Stats® Transaction Report
Prepared: 8/20/2010 2:09:44 PM (PST)

Seller Details
Target Name:	Evans Automotive Group
Business Description:	New and Used Auto Sales, BMW, Nissan
SIC:	5511 Motor Vehicle Dealers (New and Used)
NAICS:	441110 New Car Dealers
Sale Location:	Duluth, GA, United States
Years in Business:	N/A Number Employees: N/A

Source Data
Public Buyer Name:	UNITED AUTO GROUP INC
8-K Date:	N/A
8-K/A Date:	N/A
Other Filing Type:	S-1/A
Other Filing Date:	9/13/1996
CIK Code:	0001019849

Income Data
Data is "Latest Full Year" Reported	Yes
Data is Restated (see Notes for any explanation)	No
Income Statement Date	12/31/1995
Net Sales	$81,669,000
COGS	$72,459,000
Gross Profit	$9,210,000
Yearly Rent	$504,000
Owner's Compensation	N/A
Other Operating Expenses	N/A
Noncash Charges	$90,000
Total Operating Expenses	$7,842,000
Operating Profit	$1,368,000
Interest Expenses	N/A
EBT	$1,334,000
Taxes	$457,000
Net Income	$877,000

Asset Data
Data is Latest Reported	Yes
Data is "Purchase Price Allocation agreed upon by Buyer and Seller"	No
Balance Sheet Date	6/30/1996
Cash Equivalents	$701,000
Trade Receivables	$5,812,000
Inventory	$8,927,000
Other Current Assets	$81,000
Total Current Assets	$15,521,000
Fixed Assets	$335,000
Real Estate	N/A
Intangibles	N/A
Other Noncurrent Assets	$731,000
Total Assets	$16,587,000
Long-term Liabilities	$95,000
Total Liabilities	$12,646,000
Stockholder's Equity	$3,941,000

Transaction Data
Date Sale Initiated:	N/A
Date of Sale:	8/5/1996
Days to Sell:	N/A
Asking Price:	N/A
Market Value of Invested Capital*:	$12,000,000
Debt Assumed:	N/A
Employment Agreement Value:	N/A
Noncompete Value:	N/A
Amount of Down Payment:	$12,000,000
Stock or Asset Sale:	Stock
Company Type:	C Corporation
Was there an Employment/Consulting Agreement?	No
Was there an Assumed Lease in the sale?	No
Was there a Renewal Option with the Lease?	No

*Includes noncompete value and interest-bearing debt; excludes real estate, employment/consulting agreement values, and all contingent payments.

Additional Transaction Information
Was there a Note in the consideration paid? No
Terms:
Considerations paid in cash.
Assumed Lease (Months): N/A
Noncompete Length (Months): N/A
Employment/Consulting Agreement Description:
Additional Notes:
EBT includes $(34,000) Other Expense. Seller holds franchises for BMW and Nissan. Inventory stated using LIFO.

Was there a personal guarantee on the Note? No

Terms of Lease: N/A
Noncompete Description: N/A

Valuation Multiples
MVIC/Net Sales	0.15
MVIC/Gross Profit	1.30
MVIC/EBITDA	8.23
MVIC/EBIT	8.77
MVIC/Discretionary Earnings	N/A
MVIC/Book Value of Invested Capital	2.97

Profitability Ratios
Net Profit Margin	0.01
Operating Profit Margin	N/A
Gross Profit Margin	0.11
Return on Assets	0.05
Return on Equity	0.22

Leverage Ratios
Fixed Charge Coverage	N/A
Long-Term Debt to Assets	0.01
Long-Term Debt to Equity	0.02

Earnings
EBITDA	$1,458,000
Discretionary Earnings	N/A

Liquidity Ratios
Current Ratio	1.24
Quick Ratio	0.53

Activity Ratios
Total Asset Turnover	4.92
Fixed Asset Turnover	243.79
Inventory Turnover	9.15

Copyright © 2010 Business Valuation Resources, LLC. All rights reserved. www.BVResources.com(SM)
(888) BUS-VALU, (503) 291-7963

Pratt's Stats® Auto Dealership Report

Pratt's Stats® Transaction Report
Prepared: 8/20/2010 2:09:44 PM (PST)

Seller Details
Target Name:	Clearwater Dealership
Business Description:	Automobile Dealer
SIC:	5511 Motor Vehicle Dealers (New and Used)
NAICS:	441110 New Car Dealers
Sale Location:	Clearwater, FL, United States
Years in Business:	N/A
Number Employees:	N/A

Source Data
Public Buyer Name:	SONIC AUTOMOTIVE INC
8-K Date:	3/30/1998
8-K/A Date:	N/A
Other Filing Type:	N/A
Other Filing Date:	N/A
CIK Code:	0001043509

Income Data
Data is "Latest Full Year" Reported	Yes
Data is Restated (see Notes for any explanation)	No
Income Statement Date	12/31/1997
Net Sales	$121,899,000
COGS	$105,786,000
Gross Profit	$16,113,000
Yearly Rent	N/A
Owner's Compensation	N/A
Other Operating Expenses	N/A
Noncash Charges	$390,000
Total Operating Expenses	$12,616,000
Operating Profit	$3,497,000
Interest Expenses	$1,500,000
EBT	$2,191,000
Taxes	$0
Net Income	$2,191,000

Asset Data
Data is Latest Reported	Yes
Data is "Purchase Price Allocation agreed upon by Buyer and Seller"	No
Balance Sheet Date	12/31/1997
Cash Equivalents	$2,065,000
Trade Receivables	$1,138,000
Inventory	$9,215,000
Other Current Assets	$282,000
Total Current Assets	$12,700,000
Fixed Assets	$7,829,000
Real Estate	N/A
Intangibles	$1,736,000
Other Noncurrent Assets	N/A
Total Assets	$22,265,000
Long-term Liabilities	$6,117,000
Total Liabilities	$17,283,000
Stockholder's Equity	$4,982,000

Transaction Data
Date Sale Initiated:	N/A
Date of Sale:	3/24/1998
Days to Sell:	N/A
Asking Price:	N/A
Market Value of Invested Capital*:	$15,000,000
Debt Assumed:	N/A
Employment Agreement Value:	N/A
Noncompete Value:	N/A
Amount of Down Payment:	$15,000,000
Stock or Asset Sale:	Asset
Company Type:	C Corporation
Was there an Employment/Consulting Agreement?	No
Was there an Assumed Lease in the sale?	No
Was there a Renewal Option with the Lease?	No

*Includes noncompete value and interest-bearing debt; excludes real estate, employment/consulting agreement values, and all contingent payments.

Additional Transaction Information
Was there a Note in the consideration paid? No
Was there a personal guarantee on the Note? No

Terms:
Considerations paid as follows: $11,040,000 cash, 3,960 shares of purchaser's Class A Series III Convertible Preferred Stock valued at $3,960,000. Contingent payments equal to 50% of the combined pre-tax earnings for fiscal year ended 12/31/98 not to exceed $1,650,000

Assumed Lease (Months): N/A
Terms of Lease: N/A
Noncompete Length (Months): N/A
Noncompete Description: N/A
Employment/Consulting Agreement Description:
Additional Notes:
EBT includes: $194,000 other income. Cars sold include Mitsubishi, Toyota and Ford. Inventory stated using LIFO.

Valuation Multiples
MVIC/Net Sales	0.12
MVIC/Gross Profit	0.93
MVIC/EBITDA	3.86
MVIC/EBIT	4.29
MVIC/Discretionary Earnings	N/A
MVIC/Book Value of Invested Capital	1.35

Profitability Ratios
Net Profit Margin	0.02
Operating Profit Margin	0.03
Gross Profit Margin	0.13
Return on Assets	0.10
Return on Equity	0.44

Leverage Ratios
Fixed Charge Coverage	2.46
Long-Term Debt to Assets	0.27
Long-Term Debt to Equity	1.23

Earnings
EBITDA	$3,887,000
Discretionary Earnings	N/A

Liquidity Ratios
Current Ratio	1.14
Quick Ratio	0.31

Activity Ratios
Total Asset Turnover	5.47
Fixed Asset Turnover	15.57
Inventory Turnover	13.23

Copyright © 2010 Business Valuation Resources, LLC. All rights reserved. www.BVResources.com℠
(888) BUS-VALU, (503) 291-7963

Pratt's Stats® Auto Dealership Report

Pratt's Stats® Transaction Report
Prepared: 8/20/2010 2:09:44 PM (PST)

Seller Details
Target Name:	Desert Automotive Group
Business Description:	New and Used Auto Sales, GMC Trucks, Volvo, Buick
SIC:	5511 Motor Vehicle Dealers (New and Used)
NAICS:	441110 New Car Dealers
Sale Location:	Las Vegas, NV, United States
Years in Business:	N/A Number Employees: N/A

Source Data
Public Buyer Name:	REPUBLIC INDUSTRIES INC
8-K Date:	2/20/1998
8-K/A Date:	N/A
Other Filing Type:	N/A
Other Filing Date:	N/A
CIK Code:	0000350698

Income Data
Data is "Latest Full Year" Reported	Yes
Data is Restated (see Notes for any explanation)	No
Income Statement Date	12/31/1996
Net Sales	$105,540,000
COGS	$87,625,000
Gross Profit	$17,915,000
Yearly Rent	N/A
Owner's Compensation	N/A
Other Operating Expenses	N/A
Noncash Charges	$485,000
Total Operating Expenses	$12,722,000
Operating Profit	$5,193,000
Interest Expenses	$440,000
EBT	$6,032,000
Taxes	$0
Net Income	$6,032,000

Asset Data
Data is Latest Reported	Yes
Data is "Purchase Price Allocation agreed upon by Buyer and Seller"	No
Balance Sheet Date	12/31/1996
Cash Equivalents	$9,819,000
Trade Receivables	$2,586,000
Inventory	$14,679,000
Other Current Assets	$524,000
Total Current Assets	$27,608,000
Fixed Assets	$9,959,000
Real Estate	$0
Intangibles	$0
Other Noncurrent Assets	$0
Total Assets	$37,567,000
Long-term Liabilities	$4,012,000
Total Liabilities	$25,510,000
Stockholder's Equity	$12,057,000

Transaction Data
Date Sale Initiated:	N/A
Date of Sale:	9/29/1997
Days to Sell:	N/A
Asking Price:	N/A
Market Value of Invested Capital*:	$70,000,000
Debt Assumed:	N/A
Employment Agreement Value:	N/A
Noncompete Value:	N/A
Amount of Down Payment:	$70,000,000
Stock or Asset Sale:	Asset
Company Type:	S Corporation
Was there an Employment/Consulting Agreement?	No
Was there an Assumed Lease in the sale?	Yes
Was there a Renewal Option with the Lease?	No

*Includes noncompete value and interest-bearing debt; excludes real estate, employment/consulting agreement values, and all contingent payments.

Additional Transaction Information
Was there a Note in the consideration paid? No
Terms:
Consideration paid: $70,000,000 in buyer's stock.
Assumed Lease (Months): N/A
Noncompete Length (Months): N/A
Employment/Consulting Agreement Description:
Additional Notes:
EBT includes $137,000 Interest Income, $1,142,000 Miscellaneous Income. Auto inventory stated using specific identification method, parts inventory stated using FIFO.

Was there a personal guarantee on the Note? No

Terms of Lease: N/A
Noncompete Description: N/A

Valuation Multiples
MVIC/Net Sales	0.66
MVIC/Gross Profit	3.91
MVIC/EBITDA	12.33
MVIC/EBIT	13.48
MVIC/Discretionary Earnings	N/A
MVIC/Book Value of Invested Capital	4.36

Profitability Ratios
Net Profit Margin	0.06
Operating Profit Margin	0.06
Gross Profit Margin	0.17
Return on Assets	0.16
Return on Equity	0.50

Leverage Ratios
Fixed Charge Coverage	14.71
Long-Term Debt to Assets	0.11
Long-Term Debt to Equity	0.33

Earnings
EBITDA	$5,678,000
Discretionary Earnings	N/A

Liquidity Ratios
Current Ratio	1.28
Quick Ratio	0.60

Activity Ratios
Total Asset Turnover	2.81
Fixed Asset Turnover	10.60
Inventory Turnover	7.19

Copyright © 2010 Business Valuation Resources, LLC. All rights reserved. www.BVResources.com℠
(888) BUS-VALU, (503) 291-7963

Pratt's Stats® Auto Dealership Report

Pratt's Stats® Transaction Report
Prepared: 8/20/2010 2:09:44 PM (PST)

Seller Details

Target Name:	Bledsoe Dodge, Inc.
Business Description:	Owns and Operates 3 Franchised Automobile Dealerships
SIC:	5511 Motor Vehicle Dealers (New and Used)
NAICS:	441110 New Car Dealers
Sale Location:	Dallas, TX, United States
Years in Business:	N/A
Number Employees:	N/A

Source Data

Public Buyer Name:	REPUBLIC INDUSTRIES INC
8-K Date:	6/13/1997
8-K/A Date:	N/A
Other Filing Type:	N/A
Other Filing Date:	N/A
CIK Code:	0000350698

Income Data

Data is "Latest Full Year" Reported	Yes
Data is Restated (see Notes for any explanation)	No
Income Statement Date	12/31/1996
Net Sales	$154,046,407
COGS	$131,196,561
Gross Profit	$22,849,846
Yearly Rent	N/A
Owner's Compensation	N/A
Other Operating Expenses	N/A
Noncash Charges	N/A
Total Operating Expenses	$18,884,862
Operating Profit	$3,964,984
Interest Expenses	$0
EBT	$4,415,225
Taxes	$198,285
Net Income	$4,216,940

Asset Data

Data is Latest Reported	Yes
Data is "Purchase Price Allocation agreed upon by Buyer and Seller"	No
Balance Sheet Date	3/31/1997
Cash Equivalents	$7,295,544
Trade Receivables	$2,857,943
Inventory	$16,122,873
Other Current Assets	$125,737
Total Current Assets	$26,402,097
Fixed Assets	$1,479,022
Real Estate	N/A
Intangibles	N/A
Other Noncurrent Assets	$135,326
Total Assets	$28,016,445
Long-term Liabilities	$0
Total Liabilities	$18,341,736
Stockholder's Equity	$9,674,709

Transaction Data

Date Sale Initiated:	N/A
Date of Sale:	5/31/1997
Days to Sell:	N/A
Asking Price:	N/A
Market Value of Invested Capital*:	$42,000,000
Debt Assumed:	N/A
Employment Agreement Value:	N/A
Noncompete Value:	N/A
Amount of Down Payment:	$42,000,000
Stock or Asset Sale:	Stock
Company Type:	S Corporation
Was there an Employment/Consulting Agreement?	No
Was there an Assumed Lease in the sale?	No
Was there a Renewal Option with the Lease?	No

*Includes noncompete value and interest-bearing debt; excludes real estate, employment/consulting agreement values, and all contingent payments.

Additional Transaction Information

Was there a Note in the consideration paid? No
Was there a personal guarantee on the Note? No
Terms:
Consideration paid as follows: 1,700,000 shares of buyer's public company common stock valued at $42,000,000
Assumed Lease (Months): N/A
Terms of Lease: N/A
Noncompete Length (Months): N/A
Noncompete Description: N/A
Employment/Consulting Agreement Description:
Additional Notes:
EBT includes $450,241 in interest income. Company operates Dodge dealerships in Dallas, Arlington, and Duncanville, Texas.

Valuation Multiples

MVIC/Net Sales	0.27
MVIC/Gross Profit	1.84
MVIC/EBITDA	N/A
MVIC/EBIT	10.59
MVIC/Discretionary Earnings	N/A
MVIC/Book Value of Invested Capital	4.34

Profitability Ratios

Net Profit Margin	0.03
Operating Profit Margin	0.03
Gross Profit Margin	0.15
Return on Assets	0.15
Return on Equity	0.44

Leverage Ratios

Fixed Charge Coverage	N/A
Long-Term Debt to Assets	0.00
Long-Term Debt to Equity	0.00

Earnings

EBITDA	N/A
Discretionary Earnings	N/A

Liquidity Ratios

Current Ratio	1.44
Quick Ratio	0.56

Activity Ratios

Total Asset Turnover	5.50
Fixed Asset Turnover	104.15
Inventory Turnover	9.55

Copyright © 2010 Business Valuation Resources, LLC. All rights reserved. www.BVResources.com℠
(888) BUS-VALU, (503) 291-7963

Pratt's Stats® Auto Dealership Report

Pratt's Stats® Transaction Report
Prepared: 8/20/2010 2:09:44 PM (PST)

Seller Details
Target Name:	N/A
Business Description:	Auto Dealership, Ford
SIC:	5511 Motor Vehicle Dealers (New and Used)
NAICS:	441110 New Car Dealers
Sale Location:	United States
Years in Business:	N/A
Number Employees:	N/A

Source Data
Public Buyer Name:	GROUP 1 AUTOMOTIVE INC
8-K Date:	3/31/1998
8-K/A Date:	5/28/1998
Other Filing Type:	N/A
Other Filing Date:	N/A
CIK Code:	0001031203

Income Data
Data is "Latest Full Year" Reported	Yes
Data is Restated (see Notes for any explanation)	No
Income Statement Date	12/31/1997
Net Sales	$244,330,456
COGS	$210,600,138
Gross Profit	$33,730,318
Yearly Rent	$1,998,098
Owner's Compensation	N/A
Other Operating Expenses	N/A
Noncash Charges	$779,952
Total Operating Expenses	$28,775,973
Operating Profit	$4,954,345
Interest Expenses	$3,912,385
EBT	$1,041,960
Taxes	$0
Net Income	$1,041,960

Asset Data
Data is Latest Reported	Yes
Data is "Purchase Price Allocation agreed upon by Buyer and Seller"	No
Balance Sheet Date	12/31/1997
Cash Equivalents	$3,396,595
Trade Receivables	$4,737,975
Inventory	$38,384,572
Other Current Assets	$1,792,654
Total Current Assets	$48,311,796
Fixed Assets	$9,514,401
Real Estate	N/A
Intangibles	$570,052
Other Noncurrent Assets	$75,121
Total Assets	$58,471,370
Long-term Liabilities	$6,660,925
Total Liabilities	$58,796,489
Stockholder's Equity	($325,119)

Transaction Data
Date Sale Initiated:	N/A
Date of Sale:	3/16/1998
Days to Sell:	N/A
Asking Price:	N/A
Market Value of Invested Capital*:	$37,798,000
Debt Assumed:	N/A
Employment Agreement Value:	N/A
Noncompete Value:	N/A
Amount of Down Payment:	$37,798,000
Stock or Asset Sale:	Stock
Company Type:	S Corporation
Was there an Employment/Consulting Agreement?	Yes
Was there an Assumed Lease in the sale?	No
Was there a Renewal Option with the Lease?	No

*Includes noncompete value and interest-bearing debt; excludes real estate, employment/consulting agreement values, and all contingent payments.

Additional Transaction Information
Was there a Note in the consideration paid? No
Was there a personal guarantee on the Note? No

Terms:
Consideration paid as follows: $17,806,000 Cash, and 1,428,000 shares of purchaser's public company common stock guaranteed at $14 per share if sold between 3/16/99 and 3/19/03 for less than $14 per share. Stock issued in this acquisition is not permitted to be sold until 3/16/99. Additional contingent consideration in the aggregate amount not to exceed $7,500,000 payable over 5 year period beginning 1/1/99 based upon performance.

Assumed Lease (Months): N/A
Terms of Lease: N/A
Noncompete Length (Months): N/A
Noncompete Description: N/A
Employment/Consulting Agreement Description:

Additional Notes:
Two dealerships sold, one in FL, and one in GA. Noncompete signed in connection with acquisition, details not available. Inventory stated using LIFO.

Valuation Multiples
MVIC/Net Sales	0.15
MVIC/Gross Profit	1.12
MVIC/EBITDA	6.59
MVIC/EBIT	7.63
MVIC/Discretionary Earnings	N/A
MVIC/Book Value of Invested Capital	5.97

Profitability Ratios
Net Profit Margin	0.00
Operating Profit Margin	0.02
Gross Profit Margin	0.14
Return on Assets	0.02
Return on Equity	N/A

Leverage Ratios
Fixed Charge Coverage	1.27
Long-Term Debt to Assets	0.11
Long-Term Debt to Equity	N/A

Earnings
EBITDA	$5,734,297
Discretionary Earnings	N/A

Liquidity Ratios
Current Ratio	0.93
Quick Ratio	0.19

Activity Ratios
Total Asset Turnover	4.18
Fixed Asset Turnover	25.68
Inventory Turnover	6.37

Copyright © 2010 Business Valuation Resources, LLC. All rights reserved. www.BVResources.com^SM
(888) BUS-VALU, (503) 291-7963

Pratt's Stats® Auto Dealership Report

Pratt's Stats® Transaction Report
Prepared: 8/20/2010 2:09:44 PM (PST)

Seller Details
Target Name:	Courtesy Auto Group, Inc.
Business Description:	Own and Operates Auto Dealerships
SIC:	5511 Motor Vehicle Dealers (New and Used)
NAICS:	441110 New Car Dealers
Sale Location:	Orlando, FL, United States
Years in Business:	14
Number Employees:	N/A

Source Data
Public Buyer Name:	REPUBLIC INDUSTRIES INC
8-K Date:	9/16/1997
8-K/A Date:	N/A
Other Filing Type:	N/A
Other Filing Date:	N/A
CIK Code:	0000350698

Income Data
Data is "Latest Full Year" Reported	Yes
Data is Restated (see Notes for any explanation)	No
Income Statement Date	12/31/1996
Net Sales	$186,238,970
COGS	$164,241,381
Gross Profit	$21,997,589
Yearly Rent	$246,900
Owner's Compensation	N/A
Other Operating Expenses	N/A
Noncash Charges	$595,088
Total Operating Expenses	$22,019,639
Operating Profit	($22,050)
Interest Expenses	$0
EBT	$2,110,861
Taxes	$0
Net Income	$2,110,861

Asset Data
Data is Latest Reported	Yes
Data is "Purchase Price Allocation agreed upon by Buyer and Seller"	No
Balance Sheet Date	6/30/1997
Cash Equivalents	$1,394,436
Trade Receivables	$1,812,967
Inventory	$26,233,784
Other Current Assets	$1,316,105
Total Current Assets	$30,757,292
Fixed Assets	$16,375,054
Real Estate	N/A
Intangibles	N/A
Other Noncurrent Assets	$14,068
Total Assets	$47,146,414
Long-term Liabilities	$11,708,671
Total Liabilities	$44,927,503
Stockholder's Equity	$2,218,911

Transaction Data
Date Sale Initiated:	N/A
Date of Sale:	6/30/1997
Days to Sell:	N/A
Asking Price:	N/A
Market Value of Invested Capital*:	$30,000,000
Debt Assumed:	N/A
Employment Agreement Value:	N/A
Noncompete Value:	N/A
Amount of Down Payment:	$30,000,000
Stock or Asset Sale:	Asset
Company Type:	S Corporation
Was there an Employment/Consulting Agreement?	No
Was there an Assumed Lease in the sale?	Yes
Was there a Renewal Option with the Lease?	No

*Includes noncompete value and interest-bearing debt; excludes real estate, employment/consulting agreement values, and all contingent payments.

Additional Transaction Information
Was there a Note in the consideration paid? No
Was there a personal guarantee on the Note? No
Terms:
Consideration: 1,380,744 shares of buyer's public company common stock valued at $30,000,000
Assumed Lease (Months): 41
Terms of Lease: Future Minimum Lease Payments: $781,850
Noncompete Length (Months): N/A
Noncompete Description: N/A
Employment/Consulting Agreement Description:
Additional Notes:
Inventory stated at lower of cost (LIFO) or market. EBT includes $2,132,911 other income. Company operates Saturn, Pontiac, Acura, Isuzu, Suzuki, and Kia dealerships in Orlando, Florida.

Valuation Multiples
MVIC/Net Sales	0.16
MVIC/Gross Profit	1.36
MVIC/EBITDA	52.35
MVIC/EBIT	N/A
MVIC/Discretionary Earnings	N/A
MVIC/Book Value of Invested Capital	2.15

Profitability Ratios
Net Profit Margin	0.01
Operating Profit Margin	0.01
Gross Profit Margin	0.12
Return on Assets	0.04
Return on Equity	0.95

Leverage Ratios
Fixed Charge Coverage	N/A
Long-Term Debt to Assets	0.25
Long-Term Debt to Equity	5.28

Earnings
EBITDA	$573,038
Discretionary Earnings	N/A

Liquidity Ratios
Current Ratio	0.93
Quick Ratio	0.14

Activity Ratios
Total Asset Turnover	3.95
Fixed Asset Turnover	11.37
Inventory Turnover	7.10

Copyright © 2010 Business Valuation Resources, LLC. All rights reserved. www.BVResources.com^SM
(888) BUS-VALU, (503) 291-7963

Pratt's Stats® Auto Dealership Report

Pratt's Stats® Transaction Report
Prepared: 8/20/2010 2:09:44 PM (PST)

Seller Details
Target Name:	Pierce Automotive Group
Business Description:	Retail and Commercial Sales of New and Used Autos
SIC:	5511 Motor Vehicle Dealers (New and Used)
NAICS:	441110 New Car Dealers
Sale Location:	Tempe, AZ, United States
Years in Business:	N/A Number Employees: N/A

Source Data
Public Buyer Name:	REPUBLIC INDUSTRIES INC
8-K Date:	9/16/1997
8-K/A Date:	N/A
Other Filing Type:	N/A
Other Filing Date:	N/A
CIK Code:	0000350698

Income Data
Data is "Latest Full Year" Reported	Yes
Data is Restated (see Notes for any explanation)	No
Income Statement Date	12/31/1996
Net Sales	$138,636,000
COGS	$120,360,000
Gross Profit	$18,276,000
Yearly Rent	$382,000
Owner's Compensation	N/A
Other Operating Expenses	N/A
Noncash Charges	$331,000
Total Operating Expenses	$11,068,000
Operating Profit	$7,208,000
Interest Expenses	$769,000
EBT	$6,322,000
Taxes	$0
Net Income	$6,322,000

Asset Data
Data is Latest Reported	Yes
Data is "Purchase Price Allocation agreed upon by Buyer and Seller"	No
Balance Sheet Date	3/31/1997
Cash Equivalents	$3,919,000
Trade Receivables	$2,451,000
Inventory	$10,623,000
Other Current Assets	$75,000
Total Current Assets	$17,068,000
Fixed Assets	$7,853,000
Real Estate	N/A
Intangibles	N/A
Other Noncurrent Assets	$32,000
Total Assets	$24,953,000
Long-term Liabilities	$4,415,000
Total Liabilities	$19,660,000
Stockholder's Equity	$5,293,000

Transaction Data
Date Sale Initiated:	N/A
Date of Sale:	6/1/1997
Days to Sell:	N/A
Asking Price:	N/A
Market Value of Invested Capital*:	$48,000,000
Debt Assumed:	N/A
Employment Agreement Value:	N/A
Noncompete Value:	N/A
Amount of Down Payment:	$48,000,000
Stock or Asset Sale:	Asset
Company Type:	S Corporation
Was there an Employment/Consulting Agreement?	No
Was there an Assumed Lease in the sale?	Yes
Was there a Renewal Option with the Lease?	No

*Includes noncompete value and interest-bearing debt; excludes real estate, employment/consulting agreement values, and all contingent payments.

Additional Transaction Information
Was there a Note in the consideration paid? No
Terms:
Consideration paid as follows: 2,300,000 shares of public company common stock valued at $48,000,000.
Assumed Lease (Months): 6
Noncompete Length (Months): N/A
Employment/Consulting Agreement Description:
Additional Notes:
Seller operates one franchised automotive dealership and two used auto dealerships. EBT includes $117,000 other expense. Inventory stated at lower of cost (LIFO) or market.

Was there a personal guarantee on the Note? No

Terms of Lease: Future Minimum Lease Payments: $57,000
Noncompete Description: N/A

Valuation Multiples
MVIC/Net Sales	0.35
MVIC/Gross Profit	2.63
MVIC/EBITDA	6.37
MVIC/EBIT	6.66
MVIC/Discretionary Earnings	N/A
MVIC/Book Value of Invested Capital	4.94

Profitability Ratios
Net Profit Margin	0.05
Operating Profit Margin	0.05
Gross Profit Margin	0.13
Return on Assets	0.25
Return on Equity	1.19

Leverage Ratios
Fixed Charge Coverage	9.22
Long-Term Debt to Assets	0.18
Long-Term Debt to Equity	0.83

Earnings
EBITDA	$7,539,000
Discretionary Earnings	N/A

Liquidity Ratios
Current Ratio	1.12
Quick Ratio	0.42

Activity Ratios
Total Asset Turnover	5.56
Fixed Asset Turnover	17.65
Inventory Turnover	13.05

Copyright © 2010 Business Valuation Resources, LLC. All rights reserved. www.BVResources.com℠
(888) BUS-VALU, (503) 291-7963

Pratt's Stats® Auto Dealership Report

Pratt's Stats® Transaction Report
Prepared: 8/20/2010 2:09:44 PM (PST)

Seller Details
Target Name:	N/A
Business Description:	Retail Sales of Vehicles - New and Used, Parts, Service, Finance, and Warranty Products
SIC:	5511 Motor Vehicle Dealers (New and Used)
NAICS:	441110 New Car Dealers
Sale Location:	Miami, FL, United States
Years in Business:	20
Number Employees:	500

Source Data
Broker Name:	N/A
Broker Firm Name:	Morrison, Brown, Argiz, & Co., CPA

Income Data
Data is "Latest Full Year" Reported	Yes
Data is Restated (see Notes for any explanation)	No
Income Statement Date	12/31/1997
Net Sales	$220,500,000
COGS	$188,000,000
Gross Profit	$32,500,000
Yearly Rent	$311,000
Owner's Compensation	$0
Other Operating Expenses	N/A
Noncash Charges	$735,000
Total Operating Expenses	$26,800,000
Operating Profit	$5,700,000
Interest Expenses	$228,000
EBT	$5,472,000
Taxes	$0
Net Income	$5,472,000

Asset Data
Data is Latest Reported	Yes
Data is "Purchase Price Allocation agreed upon by Buyer and Seller"	No
Balance Sheet Date	12/31/1997
Cash Equivalents	$14,300,000
Trade Receivables	$6,100,000
Inventory	$29,000,000
Other Current Assets	$940,000
Total Current Assets	$50,340,000
Fixed Assets	$15,500,000
Real Estate	$11,500,000
Intangibles	$0
Other Noncurrent Assets	$0
Total Assets	$65,840,000
Long-term Liabilities	N/A
Total Liabilities	N/A
Stockholder's Equity	N/A

Transaction Data
Date Sale Initiated:	11/15/1997
Date of Sale:	1/15/1998
Days to Sell:	61
Asking Price:	N/A
Market Value of Invested Capital*:	$66,350,000
Debt Assumed:	$22,900,000
Employment Agreement Value:	N/A
Noncompete Value:	N/A
Amount of Down Payment:	$43,450,000
Stock or Asset Sale:	Asset
Company Type:	Partnership
Was there an Employment/Consulting Agreement?	Yes
Was there an Assumed Lease in the sale?	Yes
Was there a Renewal Option with the Lease?	Yes

*Includes noncompete value and interest-bearing debt; excludes real estate, employment/consulting agreement values, and all contingent payments.

Additional Transaction Information

Was there a Note in the consideration paid? No
Terms:
Assumed Lease (Months): N/A
Noncompete Length (Months): 24
Employment/Consulting Agreement Description:

Was there a personal guarantee on the Note? No

Terms of Lease: 15 years and (2) five-year options
Noncompete Description: 25 mile radius of dealership locations

Additional Notes:
There was a partner loan. Buyer assumed $5,800,000 of Accounts Payable and $22,900,000 of floor plan borrowings. Real Estate was not part of the sale and is therefore not included in the Total Assets field of the Asset Data. It was retained by the owners and leased back to the buyer (market value $20,000,000 combined at sale date). Seller consisted of 2 Chevrolet franchises and 1 warranty company.

Valuation Multiples
MVIC/Net Sales	0.30
MVIC/Gross Profit	2.04
MVIC/EBITDA	10.31
MVIC/EBIT	11.64
MVIC/Discretionary Earnings	10.31
MVIC/Book Value of Invested Capital	N/A

Profitability Ratios
Net Profit Margin	0.02
Operating Profit Margin	0.03
Gross Profit Margin	0.15
Return on Assets	0.08
Return on Equity	N/A

Leverage Ratios
Fixed Charge Coverage	25.00
Long-Term Debt to Assets	N/A
Long-Term Debt to Equity	N/A

Earnings
EBITDA	$6,435,000
Discretionary Earnings	$6,435,000

Liquidity Ratios
Current Ratio	N/A
Quick Ratio	N/A

Activity Ratios
Total Asset Turnover	3.35
Fixed Asset Turnover	14.23
Inventory Turnover	7.60

Copyright © 2010 Business Valuation Resources, LLC. All rights reserved. www.BVResources.com℠
(888) BUS-VALU, (503) 291-7963

Pratt's Stats® Auto Dealership Report

Pratt's Stats® Transaction Report
Prepared: 8/20/2010 2:09:44 PM (PST)

Seller Details
Target Name:	De la Cruz Auto Group
Business Description:	Owns and Operates 4 Franchised Auto Dealerships
SIC:	5511 Motor Vehicle Dealers (New and Used)
NAICS:	441110 New Car Dealers
Sale Location:	Miami, FL, United States
Years in Business:	7
Number Employees:	N/A

Source Data
Public Buyer Name:	REPUBLIC INDUSTRIES INC
8-K Date:	9/16/1997
8-K/A Date:	N/A
Other Filing Type:	N/A
Other Filing Date:	N/A
CIK Code:	0000350698

Income Data
Data is "Latest Full Year" Reported	Yes
Data is Restated (see Notes for any explanation)	No
Income Statement Date	12/31/1996
Net Sales	$191,858,273
COGS	$165,985,688
Gross Profit	$25,872,585
Yearly Rent	N/A
Owner's Compensation	N/A
Other Operating Expenses	N/A
Noncash Charges	$822,839
Total Operating Expenses	$20,889,656
Operating Profit	$4,982,929
Interest Expenses	$1,929,702
EBT	$3,232,713
Taxes	$0
Net Income	$3,232,713

Asset Data
Data is Latest Reported	Yes
Data is "Purchase Price Allocation agreed upon by Buyer and Seller"	No
Balance Sheet Date	6/30/1997
Cash Equivalents	$2,077,900
Trade Receivables	$4,380,285
Inventory	$26,318,898
Other Current Assets	$5,844,639
Total Current Assets	$38,621,722
Fixed Assets	$16,189,655
Real Estate	N/A
Intangibles	$1,158,998
Other Noncurrent Assets	N/A
Total Assets	$55,970,375
Long-term Liabilities	$11,574,745
Total Liabilities	$49,644,094
Stockholder's Equity	$6,326,281

Transaction Data
Date Sale Initiated:	N/A
Date of Sale:	7/1/1997
Days to Sell:	N/A
Asking Price:	N/A
Market Value of Invested Capital*:	$40,000,000
Debt Assumed:	N/A
Employment Agreement Value:	N/A
Noncompete Value:	N/A
Amount of Down Payment:	$40,000,000
Stock or Asset Sale:	Asset
Company Type:	S Corporation
Was there an Employment/Consulting Agreement?	No
Was there an Assumed Lease in the sale?	No
Was there a Renewal Option with the Lease?	No

*Includes noncompete value and interest-bearing debt; excludes real estate, employment/consulting agreement values, and all contingent payments.

Additional Transaction Information
Was there a Note in the consideration paid? No

Was there a personal guarantee on the Note? No

Terms:
Consideration paid as follows: 1,800,000 shares of buyer's public company common stock valued at $40,000,000.

Assumed Lease (Months): N/A
Terms of Lease: N/A
Noncompete Length (Months): N/A
Noncompete Description: N/A
Employment/Consulting Agreement Description:
Additional Notes:
EBT includes $179,486 interest income. Inventory valued at lower of cost (specific identification) or market. Company operates Ford, Hyundai, and Honda dealerships.

Valuation Multiples
MVIC/Net Sales	0.21
MVIC/Gross Profit	1.55
MVIC/EBITDA	6.89
MVIC/EBIT	8.03
MVIC/Discretionary Earnings	N/A
MVIC/Book Value of Invested Capital	2.23

Profitability Ratios
Net Profit Margin	0.02
Operating Profit Margin	0.03
Gross Profit Margin	0.13
Return on Assets	0.06
Return on Equity	0.51

Leverage Ratios
Fixed Charge Coverage	2.68
Long-Term Debt to Assets	0.21
Long-Term Debt to Equity	1.83

Earnings
EBITDA	$5,805,768
Discretionary Earnings	N/A

Liquidity Ratios
Current Ratio	1.01
Quick Ratio	0.32

Activity Ratios
Total Asset Turnover	3.43
Fixed Asset Turnover	11.85
Inventory Turnover	7.29

Copyright © 2010 Business Valuation Resources, LLC. All rights reserved. www.BVResources.com^{SM}
(888) BUS-VALU, (503) 291-7963

Pratt's Stats® Auto Dealership Report

Pratt's Stats® Transaction Report
Prepared: 8/20/2010 2:09:44 PM (PST)

Seller Details
Target Name:	Camp Automotive, Inc. (D/B/A Camp Chevrolet, Subaru, BMW, Volvo)
Business Description:	Leases, New and Used Autos
SIC:	5511 Motor Vehicle Dealers (New and Used)
NAICS:	441110 New Car Dealers
Sale Location:	Spokane, WA, United States
Years in Business:	N/A Number Employees: N/A

Source Data
Public Buyer Name:	LITHIA MOTORS INC
8-K Date:	10/28/1998
8-K/A Date:	12/31/1998
Other Filing Type:	N/A
Other Filing Date:	N/A
CIK Code:	0001023128

Income Data
Data is "Latest Full Year" Reported	Yes
Data is Restated (see Notes for any explanation)	No
Income Statement Date	12/31/1997
Net Sales	$87,812,136
COGS	$74,793,876
Gross Profit	$13,018,260
Yearly Rent	$227,834
Owner's Compensation	N/A
Other Operating Expenses	N/A
Noncash Charges	$1,253,297
Total Operating Expenses	$12,085,727
Operating Profit	$2,164,878
Interest Expenses	$765,407
EBT	$2,147,031
Taxes	$0
Net Income	$2,147,031

Asset Data
Data is Latest Reported	Yes
Data is "Purchase Price Allocation agreed upon by Buyer and Seller"	No
Balance Sheet Date	9/30/1998
Cash Equivalents	$1,581,791
Trade Receivables	$2,855,785
Inventory	$10,353,250
Other Current Assets	$4,559,827
Total Current Assets	$19,350,653
Fixed Assets	$4,468,632
Real Estate	N/A
Intangibles	N/A
Other Noncurrent Assets	$13,780,833
Total Assets	$37,600,118
Long-term Liabilities	$6,831,600
Total Liabilities	$26,374,576
Stockholder's Equity	$11,225,542

Transaction Data
Date Sale Initiated:	N/A
Date of Sale:	10/15/1998
Days to Sell:	N/A
Asking Price:	N/A
Market Value of Invested Capital*:	$11,000,000
Debt Assumed:	N/A
Employment Agreement Value:	N/A
Noncompete Value:	N/A
Amount of Down Payment:	$8,000,000
Stock or Asset Sale:	Stock
Company Type:	S Corporation
Was there an Employment/Consulting Agreement?	Yes
Was there an Assumed Lease in the sale?	Yes
Was there a Renewal Option with the Lease?	Yes

*Includes noncompete value and interest-bearing debt; excludes real estate, employment/consulting agreement values, and all contingent payments.

Additional Transaction Information
Was there a Note in the consideration paid? Yes
Terms:
Consideration paid: $8,000,000 cash, $2,000,000 note payable for 10 years at 7% interest.
Assumed Lease (Months): 6
Noncompete Length (Months): N/A
Employment/Consulting Agreement Description:
Additional Notes:
Operating Profit includes $1,232,345 in Miscellaneous Commissions, Rental and Lease Income, net EBT includes $820,368 Finance Income, $86,663 Miscellaneous Income, $(154,105) Loss on Repossessions, $(7,399) Loss on Disposal of Equipment. New auto and parts inventory stated using LIFO, used car inventory stated using the lower of actual or wholesale cost.

Was there a personal guarantee on the Note? No

Terms of Lease: $8,000 per month
Noncompete Description: N/A

Valuation Multiples
MVIC/Net Sales	0.13
MVIC/Gross Profit	0.84
MVIC/EBITDA	3.22
MVIC/EBIT	5.08
MVIC/Discretionary Earnings	N/A
MVIC/Book Value of Invested Capital	0.61

Profitability Ratios
Net Profit Margin	0.02
Operating Profit Margin	0.03
Gross Profit Margin	0.15
Return on Assets	0.06
Return on Equity	0.19

Leverage Ratios
Fixed Charge Coverage	3.81
Long-Term Debt to Assets	0.18
Long-Term Debt to Equity	0.61

Earnings
EBITDA	$3,418,175
Discretionary Earnings	N/A

Liquidity Ratios
Current Ratio	0.99
Quick Ratio	0.46

Activity Ratios
Total Asset Turnover	2.34
Fixed Asset Turnover	19.65
Inventory Turnover	8.48

Copyright © 2010 Business Valuation Resources, LLC. All rights reserved. www.BVResources.com℠
(888) BUS-VALU, (503) 291-7963

Pratt's Stats® Auto Dealership Report

Pratt's Stats® Transaction Report
Prepared: 8/20/2010 2:09:44 PM (PST)

Seller Details
Target Name:	Moreland Automotive Group
Business Description:	Operates New and Used Automobile Dealership
SIC:	5511 Motor Vehicle Dealers (New and Used)
NAICS:	441110 New Car Dealers
Sale Location:	CO, United States
Years in Business:	N/A
Number Employees:	N/A

Source Data
Public Buyer Name:	LITHIA MOTORS INC
8-K Date:	5/27/1999
8-K/A Date:	7/28/1999
Other Filing Type:	N/A
Other Filing Date:	N/A
CIK Code:	0001023128

Income Data
Data is "Latest Full Year" Reported	Yes
Data is Restated (see Notes for any explanation)	No
Income Statement Date	12/31/1998
Net Sales	$367,194,000
COGS	$311,333,000
Gross Profit	$55,861,000
Yearly Rent	$3,447,000
Owner's Compensation	$8,351,000
Other Operating Expenses	N/A
Noncash Charges	$594,000
Total Operating Expenses	$51,586,000
Operating Profit	$4,275,000
Interest Expenses	$735,000
EBT	$4,663,000
Taxes	$2,190,000
Net Income	$2,473,000

Asset Data
Data is Latest Reported	Yes
Data is "Purchase Price Allocation agreed upon by Buyer and Seller"	No
Balance Sheet Date	12/31/1998
Cash Equivalents	$14,370,000
Trade Receivables	$16,341,000
Inventory	$61,724,000
Other Current Assets	$3,030,000
Total Current Assets	$95,465,000
Fixed Assets	$6,851,000
Real Estate	N/A
Intangibles	N/A
Other Noncurrent Assets	$651,000
Total Assets	$102,967,000
Long-term Liabilities	$283,000
Total Liabilities	$77,714,000
Stockholder's Equity	$25,253,000

Transaction Data
Date Sale Initiated:	N/A
Date of Sale:	5/14/1999
Days to Sell:	N/A
Asking Price:	N/A
Market Value of Invested Capital*:	$66,000,000
Debt Assumed:	N/A
Employment Agreement Value:	N/A
Noncompete Value:	N/A
Amount of Down Payment:	$66,000,000
Stock or Asset Sale:	Stock
Company Type:	C Corporation
Was there an Employment/Consulting Agreement?	No
Was there an Assumed Lease in the sale?	Yes
Was there a Renewal Option with the Lease?	Yes

*Includes noncompete value and interest-bearing debt; excludes real estate, employment/consulting agreement values, and all contingent payments.

Additional Transaction Information
Was there a Note in the consideration paid? No   Was there a personal guarantee on the Note? No
Terms:
Consideration Paid: $35,700,000 in Cash, 10,360 shares of Series M preferred stock valued at $6,200,000, and 1,272,919 shares of buyers public company common stock valued at $24,100,000
Assumed Lease (Months): 60   Terms of Lease: Future Minimum Lease Payments are $11,422,000
Noncompete Length (Months): N/A   Noncompete Description: N/A
Employment/Consulting Agreement Description:
Additional Notes:
Earnings Before Tax includes $705,000 in Interest Income, and $418,000 in Other Income. Vehicle inventory stated at the lower of cost (LIFO) or market. Company sells Chyrsler, Jeep/Eagle, Subaru, and Hyundai vehicles from (7) lots located in Aurora, Englewood, and Colorado Springs, Co., and Reno NV.

Valuation Multiples
MVIC/Net Sales	0.18
MVIC/Gross Profit	1.18
MVIC/EBITDA	13.56
MVIC/EBIT	15.44
MVIC/Discretionary Earnings	4.99
MVIC/Book Value of Invested Capital	2.58

Profitability Ratios
Net Profit Margin	0.01
Operating Profit Margin	0.01
Gross Profit Margin	0.15
Return on Assets	0.02
Return on Equity	0.10

Leverage Ratios
Fixed Charge Coverage	7.34
Long-Term Debt to Assets	0.00
Long-Term Debt to Equity	0.01

Earnings
EBITDA	$4,869,000
Discretionary Earnings	$13,220,000

Liquidity Ratios
Current Ratio	1.23
Quick Ratio	0.44

Activity Ratios
Total Asset Turnover	3.57
Fixed Asset Turnover	53.60
Inventory Turnover	5.95

Copyright © 2010 Business Valuation Resources, LLC. All rights reserved. www.BVResources.com[SM]
(888) BUS-VALU, (503) 291-7963

Pratt's Stats® Auto Dealership Report

Pratt's Stats® Transaction Report
Prepared: 8/20/2010 2:09:44 PM (PST)

Seller Details
Target Name:	Vacation Motors Inc. doing business as Concord Toyota
Business Description:	New and Used Automobile Sales
SIC:	5511 Motor Vehicle Dealers (New and Used)
NAICS:	441110 New Car Dealers
Sale Location:	Concord, CA, United States
Years in Business:	N/A
Number Employees:	N/A

Source Data
Public Buyer Name:	FIRSTAMERICA AUTOMOTIVE INC /DE/
8-K Date:	10/16/1998
8-K/A Date:	12/15/1998
Other Filing Type:	N/A
Other Filing Date:	N/A
CIK Code:	0000766886

Income Data
Data is "Latest Full Year" Reported	Yes
Data is Restated (see Notes for any explanation)	No
Income Statement Date	12/31/1997
Net Sales	$69,875,000
COGS	$61,133,000
Gross Profit	$8,742,000
Yearly Rent	$134,000
Owner's Compensation	N/A
Other Operating Expenses	$6,387,000
Noncash Charges	$96,000
Total Operating Expenses	$6,617,000
Operating Profit	$2,125,000
Interest Expenses	$228,000
EBT	$2,002,000
Taxes	$30,000
Net Income	$1,972,000

Asset Data
Data is Latest Reported	Yes
Data is "Purchase Price Allocation agreed upon by Buyer and Seller"	No
Balance Sheet Date	9/30/1998
Cash Equivalents	N/A
Trade Receivables	$2,538,000
Inventory	$1,709,000
Other Current Assets	$153,000
Total Current Assets	$4,400,000
Fixed Assets	$331,000
Real Estate	N/A
Intangibles	N/A
Other Noncurrent Assets	$221,000
Total Assets	$4,952,000
Long-term Liabilities	$461,000
Total Liabilities	$3,718,000
Stockholder's Equity	$1,234,000

Transaction Data
Date Sale Initiated:	N/A
Date of Sale:	10/1/1998
Days to Sell:	N/A
Asking Price:	N/A
Market Value of Invested Capital*:	$12,000,000
Debt Assumed:	N/A
Employment Agreement Value:	N/A
Noncompete Value:	N/A
Amount of Down Payment:	$12,000,000
Stock or Asset Sale:	Stock
Company Type:	S Corporation
Was there an Employment/Consulting Agreement?	Yes
Was there an Assumed Lease in the sale?	Yes
Was there a Renewal Option with the Lease?	No

*Includes noncompete value and interest-bearing debt; excludes real estate, employment/consulting agreement values, and all contingent payments.

Additional Transaction Information
Was there a Note in the consideration paid? No
Terms:
Consideration: $12,000,000 in Cash
Assumed Lease (Months): N/A
Noncompete Length (Months): N/A
Employment/Consulting Agreement Description:
Additional Notes:
Earnings Before Tax includes $105,000 in Other Income. Inventory stated using LIFO.

Was there a personal guarantee on the Note? No
Terms of Lease: N/A
Noncompete Description: N/A

Valuation Multiples
MVIC/Net Sales	0.17
MVIC/Gross Profit	1.37
MVIC/EBITDA	5.40
MVIC/EBIT	5.65
MVIC/Discretionary Earnings	N/A
MVIC/Book Value of Invested Capital	7.08

Profitability Ratios
Net Profit Margin	0.03
Operating Profit Margin	0.03
Gross Profit Margin	0.13
Return on Assets	0.40
Return on Equity	1.60

Leverage Ratios
Fixed Charge Coverage	9.78
Long-Term Debt to Assets	0.09
Long-Term Debt to Equity	0.37

Earnings
EBITDA	$2,221,000
Discretionary Earnings	N/A

Liquidity Ratios
Current Ratio	1.35
Quick Ratio	0.83

Activity Ratios
Total Asset Turnover	14.11
Fixed Asset Turnover	211.10
Inventory Turnover	40.89

Copyright © 2010 Business Valuation Resources, LLC. All rights reserved. www.BVResources.com℠
(888) BUS-VALU, (503) 291-7963

Pratt's Stats® Auto Dealership Report

Pratt's Stats® Transaction Report
Prepared: 8/20/2010 2:09:44 PM (PST)

Seller Details
Target Name:	Burgess Honda
Business Description:	Auto Dealer
SIC:	5511 Motor Vehicle Dealers (New and Used)
NAICS:	441110 New Car Dealers
Sale Location:	Dale City, CA, United States
Years in Business:	N/A
Number Employees:	N/A

Source Data
Public Buyer Name:	FIRSTAMERICA AUTOMOTIVE INC /DE/
8-K Date:	7/6/1998
8-K/A Date:	9/4/1998
Other Filing Type:	N/A
Other Filing Date:	N/A
CIK Code:	0000766886

Income Data
Data is "Latest Full Year" Reported	Yes
Data is Restated (see Notes for any explanation)	No
Income Statement Date	9/30/1997
Net Sales	$23,923,000
COGS	$20,233,000
Gross Profit	$3,690,000
Yearly Rent	N/A
Owner's Compensation	N/A
Other Operating Expenses	$3,185,000
Noncash Charges	$59,000
Total Operating Expenses	$3,244,000
Operating Profit	$446,000
Interest Expenses	$119,000
EBT	$435,000
Taxes	$7,000
Net Income	$428,000

Asset Data
Data is Latest Reported	Yes
Data is "Purchase Price Allocation agreed upon by Buyer and Seller"	No
Balance Sheet Date	9/30/1997
Cash Equivalents	$1,463,000
Trade Receivables	$351,000
Inventory	$1,451,000
Other Current Assets	$103,000
Total Current Assets	$3,368,000
Fixed Assets	$175,000
Real Estate	N/A
Intangibles	N/A
Other Noncurrent Assets	$366,000
Total Assets	$3,909,000
Long-term Liabilities	$75,000
Total Liabilities	$1,968,000
Stockholder's Equity	$1,941,000

Transaction Data
Date Sale Initiated:	N/A
Date of Sale:	6/19/1998
Days to Sell:	N/A
Asking Price:	N/A
Market Value of Invested Capital*:	$5,600,000
Debt Assumed:	N/A
Employment Agreement Value:	N/A
Noncompete Value:	N/A
Amount of Down Payment:	$5,600,000
Stock or Asset Sale:	Asset
Company Type:	S Corporation
Was there an Employment/Consulting Agreement?	No
Was there an Assumed Lease in the sale?	No
Was there a Renewal Option with the Lease?	No

*Includes noncompete value and interest-bearing debt; excludes real estate, employment/consulting agreement values, and all contingent payments.

Additional Transaction Information
Was there a Note in the consideration paid? No
Terms:
Assumed Lease (Months): N/A
Noncompete Length (Months): N/A
Employment/Consulting Agreement Description:
Additional Notes:
Selling price includes the value of the new vehicle inventory at the date of closing totaling $1,900,000. EBT includes $90,000 interest income and $18,000 other income. Inventory stated using LIFO.

Was there a personal guarantee on the Note? No
Terms of Lease: N/A
Noncompete Description: N/A

Valuation Multiples
MVIC/Net Sales	0.23
MVIC/Gross Profit	1.52
MVIC/EBITDA	11.09
MVIC/EBIT	12.56
MVIC/Discretionary Earnings	N/A
MVIC/Book Value of Invested Capital	2.78

Profitability Ratios
Net Profit Margin	0.02
Operating Profit Margin	0.02
Gross Profit Margin	0.15
Return on Assets	0.11
Return on Equity	0.22

Leverage Ratios
Fixed Charge Coverage	4.66
Long-Term Debt to Assets	0.02
Long-Term Debt to Equity	0.04

Earnings
EBITDA	$505,000
Discretionary Earnings	N/A

Liquidity Ratios
Current Ratio	1.78
Quick Ratio	1.01

Activity Ratios
Total Asset Turnover	6.12
Fixed Asset Turnover	136.70
Inventory Turnover	16.49

Copyright © 2010 Business Valuation Resources, LLC. All rights reserved. www.BVResources.com℠
(888) BUS-VALU, (503) 291-7963

Pratt's Stats® Auto Dealership Report

Pratt's Stats® Transaction Report
Prepared: 8/20/2010 2:09:45 PM (PST)

Seller Details
Target Name:	Hatfield Automotive Group
Business Description:	Automobile Dealer
SIC:	5511 Motor Vehicle Dealers (New and Used)
NAICS:	441110 New Car Dealers
Sale Location:	Columbus, OH, United States
Years in Business:	N/A
Number Employees:	N/A

Source Data
Public Buyer Name:	SONIC AUTOMOTIVE INC
8-K Date:	7/24/1998
8-K/A Date:	8/20/1998
Other Filing Type:	N/A
Other Filing Date:	N/A
CIK Code:	0001043509

Income Data
Data is "Latest Full Year" Reported	Yes
Data is Restated (see Notes for any explanation)	No
Income Statement Date	12/31/1997
Net Sales	$275,280,000
COGS	$243,371,000
Gross Profit	$31,910,000
Yearly Rent	$2,467,000
Owner's Compensation	N/A
Other Operating Expenses	N/A
Noncash Charges	$221,000
Total Operating Expenses	$28,495,000
Operating Profit	$3,415,000
Interest Expenses	$3,663,000
EBT	($24,000)
Taxes	$0
Net Income	($24,000)

Asset Data
Data is Latest Reported	Yes
Data is "Purchase Price Allocation agreed upon by Buyer and Seller"	No
Balance Sheet Date	3/31/1998
Cash Equivalents	$14,990,000
Trade Receivables	$3,360,000
Inventory	$34,395,000
Other Current Assets	$6,610,000
Total Current Assets	$59,355,000
Fixed Assets	$1,003,000
Real Estate	N/A
Intangibles	$977,000
Other Noncurrent Assets	N/A
Total Assets	$61,335,000
Long-term Liabilities	$10,569,000
Total Liabilities	$55,013,000
Stockholder's Equity	$6,322,000

Transaction Data
Date Sale Initiated:	N/A
Date of Sale:	6/9/1998
Days to Sell:	N/A
Asking Price:	N/A
Market Value of Invested Capital*:	$48,600,000
Debt Assumed:	N/A
Employment Agreement Value:	N/A
Noncompete Value:	N/A
Amount of Down Payment:	$48,600,000
Stock or Asset Sale:	Asset
Company Type:	C Corporation
Was there an Employment/Consulting Agreement?	No
Was there an Assumed Lease in the sale?	Yes
Was there a Renewal Option with the Lease?	No

*Includes noncompete value and interest-bearing debt; excludes real estate, employment/consulting agreement values, and all contingent payments.

Additional Transaction Information
Was there a Note in the consideration paid? No
Was there a personal guarantee on the Note? No
Terms:
Considerations paid as follows: $34,600,000 cash, 14,025 shares of purchaser's Class A Preferred Stock.
Assumed Lease (Months): 60   Terms of Lease: Present value of future minimum payments: $8,027,766
Noncompete Length (Months): N/A   Noncompete Description: N/A
Employment/Consulting Agreement Description:
Additional Notes:
EBT includes $224,000 other income. Seller owns and operates 6 automobile dealerships (Toyota, Lincoln-Mercury, Dodge, Jeep, Chrysler-Plymouth, Hyundai, Kia and VW) and a body shop. Seller leases its facilities from a company stockholder. Inventory stated using LIFO.

Valuation Multiples
MVIC/Net Sales	0.18
MVIC/Gross Profit	1.52
MVIC/EBITDA	13.37
MVIC/EBIT	14.23
MVIC/Discretionary Earnings	N/A
MVIC/Book Value of Invested Capital	2.88

Profitability Ratios
Net Profit Margin	-0.00
Operating Profit Margin	0.01
Gross Profit Margin	0.12
Return on Assets	-0.00
Return on Equity	-0.00

Leverage Ratios
Fixed Charge Coverage	0.99
Long-Term Debt to Assets	0.17
Long-Term Debt to Equity	1.67

Earnings
EBITDA	$3,636,000
Discretionary Earnings	N/A

Liquidity Ratios
Current Ratio	1.34
Quick Ratio	0.56

Activity Ratios
Total Asset Turnover	4.49
Fixed Asset Turnover	274.46
Inventory Turnover	8.00

Copyright © 2010 Business Valuation Resources, LLC. All rights reserved. www.BVResources.com^SM
(888) BUS-VALU, (503) 291-7963

Pratt's Stats® Auto Dealership Report

Pratt's Stats® Transaction Report
Prepared: 8/20/2010 2:09:45 PM (PST)

Seller Details

Target Name:	Regent Auto Leasing and Sales, Inc.
Business Description:	Auto Broker
SIC:	5511 Motor Vehicle Dealers (New and Used)
NAICS:	441110 New Car Dealers
Sale Location:	Delray Beach, FL, United States
Years in Business:	17
Number Employees:	5

Source Data

Broker Name:	Cagnetta, Andrew
Broker Firm Name:	Transworld Business Brokers

Income Data

Data is "Latest Full Year" Reported	Yes
Data is Restated (see Notes for any explanation)	No
Income Statement Date	12/31/2001
Net Sales	$422,248
COGS	$0
Gross Profit	$422,248
Yearly Rent	$23,677
Owner's Compensation	$66,330
Other Operating Expenses	$199,368
Noncash Charges	$1,145
Total Operating Expenses	$290,520
Operating Profit	$131,728
Interest Expenses	$1,234
EBT	$126,970
Taxes	$0
Net Income	$126,970

Asset Data

Data is Latest Reported	Yes
Data is "Purchase Price Allocation agreed upon by Buyer and Seller"	No
Balance Sheet Date	12/31/2001
Cash Equivalents	$0
Trade Receivables	$0
Inventory	$0
Other Current Assets	$0
Total Current Assets	$0
Fixed Assets	$25,000
Real Estate	$0
Intangibles	$0
Other Noncurrent Assets	$0
Total Assets	$25,000
Long-term Liabilities	N/A
Total Liabilities	N/A
Stockholder's Equity	N/A

Transaction Data

Date Sale Initiated:	1/25/2002
Date of Sale:	5/22/2002
Days to Sell:	117
Asking Price:	$299,000
Market Value of Invested Capital*:	$275,000
Debt Assumed:	N/A
Employment Agreement Value:	N/A
Noncompete Value:	N/A
Amount of Down Payment:	$175,000
Stock or Asset Sale:	Asset
Company Type:	S Corporation
Was there an Employment/Consulting Agreement?	Yes
Was there an Assumed Lease in the sale?	Yes
Was there a Renewal Option with the Lease?	No

*Includes noncompete value and interest-bearing debt; excludes real estate, employment/consulting agreement values, and all contingent payments.

Additional Transaction Information

Was there a Note in the consideration paid? Yes
Was there a personal guarantee on the Note? Yes
Terms:
Consideration: $100,000 at 8% interest over 24 months subject to adjustment based on performance.
Assumed Lease (Months): 7
Terms of Lease: N/A
Noncompete Length (Months): 60
Noncompete Description: 60 miles
Employment/Consulting Agreement Description: 2 years of employment as a salesperson.
Additional Notes:
EBT includes other expenses of $3,524.

Valuation Multiples

MVIC/Net Sales	0.65
MVIC/Gross Profit	0.65
MVIC/EBITDA	2.07
MVIC/EBIT	2.09
MVIC/Discretionary Earnings	1.38
MVIC/Book Value of Invested Capital	N/A

Profitability Ratios

Net Profit Margin	0.30
Operating Profit Margin	0.30
Gross Profit Margin	1.00
Return on Assets	5.08
Return on Equity	N/A

Leverage Ratios

Fixed Charge Coverage	103.89
Long-Term Debt to Assets	N/A
Long-Term Debt to Equity	N/A

Earnings

EBITDA	$132,873
Discretionary Earnings	$199,203

Liquidity Ratios

Current Ratio	N/A
Quick Ratio	N/A

Activity Ratios

Total Asset Turnover	16.89
Fixed Asset Turnover	16.89
Inventory Turnover	N/A

Copyright © 2010 Business Valuation Resources, LLC. All rights reserved. www.BVResources.com℠
(888) BUS-VALU, (503) 291-7963

Pratt's Stats® Auto Dealership Report

Pratt's Stats® Transaction Report
Prepared: 8/20/2010 2:09:45 PM (PST)

Seller Details
Target Name:	Sierra Freightliner
Business Description:	Freightliner Dealership
SIC:	5511 Motor Vehicle Dealers (New and Used)
NAICS:	441110 New Car Dealers
Sale Location:	Sparks, NV, United States
Years in Business:	8
Number Employees:	35

Source Data
Broker Name:	Loftin, Katrina
Broker Firm Name:	BTI Group/ Business Team

Income Data
Data is "Latest Full Year" Reported	Yes
Data is Restated (see Notes for any explanation)	No
Income Statement Date	10/31/2003
Net Sales	$8,762,486
COGS	$5,809,133
Gross Profit	$2,953,353
Yearly Rent	N/A
Owner's Compensation	N/A
Other Operating Expenses	N/A
Noncash Charges	N/A
Total Operating Expenses	$3,455,159
Operating Profit	($501,806)
Interest Expenses	$16,382
EBT	($518,188)
Taxes	$0
Net Income	($518,188)

Asset Data
Data is Latest Reported	Yes
Data is "Purchase Price Allocation agreed upon by Buyer and Seller"	No
Balance Sheet Date	10/31/2003
Cash Equivalents	$68,484
Trade Receivables	$766,273
Inventory	$2,020,786
Other Current Assets	$2,173,184
Total Current Assets	$5,028,727
Fixed Assets	$0
Real Estate	$0
Intangibles	$0
Other Noncurrent Assets	$0
Total Assets	$5,028,727
Long-term Liabilities	N/A
Total Liabilities	$9,209,466
Stockholder's Equity	($4,180,739)

Transaction Data
Date Sale Initiated:	10/13/2004
Date of Sale:	12/17/2004
Days to Sell:	65
Asking Price:	N/A
Market Value of Invested Capital*:	$2,318,445
Debt Assumed:	$0
Employment Agreement Value:	$0
Noncompete Value:	N/A
Amount of Down Payment:	$2,318,445
Stock or Asset Sale:	Asset
Company Type:	S Corporation
Was there an Employment/Consulting Agreement?	No
Was there an Assumed Lease in the sale?	Yes
Was there a Renewal Option with the Lease?	Yes

*Includes noncompete value and interest-bearing debt; excludes real estate, employment/consulting agreement values, and all contingent payments.

Additional Transaction Information
Was there a Note in the consideration paid? No
Terms:
Assumed Lease (Months): 132
Noncompete Length (Months): N/A
Employment/Consulting Agreement Description:
Additional Notes:

Was there a personal guarantee on the Note? No

Terms of Lease: $34,450 per month
Noncompete Description: N/A

Valuation Multiples
MVIC/Net Sales	0.26
MVIC/Gross Profit	0.79
MVIC/EBITDA	N/A
MVIC/EBIT	N/A
MVIC/Discretionary Earnings	N/A
MVIC/Book Value of Invested Capital	N/A

Profitability Ratios
Net Profit Margin	-0.06
Operating Profit Margin	-0.06
Gross Profit Margin	0.34
Return on Assets	-0.10
Return on Equity	N/A

Leverage Ratios
Fixed Charge Coverage	-30.63
Long-Term Debt to Assets	N/A
Long-Term Debt to Equity	N/A

Earnings
EBITDA	N/A
Discretionary Earnings	N/A

Liquidity Ratios
Current Ratio	N/A
Quick Ratio	N/A

Activity Ratios
Total Asset Turnover	1.74
Fixed Asset Turnover	N/A
Inventory Turnover	4.34

Copyright © 2010 Business Valuation Resources, LLC. All rights reserved. www.BVResources.com℠
(888) BUS-VALU, (503) 291-7963

Pratt's Stats® Auto Dealership Report

Pratt's Stats® Transaction Report
Prepared: 8/20/2010 2:09:45 PM (PST)

Seller Details
Target Name:	E-Z Plan, Inc.
Business Description:	Automobile Sales and Financing
SIC:	5511 Motor Vehicle Dealers (New and Used)
NAICS:	441110 New Car Dealers
Sale Location:	United States
Years in Business:	N/A
Number Employees:	N/A

Source Data
Public Buyer Name:	UGLY DUCKLING CORP
8-K Date:	N/A
8-K/A Date:	6/11/1997
Other Filing Type:	N/A
Other Filing Date:	N/A
CIK Code:	0001012704

Income Data
Data is "Latest Full Year" Reported	Yes
Data is Restated (see Notes for any explanation)	No
Income Statement Date	12/31/1996
Net Sales	$42,302,699
COGS	$35,312,366
Gross Profit	$6,990,333
Yearly Rent	$1,061,000
Owner's Compensation	N/A
Other Operating Expenses	N/A
Noncash Charges	$226,760
Total Operating Expenses	$4,256,085
Operating Profit	$2,734,248
Interest Expenses	$1,880,125
EBT	$201,717
Taxes	$0
Net Income	$201,717

Asset Data
Data is Latest Reported	Yes
Data is "Purchase Price Allocation agreed upon by Buyer and Seller"	No
Balance Sheet Date	3/31/1997
Cash Equivalents	$1,272,000
Trade Receivables	$21,921,000
Inventory	$2,791,000
Other Current Assets	$2,096,000
Total Current Assets	$28,080,000
Fixed Assets	$838,000
Real Estate	$0
Intangibles	$0
Other Noncurrent Assets	$967,000
Total Assets	$29,885,000
Long-term Liabilities	$0
Total Liabilities	$23,439,000
Stockholder's Equity	$6,446,000

Transaction Data
Date Sale Initiated:	N/A
Date of Sale:	4/1/1997
Days to Sell:	N/A
Asking Price:	N/A
Market Value of Invested Capital*:	$26,251,000
Debt Assumed:	N/A
Employment Agreement Value:	N/A
Noncompete Value:	N/A
Amount of Down Payment:	$26,251,000
Stock or Asset Sale:	Asset
Company Type:	S Corporation
Was there an Employment/Consulting Agreement?	No
Was there an Assumed Lease in the sale?	Yes
Was there a Renewal Option with the Lease?	No

*Includes noncompete value and interest-bearing debt; excludes real estate, employment/consulting agreement values, and all contingent payments.

Additional Transaction Information

Was there a Note in the consideration paid? No
Terms:
Consideration: $26,251,000 in cash.
Assumed Lease (Months): 48
Noncompete Length (Months): N/A
Employment/Consulting Agreement Description:
Additional Notes:
EBT includes Interest Income of $43,370 and Key man life insurance expense of ($695,776).

Purchase Price Allocation: Finance Receivables $19,562,000, Inventory $1,205,000, Property and Equipment $416,000, Prepaid Rent $40,000, Deposits $6,000, Petty Cash $2,000, Property taxes ($24,000), Total Fair Value $21,207,000, Consideration Exchanged $26,251,000, Excess of Purchase Price over Fair Value of Assets Acquired (Goodwill) $5,044,000.

Was there a personal guarantee on the Note? No

Terms of Lease: Future minimum lease payments total $2,305,333 through 12/31/2000
Noncompete Description: N/A

E-Z Plan, Inc. (the Company) began operations in January 1990 with the opening of its first used automobile retail sales facility in San Antonio, Texas. As of December 31, 1996, fourteen retail sales facilities were operating under the names E-Z Motors, Red McCombs Superstores, and Red McCombs Star Cars primarily in the San Antonio and central Texas areas. In addition to automobile sales, the Company provides financing to its retail customers with terms generally averaging 24 -36 months at annual interest rates ranging from 18% to 26%. The Company retains a security interest in the related vehicles. During 1995 the Company also served as a financing source for motor vehicle contracts arising from automobile sales by affiliated dealerships. Consideration paid by the Company to these dealerships for such contracts was either 90% of the principal financed on a non-recourse basis; or 100% of the principal financed less a $200 fee on a recourse basis.

Valuation Multiples
MVIC/Net Sales	0.62
MVIC/Gross Profit	3.76
MVIC/EBITDA	8.87
MVIC/EBIT	9.60
MVIC/Discretionary Earnings	N/A
MVIC/Book Value of Invested Capital	4.07

Profitability Ratios
Net Profit Margin	0.00
Operating Profit Margin	0.05
Gross Profit Margin	0.17
Return on Assets	0.01
Return on Equity	0.03

Leverage Ratios
Fixed Charge Coverage	1.11
Long-Term Debt to Assets	0.00
Long-Term Debt to Equity	0.00

Earnings
Liquidity Ratios
Activity Ratios

Pratt's Stats® Auto Dealership Report

Pratt's Stats® Transaction Report
Prepared: 8/20/2010 2:09:45 PM (PST)

Seller Details
Target Name:	Manhattan Automotive Group
Business Description:	Automobile Dealership - New and Used
SIC:	5511 Motor Vehicle Dealers (New and Used)
NAICS:	441110 New Car Dealers
Sale Location:	DC, United States
Years in Business:	N/A Number Employees: N/A

Source Data
Public Buyer Name:	SONIC AUTOMOTIVE INC
8-K Date:	11/19/1999
8-K/A Date:	1/18/2000
Other Filing Type:	N/A
Other Filing Date:	N/A
CIK Code:	0001043509

Income Data
Data is "Latest Full Year" Reported	Yes
Data is Restated (see Notes for any explanation)	No
Income Statement Date	12/31/1998
Net Sales	$154,821,083
COGS	$133,975,188
Gross Profit	$20,845,895
Yearly Rent	N/A
Owner's Compensation	N/A
Other Operating Expenses	N/A
Noncash Charges	$174,835
Total Operating Expenses	$14,704,949
Operating Profit	$6,140,946
Interest Expenses	$513,786
EBT	$5,983,281
Taxes	$527,000
Net Income	$5,456,281

Asset Data
Data is Latest Reported	Yes
Data is "Purchase Price Allocation agreed upon by Buyer and Seller"	No
Balance Sheet Date	6/30/1999
Cash Equivalents	$6,590,534
Trade Receivables	$3,444,428
Inventory	$11,886,336
Other Current Assets	$58,687
Total Current Assets	$21,979,985
Fixed Assets	$657,197
Real Estate	$0
Intangibles	$0
Other Noncurrent Assets	$3,021,776
Total Assets	$25,658,958
Long-term Liabilities	$0
Total Liabilities	$13,115,460
Stockholder's Equity	$12,543,498

Transaction Data
Date Sale Initiated:	N/A
Date of Sale:	8/3/1999
Days to Sell:	N/A
Asking Price:	N/A
Market Value of Invested Capital*:	$51,000,000
Debt Assumed:	N/A
Employment Agreement Value:	N/A
Noncompete Value:	N/A
Amount of Down Payment:	$51,000,000
Stock or Asset Sale:	Asset
Company Type:	S Corporation
Was there an Employment/Consulting Agreement?	No
Was there an Assumed Lease in the sale?	No
Was there a Renewal Option with the Lease?	No

*Includes noncompete value and interest-bearing debt; excludes real estate, employment/consulting agreement values, and all contingent payments.

Additional Transaction Information

Was there a Note in the consideration paid? No   Was there a personal guarantee on the Note? No

Terms:
Consideration: Cash in the amount of $31,000,000 and 1,574,932 shares of the Buyer's Class A common stock having a fair value of $20,000,000.

Assumed Lease (Months): N/A   Terms of Lease: N/A
Noncompete Length (Months): N/A   Noncompete Description: N/A
Employment/Consulting Agreement Description:
Additional Notes:
EBT includes Interest Income of $236,820 and Other Income of $119,301.

Manhattan Automotive Group (the "Company") operates four automobile dealerships in the Washington, D.C. area. The Company sells new and used cars and light trucks, sells replacement parts, provides maintenance, warranty services, paint and repair services and arranges related financing and insurance. The Company's four vehicle dealership locations sell new vehicles manufactured by Lexus, BMW, Porche, Audi, Nissan and Jeep.

Valuation Multiples
MVIC/Net Sales	0.33
MVIC/Gross Profit	2.45
MVIC/EBITDA	8.08
MVIC/EBIT	8.30
MVIC/Discretionary Earnings	N/A
MVIC/Book Value of Invested Capital	4.07

Profitability Ratios
Net Profit Margin	0.04
Operating Profit Margin	0.04
Gross Profit Margin	0.13
Return on Assets	0.21
Return on Equity	0.43

Leverage Ratios
Fixed Charge Coverage	12.65
Long-Term Debt to Assets	0.00
Long-Term Debt to Equity	0.00

Earnings
EBITDA	$6,315,781
Discretionary Earnings	N/A

Liquidity Ratios
Current Ratio	1.68
Quick Ratio	0.77

Activity Ratios
Total Asset Turnover	6.03
Fixed Asset Turnover	235.58
Inventory Turnover	13.03

Copyright © 2010 Business Valuation Resources, LLC. All rights reserved. www.BVResources.com℠
(888) BUS-VALU, (503) 291-7963

Pratt's Stats® Auto Dealership Report

Pratt's Stats® Transaction Report
Prepared: 8/20/2010 2:09:45 PM (PST)

Seller Details
Target Name:	N/A
Business Description:	New Car Dealership
SIC:	5511 Motor Vehicle Dealers (New and Used)
NAICS:	441110 New Car Dealers
Sale Location:	IA, United States
Years in Business:	18
Number Employees:	N/A

Source Data
Broker Name:	Zipursky, Jim
Broker Firm Name:	Corporate Finance Associates

Income Data
Data is "Latest Full Year" Reported	Yes
Data is Restated (see Notes for any explanation)	No
Income Statement Date	9/30/2004
Net Sales	$2,352,105
COGS	$2,203,173
Gross Profit	$148,932
Yearly Rent	N/A
Owner's Compensation	N/A
Other Operating Expenses	N/A
Noncash Charges	N/A
Total Operating Expenses	$125,076
Operating Profit	$23,856
Interest Expenses	$0
EBT	$23,856
Taxes	$0
Net Income	$23,856

Asset Data
Data is Latest Reported	Yes
Data is "Purchase Price Allocation agreed upon by Buyer and Seller"	No
Balance Sheet Date	9/30/2004
Cash Equivalents	$0
Trade Receivables	$0
Inventory	$25,000
Other Current Assets	$0
Total Current Assets	$25,000
Fixed Assets	$100,000
Real Estate	$0
Intangibles	$0
Other Noncurrent Assets	$0
Total Assets	$125,000
Long-term Liabilities	N/A
Total Liabilities	N/A
Stockholder's Equity	N/A

Transaction Data
Date Sale Initiated:	8/1/2002
Date of Sale:	10/10/2004
Days to Sell:	801
Asking Price:	N/A
Market Value of Invested Capital*:	$250,000
Debt Assumed:	N/A
Employment Agreement Value:	$150,000
Noncompete Value:	N/A
Amount of Down Payment:	N/A
Stock or Asset Sale:	Asset
Company Type:	S Corporation
Was there an Employment/Consulting Agreement?	Yes
Was there an Assumed Lease in the sale?	No
Was there a Renewal Option with the Lease?	No

*Includes noncompete value and interest-bearing debt; excludes real estate, employment/consulting agreement values, and all contingent payments.

Additional Transaction Information
Was there a Note in the consideration paid? No

Was there a personal guarantee on the Note? No

Terms:
Consideration: $400,000 in cash with a $600,000 no interest, no guarantee earnout paid at $150 per new auto sold in the first 3 years of business.

Assumed Lease (Months): N/A

Terms of Lease: N/A

Noncompete Length (Months): N/A

Noncompete Description: N/A

Employment/Consulting Agreement Description:

Additional Notes:
The employment agreement value of $150,000 was subtracted from the selling price.

Valuation Multiples
MVIC/Net Sales	0.11
MVIC/Gross Profit	1.68
MVIC/EBITDA	N/A
MVIC/EBIT	10.48
MVIC/Discretionary Earnings	N/A
MVIC/Book Value of Invested Capital	N/A

Profitability Ratios
Net Profit Margin	0.01
Operating Profit Margin	0.01
Gross Profit Margin	0.06
Return on Assets	0.19
Return on Equity	N/A

Leverage Ratios
Fixed Charge Coverage	N/A
Long-Term Debt to Assets	N/A
Long-Term Debt to Equity	N/A

Earnings
EBITDA	N/A
Discretionary Earnings	N/A

Liquidity Ratios
Current Ratio	N/A
Quick Ratio	N/A

Activity Ratios
Total Asset Turnover	18.82
Fixed Asset Turnover	23.52
Inventory Turnover	94.08

Copyright © 2010 Business Valuation Resources, LLC. All rights reserved. www.BVResources.com^SM
(888) BUS-VALU, (503) 291-7963

# Pratt's Stats® Auto Dealership Report

Pratt's Stats® Transaction Report
Prepared: 8/20/2010 2:09:45 PM (PST)

Seller Details
Target Name:	King's Auto Sales and Service, Inc.
Business Description:	Automobile Sales, Service, Repair and Rental
SIC:	5511 Motor Vehicle Dealers (New and Used)
NAICS:	441120 Used Car Dealers
Sale Location:	Fort Collins, CO, United States
Years in Business:	36
Number Employees:	6

Source Data
Broker Name:	N/A
Broker Firm Name:	VR Business Brokers

Income Data
Data is "Latest Full Year" Reported	Yes
Data is Restated (see Notes for any explanation)	No
Income Statement Date	12/31/2004
Net Sales	$1,548,643
COGS	$962,950
Gross Profit	$585,693
Yearly Rent	$30,176
Owner's Compensation	$30,611
Other Operating Expenses	N/A
Noncash Charges	N/A
Total Operating Expenses	$588,321
Operating Profit	($2,628)
Interest Expenses	$10,228
EBT	($12,856)
Taxes	$0
Net Income	($12,856)

Asset Data
Data is Latest Reported	Yes
Data is "Purchase Price Allocation agreed upon by Buyer and Seller"	No
Balance Sheet Date	10/31/2004
Cash Equivalents	$46,319
Trade Receivables	$15,594
Inventory	$509,351
Other Current Assets	$29,801
Total Current Assets	$601,065
Fixed Assets	$13,584
Real Estate	$0
Intangibles	$0
Other Noncurrent Assets	$0
Total Assets	$614,649
Long-term Liabilities	$258,104
Total Liabilities	$595,249
Stockholder's Equity	$19,400

Transaction Data
Date Sale Initiated:	10/23/2002
Date of Sale:	4/15/2005
Days to Sell:	905
Asking Price:	$350,000
Market Value of Invested Capital*:	$240,000
Debt Assumed:	$0
Employment Agreement Value:	N/A
Noncompete Value:	N/A
Amount of Down Payment:	$240,000
Stock or Asset Sale:	Asset
Company Type:	C Corporation
Was there an Employment/Consulting Agreement?	Yes
Was there an Assumed Lease in the sale?	No
Was there a Renewal Option with the Lease?	No

*Includes noncompete value and interest-bearing debt; excludes real estate, employment/consulting agreement values, and all contingent payments.

Additional Transaction Information
Was there a Note in the consideration paid? No
Terms:
Consideration: Cash in the amount of $240,000. The Buyer assumed the Seller's flooring.
Assumed Lease (Months): N/A
Noncompete Length (Months): 60
Employment/Consulting Agreement Description: 4 weeks training
Additional Notes:
This business sells, rents, services, and repairs cars. The customer base is mostly local with some customers from neighboring states. Marketing efforts include yellow pages, Wheels, and the internet. Their strengths include longevity and reputation, service, and growth. The business has a trained staff in place with a full-time service manager and a full-time general manager.

Was there a personal guarantee on the Note? No
Terms of Lease: N/A
Noncompete Description: 100 miles

Valuation Multiples
MVIC/Net Sales	0.15
MVIC/Gross Profit	0.41
MVIC/EBITDA	N/A
MVIC/EBIT	N/A
MVIC/Discretionary Earnings	N/A
MVIC/Book Value of Invested Capital	0.86

Profitability Ratios
Net Profit Margin	-0.01
Operating Profit Margin	-0.00
Gross Profit Margin	0.38
Return on Assets	-0.02
Return on Equity	-0.66

Leverage Ratios
Fixed Charge Coverage	-0.26
Long-Term Debt to Assets	0.42
Long-Term Debt to Equity	13.30

Earnings
EBITDA	N/A
Discretionary Earnings	N/A

Liquidity Ratios
Current Ratio	1.78
Quick Ratio	0.27

Activity Ratios
Total Asset Turnover	2.52
Fixed Asset Turnover	114.00
Inventory Turnover	3.04

Copyright © 2010 Business Valuation Resources, LLC. All rights reserved. www.BVResources.com℠
(888) BUS-VALU, (503) 291-7963

Pratt's Stats® Auto Dealership Report

Pratt's Stats® Transaction Report
Prepared: 8/20/2010 2:09:45 PM (PST)

Seller Details

Target Name:	Freeland Automotive (a business unit of South Gate Motors, Inc.)
Business Description:	Sells New and Used Cars and Light Trucks, Sells Replacement Parts, Provides Maintenance, Warranty Services, and Arranges Related Financing and Insurance
SIC:	5511 Motor Vehicle Dealers (New and Used)
NAICS:	441110 New Car Dealers
Sale Location:	Fort Myers, FL, United States
Years in Business:	N/A Number Employees: N/A

Source Data

Public Buyer Name:	SONIC AUTOMOTIVE INC
8-K Date:	11/19/1999
8-K/A Date:	1/18/2000
Other Filing Type:	N/A
Other Filing Date:	N/A
CIK Code:	0001043509

Income Data

Data is "Latest Full Year" Reported	Yes
Data is Restated (see Notes for any explanation)	No
Income Statement Date	12/31/1998
Net Sales	$125,225,996
COGS	$108,740,505
Gross Profit	$16,485,491
Yearly Rent	$151,000
Owner's Compensation	N/A
Other Operating Expenses	N/A
Noncash Charges	$330,151
Total Operating Expenses	$14,282,941
Operating Profit	$2,202,550
Interest Expenses	$1,915,803
EBT	$279,005
Taxes	$0
Net Income	$279,005

Asset Data

Data is Latest Reported	Yes
Data is "Purchase Price Allocation agreed upon by Buyer and Seller"	No
Balance Sheet Date	9/30/1999
Cash Equivalents	$2,155,473
Trade Receivables	$1,011,582
Inventory	$12,828,255
Other Current Assets	$469,205
Total Current Assets	$16,464,515
Fixed Assets	$8,214,373
Real Estate	$0
Intangibles	$0
Other Noncurrent Assets	$2,757,433
Total Assets	$27,436,321
Long-term Liabilities	$8,291,916
Total Liabilities	$25,379,331
Stockholder's Equity	$2,056,990

Transaction Data

Date Sale Initiated:	N/A
Date of Sale:	11/4/1999
Days to Sell:	N/A
Asking Price:	N/A
Market Value of Invested Capital*:	$25,000,000
Debt Assumed:	N/A
Employment Agreement Value:	N/A
Noncompete Value:	N/A
Amount of Down Payment:	$25,000,000
Stock or Asset Sale:	Asset
Company Type:	S Corporation
Was there an Employment/Consulting Agreement?	No
Was there an Assumed Lease in the sale?	Yes
Was there a Renewal Option with the Lease?	No

*Includes noncompete value and interest-bearing debt; excludes real estate, employment/consulting agreement values, and all contingent payments.

Additional Transaction Information

Was there a Note in the consideration paid? No
Terms:
Consideration: Cash in the amount of $25,000,000.
Assumed Lease (Months): 84
Noncompete Length (Months): N/A
Employment/Consulting Agreement Description:
Additional Notes:
EBT includes Other Expenses of $7,742.

Was there a personal guarantee on the Note? No

Terms of Lease: Future minimum lease payments total $651,900 through 12/31/2005
Noncompete Description: N/A

Freeland Automotive ("Freeland") is a business unit of South Gate Motors, Inc. Freeland operates five automobile franchises in the Fort Myers, Florida area. Freeland sells new and used cars and light trucks, sells replacement parts, provides maintenance, warranty services, and arranges related financing and insurance. Freeland's five dealership franchises sells new vehicles manufactured by Mercedes, BMW, Honda, Volkswagon and Nissan.

Valuation Multiples

MVIC/Net Sales	0.20
MVIC/Gross Profit	1.52
MVIC/EBITDA	9.87
MVIC/EBIT	11.35
MVIC/Discretionary Earnings	N/A
MVIC/Book Value of Invested Capital	2.42

Profitability Ratios

Net Profit Margin	0.00
Operating Profit Margin	0.02
Gross Profit Margin	0.13
Return on Assets	0.01
Return on Equity	0.14

Leverage Ratios

Fixed Charge Coverage	1.15
Long-Term Debt to Assets	0.30
Long-Term Debt to Equity	4.03

Earnings

EBITDA	$2,532,701
Discretionary Earnings	N/A

Liquidity Ratios

Current Ratio	0.96
Quick Ratio	0.21

Activity Ratios

Total Asset Turnover	4.56
Fixed Asset Turnover	15.24
Inventory Turnover	9.76

Pratt's Stats® Auto Dealership Report

Pratt's Stats® Transaction Report
Prepared: 8/20/2010 2:09:45 PM (PST)

Seller Details
Target Name:	N/A
Business Description:	Auto Dealership
SIC:	5511 Motor Vehicle Dealers (New and Used)
NAICS:	441110 New Car Dealers
Sale Location:	Naples, FL, United States
Years in Business:	8
Number Employees:	9

Source Data
Broker Name:	Cagnetta, Andrew
Broker Firm Name:	Transworld Business Brokers

Income Data
Data is "Latest Full Year" Reported	Yes
Data is Restated (see Notes for any explanation)	No
Income Statement Date	12/31/2006
Net Sales	$6,665,780
COGS	$4,356,897
Gross Profit	$2,308,883
Yearly Rent	$60,000
Owner's Compensation	$885,000
Other Operating Expenses	N/A
Noncash Charges	N/A
Total Operating Expenses	$1,423,883
Operating Profit	$885,000
Interest Expenses	$0
EBT	$885,000
Taxes	$0
Net Income	$885,000

Asset Data
Data is Latest Reported	Yes
Data is "Purchase Price Allocation agreed upon by Buyer and Seller"	No
Balance Sheet Date	12/31/2006
Cash Equivalents	$0
Trade Receivables	$0
Inventory	$35,000
Other Current Assets	$0
Total Current Assets	$35,000
Fixed Assets	$200,000
Real Estate	$0
Intangibles	$0
Other Noncurrent Assets	$0
Total Assets	$235,000
Long-term Liabilities	N/A
Total Liabilities	N/A
Stockholder's Equity	N/A

Transaction Data
Date Sale Initiated:	7/1/2007
Date of Sale:	11/20/2007
Days to Sell:	142
Asking Price:	$1,250,000
Market Value of Invested Capital*:	$1,250,000
Debt Assumed:	N/A
Employment Agreement Value:	N/A
Noncompete Value:	N/A
Amount of Down Payment:	$271,468
Stock or Asset Sale:	Stock
Company Type:	N/A
Was there an Employment/Consulting Agreement?	Yes
Was there an Assumed Lease in the sale?	No
Was there a Renewal Option with the Lease?	Yes

*Includes noncompete value and interest-bearing debt; excludes real estate, employment/consulting agreement values, and all contingent payments.

Additional Transaction Information
Was there a Note in the consideration paid? Yes
Terms:
Consideration: SBA loan.
Assumed Lease (Months): N/A
Noncompete Length (Months): 60
Employment/Consulting Agreement Description:
Additional Notes:

Was there a personal guarantee on the Note? Yes

Terms of Lease: N/A
Noncompete Description: 50 miles

Valuation Multiples
MVIC/Net Sales	0.19
MVIC/Gross Profit	0.54
MVIC/EBITDA	N/A
MVIC/EBIT	1.41
MVIC/Discretionary Earnings	N/A
MVIC/Book Value of Invested Capital	N/A

Profitability Ratios
Net Profit Margin	0.13
Operating Profit Margin	0.13
Gross Profit Margin	0.35
Return on Assets	3.77
Return on Equity	N/A

Leverage Ratios
Fixed Charge Coverage	N/A
Long-Term Debt to Assets	N/A
Long-Term Debt to Equity	N/A

Earnings
EBITDA	N/A
Discretionary Earnings	N/A

Liquidity Ratios
Current Ratio	N/A
Quick Ratio	N/A

Activity Ratios
Total Asset Turnover	28.37
Fixed Asset Turnover	33.33
Inventory Turnover	190.45

Copyright © 2010 Business Valuation Resources, LLC. All rights reserved. www.BVResources.com^SM
(888) BUS-VALU, (503) 291-7963

Pratt's Stats® Auto Dealership Report

Pratt's Stats® Transaction Report
Prepared: 8/20/2010 2:09:45 PM (PST)

Seller Details
Target Name:	N/A
Business Description:	Sells Wheelchair Accessible Vans and Driving Aids
SIC:	5511 Motor Vehicle Dealers (New and Used)
NAICS:	441110 New Car Dealers
Sale Location:	Edmonds, WA, United States
Years in Business:	19
Number Employees:	N/A

Source Data
Broker Name:	Tveidt, C. Jay
Broker Firm Name:	VR Tveidt & Associates, Inc.

Income Data
Data is "Latest Full Year" Reported	Yes
Data is Restated (see Notes for any explanation)	No
Income Statement Date	12/31/2000
Net Sales	$3,435,294
COGS	$2,927,994
Gross Profit	$507,300
Yearly Rent	$54,857
Owner's Compensation	$48,000
Other Operating Expenses	$324,320
Noncash Charges	$7,094
Total Operating Expenses	$434,271
Operating Profit	$73,029
Interest Expenses	$14,303
EBT	$81,459
Taxes	$0
Net Income	$81,459

Asset Data
Data is Latest Reported	No
Data is "Purchase Price Allocation agreed upon by Buyer and Seller"	No
Balance Sheet Date	12/31/2000
Cash Equivalents	$82,333
Trade Receivables	$200,443
Inventory	$541,307
Other Current Assets	$14,720
Total Current Assets	$838,803
Fixed Assets	$172,852
Real Estate	$0
Intangibles	$0
Other Noncurrent Assets	$21,638
Total Assets	$1,033,293
Long-term Liabilities	$65,839
Total Liabilities	$596,938
Stockholder's Equity	$436,355

Transaction Data
Date Sale Initiated:	N/A
Date of Sale:	7/29/2002
Days to Sell:	N/A
Asking Price:	N/A
Market Value of Invested Capital*:	$750,000
Debt Assumed:	N/A
Employment Agreement Value:	N/A
Noncompete Value:	N/A
Amount of Down Payment:	$750,000
Stock or Asset Sale:	Asset
Company Type:	C Corporation
Was there an Employment/Consulting Agreement?	No
Was there an Assumed Lease in the sale?	No
Was there a Renewal Option with the Lease?	No

*Includes noncompete value and interest-bearing debt; excludes real estate, employment/consulting agreement values, and all contingent payments.

Additional Transaction Information
Was there a Note in the consideration paid? No
Terms:
Consideration: $750,000 in cash.
Assumed Lease (Months): N/A
Noncompete Length (Months): 60
Employment/Consulting Agreement Description:
Additional Notes:
EBT includes interest and other income of $22,733. Purchase Price Allocation: $300,000 inventory, $43,300 furniture and equipment, $14,000 vehicles, $54,000 software, $5,000 fixtures and improvements, $210,000 rental inventory, $124,350 goodwill.

Was there a personal guarantee on the Note? No

Terms of Lease: N/A
Noncompete Description: Washington, Oregon, Idado, and Alaska

Valuation Multiples
MVIC/Net Sales	0.22
MVIC/Gross Profit	1.48
MVIC/EBITDA	9.36
MVIC/EBIT	10.27
MVIC/Discretionary Earnings	5.85
MVIC/Book Value of Invested Capital	1.49

Profitability Ratios
Net Profit Margin	0.02
Operating Profit Margin	0.03
Gross Profit Margin	0.15
Return on Assets	0.08
Return on Equity	0.19

Leverage Ratios
Fixed Charge Coverage	6.70
Long-Term Debt to Assets	0.06
Long-Term Debt to Equity	0.15

Earnings
EBITDA	$80,123
Discretionary Earnings	$128,123

Liquidity Ratios
Current Ratio	1.58
Quick Ratio	0.56

Activity Ratios
Total Asset Turnover	3.32
Fixed Asset Turnover	19.87
Inventory Turnover	6.35

Copyright © 2010 Business Valuation Resources, LLC. All rights reserved. www.BVResources.com(SM)
(888) BUS-VALU, (503) 291-7963

Pratt's Stats® Auto Dealership Report

Pratt's Stats® Transaction Report
Prepared: 8/20/2010 2:09:45 PM (PST)

Seller Details
Target Name:	L & B Truck Services, Inc.
Business Description:	New Truck Sales and Service (Class 5 - 8)
SIC:	5511 Motor Vehicle Dealers (New and Used)
NAICS:	441110 New Car Dealers
Sale Location:	United States
Years in Business:	27
Number Employees:	60

Source Data
Broker Name:	Steckler, Philip
Broker Firm Name:	Country Business, Inc.

Income Data
Data is "Latest Full Year" Reported	No
Data is Restated (see Notes for any explanation)	Yes
Income Statement Date	12/31/2007
Net Sales	$16,000,000
COGS	$12,500,000
Gross Profit	$3,500,000
Yearly Rent	$0
Owner's Compensation	$96,000
Other Operating Expenses	$2,365,800
Noncash Charges	$260,000
Total Operating Expenses	$2,721,800
Operating Profit	$778,200
Interest Expenses	$19,500
EBT	$758,700
Taxes	$0
Net Income	$758,700

Asset Data
Data is Latest Reported	No
Data is "Purchase Price Allocation agreed upon by Buyer and Seller"	Yes
Balance Sheet Date	5/1/2008
Cash Equivalents	$90,000
Trade Receivables	$476,600
Inventory	$893,800
Other Current Assets	$23,800
Total Current Assets	$1,484,200
Fixed Assets	$3,255,000
Real Estate	$1,900,000
Intangibles	$350,000
Other Noncurrent Assets	$0
Total Assets	$6,989,200
Long-term Liabilities	N/A
Total Liabilities	N/A
Stockholder's Equity	N/A

Transaction Data
Date Sale Initiated:	N/A
Date of Sale:	5/1/2008
Days to Sell:	N/A
Asking Price:	N/A
Market Value of Invested Capital*:	$5,089,200
Debt Assumed:	$50,000
Employment Agreement Value:	$96,000
Noncompete Value:	$0
Amount of Down Payment:	$800,000
Stock or Asset Sale:	Asset
Company Type:	S Corporation
Was there an Employment/Consulting Agreement?	Yes
Was there an Assumed Lease in the sale?	No
Was there a Renewal Option with the Lease?	No

*Includes noncompete value and interest-bearing debt; excludes real estate, employment/consulting agreement values, and all contingent payments.

Additional Transaction Information
Was there a Note in the consideration paid? Yes

Was there a personal guarantee on the Note? Yes

Terms:
Consideration: $1,000,000 with no payments for 12 months with a 10-year amortization at around 3% interest.

Assumed Lease (Months): N/A

Terms of Lease: N/A

Noncompete Length (Months): 60

Noncompete Description: 100 miles

Employment/Consulting Agreement Description: One year at $96,000.

Additional Notes:
Sales range from $15,000,000 to $22,000,000. Emission regulators influence these type of businesses. The income statement is somewhat of a normalized average. EBIDT over the past five years has generally been $1,000,000 but has ranged from $735,000 to $1,300,000. The focus of the company has always been on service and parts.

Valuation Multiples
MVIC/Net Sales	0.32
MVIC/Gross Profit	1.45
MVIC/EBITDA	4.90
MVIC/EBIT	6.54
MVIC/Discretionary Earnings	4.49
MVIC/Book Value of Invested Capital	N/A

Profitability Ratios
Net Profit Margin	0.05
Operating Profit Margin	0.05
Gross Profit Margin	0.22
Return on Assets	0.11
Return on Equity	N/A

Leverage Ratios
Fixed Charge Coverage	39.91
Long-Term Debt to Assets	N/A
Long-Term Debt to Equity	N/A

Earnings
EBITDA	$1,038,200
Discretionary Earnings	$1,134,200

Liquidity Ratios
Current Ratio	N/A
Quick Ratio	N/A

Activity Ratios
Total Asset Turnover	2.29
Fixed Asset Turnover	4.92
Inventory Turnover	17.90

Copyright © 2010 Business Valuation Resources, LLC. All rights reserved. www.BVResources.com℠
(888) BUS-VALU, (503) 291-7963

Pratt's Stats® Auto Dealership Report

Pratt's Stats® Transaction Report
Prepared: 8/20/2010 2:09:45 PM (PST)

Seller Details
Target Name:	N/A
Business Description:	Used Auto Dealer
SIC:	5511 Motor Vehicle Dealers (New and Used)
NAICS:	441110 New Car Dealers
Sale Location:	Satellite Beach, FL, United States
Years in Business:	3
Number Employees:	1

Source Data
Broker Name:	Vescio, Lou
Broker Firm Name:	Sunbelt Business Brokers of Vero, Inc.

Income Data
Data is "Latest Full Year" Reported	Yes
Data is Restated (see Notes for any explanation)	No
Income Statement Date	12/31/2006
Net Sales	$2,429,728
COGS	$2,027,996
Gross Profit	$401,732
Yearly Rent	$24,000
Owner's Compensation	$41,000
Other Operating Expenses	$266,987
Noncash Charges	$1,361
Total Operating Expenses	$333,348
Operating Profit	$68,384
Interest Expenses	$0
EBT	$68,384
Taxes	$0
Net Income	$68,384

Asset Data
Data is Latest Reported	No
Data is "Purchase Price Allocation agreed upon by Buyer and Seller"	No
Balance Sheet Date	N/A
Cash Equivalents	N/A
Trade Receivables	N/A
Inventory	N/A
Other Current Assets	N/A
Total Current Assets	N/A
Fixed Assets	N/A
Real Estate	N/A
Intangibles	N/A
Other Noncurrent Assets	N/A
Total Assets	N/A
Long-term Liabilities	N/A
Total Liabilities	N/A
Stockholder's Equity	N/A

Transaction Data
Date Sale Initiated:	8/21/2007
Date of Sale:	9/20/2007
Days to Sell:	30
Asking Price:	$225,000
Market Value of Invested Capital*:	$190,000
Debt Assumed:	$0
Employment Agreement Value:	$0
Noncompete Value:	N/A
Amount of Down Payment:	$190,000
Stock or Asset Sale:	Asset
Company Type:	S Corporation
Was there an Employment/Consulting Agreement?	No
Was there an Assumed Lease in the sale?	No
Was there a Renewal Option with the Lease?	No

*Includes noncompete value and interest-bearing debt; excludes real estate, employment/consulting agreement values, and all contingent payments.

Additional Transaction Information

Was there a Note in the consideration paid? No
Terms:
Assumed Lease (Months): N/A
Noncompete Length (Months): 24
Employment/Consulting Agreement Description: 2 weeks/no compensation
Additional Notes:
The balance sheet was unavailable. A new lease was written to accomodate the buyer. Listed with $25,000 in inventory, but sold with $2500 in inventory.

Was there a personal guarantee on the Note? No

Terms of Lease: 1 year lease
Noncompete Description: 8 miles

Valuation Multiples
MVIC/Net Sales	0.08
MVIC/Gross Profit	0.47
MVIC/EBITDA	2.72
MVIC/EBIT	2.78
MVIC/Discretionary Earnings	1.72
MVIC/Book Value of Invested Capital	N/A

Profitability Ratios
Net Profit Margin	0.03
Operating Profit Margin	0.03
Gross Profit Margin	0.17
Return on Assets	N/A
Return on Equity	N/A

Leverage Ratios
Fixed Charge Coverage	N/A
Long-Term Debt to Assets	N/A
Long-Term Debt to Equity	N/A

Earnings
EBITDA	$69,745
Discretionary Earnings	$110,745

Liquidity Ratios
Current Ratio	N/A
Quick Ratio	N/A

Activity Ratios
Total Asset Turnover	N/A
Fixed Asset Turnover	N/A
Inventory Turnover	N/A

Copyright © 2010 Business Valuation Resources, LLC. All rights reserved. www.BVResources.com^SM
(888) BUS-VALU, (503) 291-7963

Pratt's Stats® Auto Dealership Report

Pratt's Stats® Transaction Report
Prepared: 8/20/2010 2:09:45 PM (PST)

Seller Details
Target Name:	Total Leasing and Sales
Business Description:	New and Used Automobile Brokerage
SIC:	5511 Motor Vehicle Dealers (New and Used)
NAICS:	441110 New Car Dealers
Sale Location:	Chattanooga, TN, United States
Years in Business:	26
Number Employees:	3

Source Data
Broker Name:	Seitz, Patrick
Broker Firm Name:	Sunbelt Business Advisors

Income Data
Data is "Latest Full Year" Reported	Yes
Data is Restated (see Notes for any explanation)	No
Income Statement Date	12/31/2007
Net Sales	$4,356,000
COGS	$4,011,000
Gross Profit	$345,000
Yearly Rent	$18,000
Owner's Compensation	$110,000
Other Operating Expenses	$157,000
Noncash Charges	$3,000
Total Operating Expenses	$288,000
Operating Profit	$57,000
Interest Expenses	$0
EBT	$57,000
Taxes	$0
Net Income	$57,000

Asset Data
Data is Latest Reported	No
Data is "Purchase Price Allocation agreed upon by Buyer and Seller"	Yes
Balance Sheet Date	4/30/2008
Cash Equivalents	N/A
Trade Receivables	N/A
Inventory	N/A
Other Current Assets	N/A
Total Current Assets	N/A
Fixed Assets	N/A
Real Estate	N/A
Intangibles	$300,000
Other Noncurrent Assets	N/A
Total Assets	N/A
Long-term Liabilities	N/A
Total Liabilities	N/A
Stockholder's Equity	N/A

Transaction Data
Date Sale Initiated:	4/12/2007
Date of Sale:	4/30/2008
Days to Sell:	384
Asking Price:	$395,000
Market Value of Invested Capital*:	$300,000
Debt Assumed:	$0
Employment Agreement Value:	$0
Noncompete Value:	$0
Amount of Down Payment:	$100,000
Stock or Asset Sale:	Stock
Company Type:	LLC
Was there an Employment/Consulting Agreement?	Yes
Was there an Assumed Lease in the sale?	Yes
Was there a Renewal Option with the Lease?	No

*Includes noncompete value and interest-bearing debt; excludes real estate, employment/consulting agreement values, and all contingent payments.

Additional Transaction Information
Was there a Note in the consideration paid? Yes
Terms:
Consideration: $100,000 in cash and a $200,000 note at 5% interest over 6 years with monthly payments of $3,221 with the first payment due on July 30, 2008.
Assumed Lease (Months): N/A
Noncompete Length (Months): 60
Employment/Consulting Agreement Description: 3 months of full-time training and transition.
Additional Notes:
Licensed dealership with sales only. Carried zero inventory. Located vehicles for customers via online auctions, at auctions, or new vehicle dealerships. Owner's compensation is SDE and includes seller's benefits and perks. Business may be relocated.

Was there a personal guarantee on the Note? No
Terms of Lease: Month to month
Noncompete Description: 500 mile radius

Valuation Multiples
MVIC/Net Sales	0.07
MVIC/Gross Profit	0.87
MVIC/EBITDA	5.00
MVIC/EBIT	5.26
MVIC/Discretionary Earnings	1.76
MVIC/Book Value of Invested Capital	N/A

Profitability Ratios
Net Profit Margin	0.01
Operating Profit Margin	0.01
Gross Profit Margin	0.08
Return on Assets	N/A
Return on Equity	N/A

Leverage Ratios
Fixed Charge Coverage	N/A
Long-Term Debt to Assets	N/A
Long-Term Debt to Equity	N/A

Earnings
EBITDA	$60,000
Discretionary Earnings	$170,000

Liquidity Ratios
Current Ratio	N/A
Quick Ratio	N/A

Activity Ratios
Total Asset Turnover	N/A
Fixed Asset Turnover	N/A
Inventory Turnover	N/A

Copyright © 2010 Business Valuation Resources, LLC. All rights reserved. www.BVResources.com^{SM}
(888) BUS-VALU, (503) 291-7963

Pratt's Stats® Auto Dealership Report

Pratt's Stats® Transaction Report
Prepared: 8/20/2010 2:09:45 PM (PST)

Seller Details
Target Name:	N/A
Business Description:	Auto Broker
SIC:	5511 Motor Vehicle Dealers (New and Used)
NAICS:	441110 New Car Dealers
Sale Location:	GA, United States
Years in Business:	7
Number Employees:	1

Source Data
Broker Name:	N/A
Broker Firm Name:	N/A

Income Data
Data is "Latest Full Year" Reported	Yes
Data is Restated (see Notes for any explanation)	No
Income Statement Date	12/31/2006
Net Sales	$7,091,830
COGS	$6,622,038
Gross Profit	$469,792
Yearly Rent	N/A
Owner's Compensation	$0
Other Operating Expenses	N/A
Noncash Charges	$0
Total Operating Expenses	$753,591
Operating Profit	($283,799)
Interest Expenses	$0
EBT	($283,799)
Taxes	$0
Net Income	($283,799)

Asset Data
Data is Latest Reported	No
Data is "Purchase Price Allocation agreed upon by Buyer and Seller"	Yes
Balance Sheet Date	2/29/2008
Cash Equivalents	N/A
Trade Receivables	N/A
Inventory	N/A
Other Current Assets	N/A
Total Current Assets	N/A
Fixed Assets	$172,800
Real Estate	$1,100,000
Intangibles	$10,386
Other Noncurrent Assets	N/A
Total Assets	N/A
Long-term Liabilities	N/A
Total Liabilities	N/A
Stockholder's Equity	N/A

Transaction Data
Date Sale Initiated:	1/29/2007
Date of Sale:	2/29/2008
Days to Sell:	396
Asking Price:	$1,800,000
Market Value of Invested Capital*:	$183,186
Debt Assumed:	N/A
Employment Agreement Value:	N/A
Noncompete Value:	N/A
Amount of Down Payment:	N/A
Stock or Asset Sale:	Asset
Company Type:	C Corporation
Was there an Employment/Consulting Agreement?	No
Was there an Assumed Lease in the sale?	No
Was there a Renewal Option with the Lease?	No

*Includes noncompete value and interest-bearing debt; excludes real estate, employment/consulting agreement values, and all contingent payments.

Additional Transaction Information
Was there a Note in the consideration paid? No
Terms:
Assumed Lease (Months): N/A
Noncompete Length (Months): 24
Employment/Consulting Agreement Description:
Additional Notes:
Transaction was submitted by the GABB (3/2009). The real estate value of $1,100,000 was subtracted from the selling price.

Was there a personal guarantee on the Note? No
Terms of Lease: N/A
Noncompete Description: 50 miles

Valuation Multiples
MVIC/Net Sales	0.03
MVIC/Gross Profit	0.39
MVIC/EBITDA	N/A
MVIC/EBIT	N/A
MVIC/Discretionary Earnings	N/A
MVIC/Book Value of Invested Capital	N/A

Profitability Ratios
Net Profit Margin	-0.04
Operating Profit Margin	-0.04
Gross Profit Margin	0.07
Return on Assets	N/A
Return on Equity	N/A

Leverage Ratios
Fixed Charge Coverage	N/A
Long-Term Debt to Assets	N/A
Long-Term Debt to Equity	N/A

Earnings
EBITDA	($283,799)
Discretionary Earnings	($283,799)

Liquidity Ratios
Current Ratio	N/A
Quick Ratio	N/A

Activity Ratios
Total Asset Turnover	N/A
Fixed Asset Turnover	41.04
Inventory Turnover	N/A

Copyright © 2010 Business Valuation Resources, LLC. All rights reserved. www.BVResources.com[SM]
(888) BUS-VALU, (503) 291-7963

Pratt's Stats® Auto Dealership Report

Pratt's Stats® Transaction Report
Prepared: 8/20/2010 2:09:45 PM (PST)

Seller Details
Target Name:	N/A
Business Description:	Retail and Wholesale of Heavy Duty Truck and Trailer Parts
SIC:	5511 Motor Vehicle Dealers (New and Used)
NAICS:	441110 New Car Dealers
Sale Location:	Raleigh, NC, United States
Years in Business:	18
Number Employees:	6

Source Data
Broker Name:	Guertin, Tom
Broker Firm Name:	Sunbelt Business Advisors

Income Data
Data is "Latest Full Year" Reported	Yes
Data is Restated (see Notes for any explanation)	No
Income Statement Date	3/31/2004
Net Sales	$944,084
COGS	$599,894
Gross Profit	$344,190
Yearly Rent	$32,593
Owner's Compensation	$50,136
Other Operating Expenses	$240,822
Noncash Charges	$14,113
Total Operating Expenses	$337,664
Operating Profit	$6,526
Interest Expenses	$3,801
EBT	$2,725
Taxes	$0
Net Income	$2,725

Asset Data
Data is Latest Reported	No
Data is "Purchase Price Allocation agreed upon by Buyer and Seller"	Yes
Balance Sheet Date	1/31/2005
Cash Equivalents	N/A
Trade Receivables	N/A
Inventory	$240,000
Other Current Assets	N/A
Total Current Assets	N/A
Fixed Assets	$200,000
Real Estate	N/A
Intangibles	$5,000
Other Noncurrent Assets	N/A
Total Assets	N/A
Long-term Liabilities	N/A
Total Liabilities	N/A
Stockholder's Equity	N/A

Transaction Data
Date Sale Initiated:	11/4/2004
Date of Sale:	1/31/2005
Days to Sell:	88
Asking Price:	N/A
Market Value of Invested Capital*:	$459,000
Debt Assumed:	$60,000
Employment Agreement Value:	N/A
Noncompete Value:	$14,000
Amount of Down Payment:	$65,000
Stock or Asset Sale:	Asset
Company Type:	C Corporation
Was there an Employment/Consulting Agreement?	No
Was there an Assumed Lease in the sale?	No
Was there a Renewal Option with the Lease?	No

*Includes noncompete value and interest-bearing debt; excludes real estate, employment/consulting agreement values, and all contingent payments.

Additional Transaction Information
Was there a Note in the consideration paid? Yes
Was there a personal guarantee on the Note? No

Terms: Consideration: $65,000 in cash, a $334,000 promissory note at 8% interest over 84 months with monthly payments of $5,205, and the assumption of $60,000 in the seller's business loan.

Assumed Lease (Months): N/A
Terms of Lease: N/A
Noncompete Length (Months): 120
Noncompete Description: North Carolina, South Carolina, and Virginia
Employment/Consulting Agreement Description:
Additional Notes: The reason for selling was retirement.

Valuation Multiples
MVIC/Net Sales	0.49
MVIC/Gross Profit	1.33
MVIC/EBITDA	22.24
MVIC/EBIT	70.33
MVIC/Discretionary Earnings	6.49
MVIC/Book Value of Invested Capital	N/A

Profitability Ratios
Net Profit Margin	0.00
Operating Profit Margin	0.01
Gross Profit Margin	0.36
Return on Assets	N/A
Return on Equity	N/A

Leverage Ratios
Fixed Charge Coverage	1.72
Long-Term Debt to Assets	N/A
Long-Term Debt to Equity	N/A

Earnings
EBITDA	$20,639
Discretionary Earnings	$70,775

Liquidity Ratios
Current Ratio	N/A
Quick Ratio	N/A

Activity Ratios
Total Asset Turnover	N/A
Fixed Asset Turnover	4.72
Inventory Turnover	3.93

Copyright © 2010 Business Valuation Resources, LLC. All rights reserved. www.BVResources.com℠
(888) BUS-VALU, (503) 291-7963

Pratt's Stats® Auto Dealership Report

Pratt's Stats® Transaction Report
Prepared: 8/20/2010 2:09:45 PM (PST)

Seller Details
Target Name:	Liberty Finance Company, Inc.
Business Description:	Retail Sales and Financing of Used Automobiles
SIC:	5521 Motor Vehicle Dealers (Used Only)
NAICS:	441120 Used Car Dealers
Sale Location:	FL, United States
Years in Business:	N/A
Number Employees:	N/A

Source Data
Public Buyer Name:	SMART CHOICE AUTOMOTIVE GROUP INC
8-K Date:	N/A
8-K/A Date:	N/A
Other Filing Type:	S-1
Other Filing Date:	7/17/1998
CIK Code:	0000949091

Income Data
Data is "Latest Full Year" Reported	Yes
Data is Restated (see Notes for any explanation)	No
Income Statement Date	12/31/1996
Net Sales	$18,639,749
COGS	$16,122,778
Gross Profit	$2,516,971
Yearly Rent	$512,008
Owner's Compensation	N/A
Other Operating Expenses	N/A
Noncash Charges	$73,398
Total Operating Expenses	$4,852,529
Operating Profit	($2,335,558)
Interest Expenses	$1,324,437
EBT	($612,326)
Taxes	$0
Net Income	($612,326)

Asset Data
Data is Latest Reported	Yes
Data is "Purchase Price Allocation agreed upon by Buyer and Seller"	No
Balance Sheet Date	12/31/1996
Cash Equivalents	$163,184
Trade Receivables	$11,383,431
Inventory	$2,861,848
Other Current Assets	N/A
Total Current Assets	$14,408,463
Fixed Assets	$272,543
Real Estate	$1,050,000
Intangibles	N/A
Other Noncurrent Assets	$87,908
Total Assets	$15,818,914
Long-term Liabilities	$0
Total Liabilities	$15,338,765
Stockholder's Equity	$480,149

Transaction Data
Date Sale Initiated:	N/A
Date of Sale:	2/12/1997
Days to Sell:	N/A
Asking Price:	N/A
Market Value of Invested Capital*:	$2,688,527
Debt Assumed:	N/A
Employment Agreement Value:	N/A
Noncompete Value:	N/A
Amount of Down Payment:	$1,188,527
Stock or Asset Sale:	Stock
Company Type:	S Corporation
Was there an Employment/Consulting Agreement?	No
Was there an Assumed Lease in the sale?	Yes
Was there a Renewal Option with the Lease?	Yes

*Includes noncompete value and interest-bearing debt; excludes real estate, employment/consulting agreement values, and all contingent payments.

Additional Transaction Information
Was there a Note in the consideration paid? Yes
Was there a personal guarantee on the Note? No
Terms:
Consideration Paid: 352,156 shares of public company common stock valued at $1,188,527, and a $1,500,000 Note Payable
Assumed Lease (Months): 60
Terms of Lease: Future Minimum Lease Payments $411,053
Noncompete Length (Months): N/A
Noncompete Description: N/A
Employment/Consulting Agreement Description:
Additional Notes:
Earnings Before Tax includes $3,047,669 of Interest Income. Inventory stated at the lower of cost (specific identification) or market. The company operates eight used car dealerships in central Florida. 8/2003 – Buyer purchased the real estate listed in the Asset Data (and the real estate value is included in the sale price), but, because this is a stock sale, there was no allocation regarding the market value of the real estate.

Valuation Multiples
MVIC/Net Sales	0.14
MVIC/Gross Profit	1.07
MVIC/EBITDA	N/A
MVIC/EBIT	N/A
MVIC/Discretionary Earnings	N/A
MVIC/Book Value of Invested Capital	5.60

Profitability Ratios
Net Profit Margin	-0.03
Operating Profit Margin	0.04
Gross Profit Margin	0.14
Return on Assets	-0.04
Return on Equity	-1.28

Leverage Ratios
Fixed Charge Coverage	0.54
Long-Term Debt to Assets	0.00
Long-Term Debt to Equity	0.00

Earnings
EBITDA	($2,262,160)
Discretionary Earnings	N/A

Liquidity Ratios
Current Ratio	0.94
Quick Ratio	0.75

Activity Ratios
Total Asset Turnover	1.18
Fixed Asset Turnover	68.39
Inventory Turnover	6.51

Copyright © 2010 Business Valuation Resources, LLC. All rights reserved. www.BVResources.com^SM
(888) BUS-VALU, (503) 291-7963

Pratt's Stats® Auto Dealership Report

Pratt's Stats® Transaction Report
Prepared: 8/20/2010 2:09:45 PM (PST)

Seller Details
Target Name:	ValCar Rental Car Sales Inc.
Business Description:	Used Vehicle Sales Facilities
SIC:	5521 Motor Vehicle Dealers (Used Only)
NAICS:	441110 New Car Dealers
Sale Location:	Indianapolis, IN, United States
Years in Business:	6
Number Employees:	N/A

Source Data
Public Buyer Name:	TEAM RENTAL GROUP INC
8-K Date:	8/16/1996
8-K/A Date:	11/13/1996
Other Filing Type:	N/A
Other Filing Date:	N/A
CIK Code:	0000922471

Income Data
Data is "Latest Full Year" Reported	Yes
Data is Restated (see Notes for any explanation)	No
Income Statement Date	12/31/1995
Net Sales	$64,171,056
COGS	$52,430,044
Gross Profit	$11,741,012
Yearly Rent	N/A
Owner's Compensation	N/A
Other Operating Expenses	N/A
Noncash Charges	$140,270
Total Operating Expenses	$12,666,172
Operating Profit	($925,160)
Interest Expenses	$544,918
EBT	($1,470,078)
Taxes	$0
Net Income	($1,470,078)

Asset Data
Data is Latest Reported	Yes
Data is "Purchase Price Allocation agreed upon by Buyer and Seller"	No
Balance Sheet Date	12/31/1995
Cash Equivalents	$61,587
Trade Receivables	N/A
Inventory	$7,129,734
Other Current Assets	$1,144,864
Total Current Assets	$8,336,185
Fixed Assets	$965,276
Real Estate	N/A
Intangibles	N/A
Other Noncurrent Assets	$2,618
Total Assets	$9,304,079
Long-term Liabilities	$1,577,438
Total Liabilities	$9,446,720
Stockholder's Equity	($142,641)

Transaction Data
Date Sale Initiated:	N/A
Date of Sale:	8/1/1996
Days to Sell:	N/A
Asking Price:	N/A
Market Value of Invested Capital*:	$400,000
Debt Assumed:	N/A
Employment Agreement Value:	N/A
Noncompete Value:	N/A
Amount of Down Payment:	$400,000
Stock or Asset Sale:	Stock
Company Type:	S Corporation
Was there an Employment/Consulting Agreement?	No
Was there an Assumed Lease in the sale?	No
Was there a Renewal Option with the Lease?	No

*Includes noncompete value and interest-bearing debt; excludes real estate, employment/consulting agreement values, and all contingent payments.

Additional Transaction Information
Was there a Note in the consideration paid? No
Terms:
Assumed Lease (Months): N/A
Noncompete Length (Months): N/A
Employment/Consulting Agreement Description:
Additional Notes:
Inventory stated using the specific-unit identification method.

Was there a personal guarantee on the Note? No

Terms of Lease: N/A
Noncompete Description: N/A

Valuation Multiples
MVIC/Net Sales	0.01
MVIC/Gross Profit	0.03
MVIC/EBITDA	N/A
MVIC/EBIT	N/A
MVIC/Discretionary Earnings	N/A
MVIC/Book Value of Invested Capital	0.28

Profitability Ratios
Net Profit Margin	-0.02
Operating Profit Margin	-0.01
Gross Profit Margin	0.18
Return on Assets	-0.16
Return on Equity	N/A

Leverage Ratios
Fixed Charge Coverage	-1.70
Long-Term Debt to Assets	0.17
Long-Term Debt to Equity	N/A

Earnings
EBITDA	($784,890)
Discretionary Earnings	N/A

Liquidity Ratios
Current Ratio	1.06
Quick Ratio	0.15

Activity Ratios
Total Asset Turnover	6.90
Fixed Asset Turnover	66.48
Inventory Turnover	9.00

Copyright © 2010 Business Valuation Resources, LLC. All rights reserved. www.BVResources.com^SM
(888) BUS-VALU, (503) 291-7963

Pratt's Stats® Auto Dealership Report

Pratt's Stats® Transaction Report
Prepared: 8/20/2010 2:09:45 PM (PST)

Seller Details
Target Name:	N/A
Business Description:	Used Car Dealership
SIC:	5521 Motor Vehicle Dealers (Used Only)
NAICS:	441120 Used Car Dealers
Sale Location:	Columbia, SC, United States
Years in Business:	10
Number Employees:	6

Source Data
Broker Name:	Gunderson, Eric
Broker Firm Name:	Empire Business Brokers-SE

Income Data
Data is "Latest Full Year" Reported	Yes
Data is Restated (see Notes for any explanation)	No
Income Statement Date	12/31/2003
Net Sales	$10,276,919
COGS	$9,737,382
Gross Profit	$539,537
Yearly Rent	$42,000
Owner's Compensation	$197,167
Other Operating Expenses	N/A
Noncash Charges	N/A
Total Operating Expenses	$300,370
Operating Profit	$239,167
Interest Expenses	$0
EBT	$239,167
Taxes	$0
Net Income	$239,167

Asset Data
Data is Latest Reported	No
Data is "Purchase Price Allocation agreed upon by Buyer and Seller"	No
Balance Sheet Date	N/A
Cash Equivalents	N/A
Trade Receivables	N/A
Inventory	N/A
Other Current Assets	N/A
Total Current Assets	N/A
Fixed Assets	N/A
Real Estate	N/A
Intangibles	N/A
Other Noncurrent Assets	N/A
Total Assets	N/A
Long-term Liabilities	N/A
Total Liabilities	N/A
Stockholder's Equity	N/A

Transaction Data
Date Sale Initiated:	8/3/2003
Date of Sale:	2/27/2004
Days to Sell:	208
Asking Price:	$325,000
Market Value of Invested Capital*:	$300,000
Debt Assumed:	N/A
Employment Agreement Value:	N/A
Noncompete Value:	N/A
Amount of Down Payment:	N/A
Stock or Asset Sale:	Asset
Company Type:	S Corporation
Was there an Employment/Consulting Agreement?	No
Was there an Assumed Lease in the sale?	No
Was there a Renewal Option with the Lease?	No

*Includes noncompete value and interest-bearing debt; excludes real estate, employment/consulting agreement values, and all contingent payments.

Additional Transaction Information

Was there a Note in the consideration paid? No
Terms:
Assumed Lease (Months): N/A
Noncompete Length (Months): 60
Employment/Consulting Agreement Description:
Additional Notes:
The balance sheet was unavailable.

Was there a personal guarantee on the Note? No

Terms of Lease: N/A
Noncompete Description: Within two surrounding counties

Valuation Multiples
MVIC/Net Sales	0.03
MVIC/Gross Profit	0.56
MVIC/EBITDA	N/A
MVIC/EBIT	1.25
MVIC/Discretionary Earnings	N/A
MVIC/Book Value of Invested Capital	N/A

Profitability Ratios
Net Profit Margin	0.02
Operating Profit Margin	0.02
Gross Profit Margin	0.05
Return on Assets	N/A
Return on Equity	N/A

Leverage Ratios
Fixed Charge Coverage	N/A
Long-Term Debt to Assets	N/A
Long-Term Debt to Equity	N/A

Earnings
EBITDA	N/A
Discretionary Earnings	N/A

Liquidity Ratios
Current Ratio	N/A
Quick Ratio	N/A

Activity Ratios
Total Asset Turnover	N/A
Fixed Asset Turnover	N/A
Inventory Turnover	N/A

Copyright © 2010 Business Valuation Resources, LLC. All rights reserved. www.BVResources.com[SM]
(888) BUS-VALU, (503) 291-7963

Pratt's Stats® Auto Dealership Report

Pratt's Stats® Transaction Report
Prepared: 8/20/2010 2:09:45 PM (PST)

Seller Details
Target Name:	Jenson Motors
Business Description:	Used Car Sales
SIC:	5521 Motor Vehicle Dealers (Used Only)
NAICS:	441120 Used Car Dealers
Sale Location:	Loveland, CO, United States
Years in Business:	14
Number Employees:	1

Source Data
Broker Name:	N/A
Broker Firm Name:	VR Business Brokers

Income Data
Data is "Latest Full Year" Reported	Yes
Data is Restated (see Notes for any explanation)	No
Income Statement Date	12/31/2001
Net Sales	$1,552,221
COGS	$1,407,626
Gross Profit	$144,595
Yearly Rent	$23,527
Owner's Compensation	N/A
Other Operating Expenses	N/A
Noncash Charges	$111
Total Operating Expenses	$52,593
Operating Profit	$92,002
Interest Expenses	$16,337
EBT	$75,665
Taxes	$0
Net Income	$75,665

Asset Data
Data is Latest Reported	Yes
Data is "Purchase Price Allocation agreed upon by Buyer and Seller"	No
Balance Sheet Date	7/31/2002
Cash Equivalents	$23,482
Trade Receivables	$64,183
Inventory	$110,096
Other Current Assets	$500
Total Current Assets	$198,261
Fixed Assets	$6,655
Real Estate	$0
Intangibles	$0
Other Noncurrent Assets	$0
Total Assets	$204,916
Long-term Liabilities	$91,994
Total Liabilities	$183,851
Stockholder's Equity	$21,065

Transaction Data
Date Sale Initiated:	2/15/2002
Date of Sale:	11/8/2002
Days to Sell:	266
Asking Price:	$460,000
Market Value of Invested Capital*:	$355,300
Debt Assumed:	$0
Employment Agreement Value:	N/A
Noncompete Value:	N/A
Amount of Down Payment:	N/A
Stock or Asset Sale:	Asset
Company Type:	Sole Proprietorship
Was there an Employment/Consulting Agreement?	No
Was there an Assumed Lease in the sale?	Yes
Was there a Renewal Option with the Lease?	Yes

*Includes noncompete value and interest-bearing debt; excludes real estate, employment/consulting agreement values, and all contingent payments.

Additional Transaction Information
Was there a Note in the consideration paid? No
Terms:
Assumed Lease (Months): N/A
Noncompete Length (Months): N/A
Employment/Consulting Agreement Description:
Additional Notes:
This business sells used cars. The facility has a showroom, offices, and its own wash bays. The business is in a lease which expires 10/31/2012 and has a monthly rent expense of $1,874. The lease has four additional options at five years each.

Was there a personal guarantee on the Note? No
Terms of Lease: N/A
Noncompete Description: N/A

Valuation Multiples
MVIC/Net Sales	0.23
MVIC/Gross Profit	2.46
MVIC/EBITDA	3.86
MVIC/EBIT	3.86
MVIC/Discretionary Earnings	N/A
MVIC/Book Value of Invested Capital	3.14

Profitability Ratios
Net Profit Margin	0.05
Operating Profit Margin	0.06
Gross Profit Margin	0.09
Return on Assets	0.37
Return on Equity	3.59

Leverage Ratios
Fixed Charge Coverage	5.63
Long-Term Debt to Assets	0.45
Long-Term Debt to Equity	4.37

Earnings
EBITDA	$92,113
Discretionary Earnings	N/A

Liquidity Ratios
Current Ratio	2.16
Quick Ratio	0.96

Activity Ratios
Total Asset Turnover	7.57
Fixed Asset Turnover	233.24
Inventory Turnover	14.10

Copyright © 2010 Business Valuation Resources, LLC. All rights reserved. www.BVResources.com[SM]
(888) BUS-VALU, (503) 291-7963

Pratt's Stats® Auto Dealership Report

Pratt's Stats® Transaction Report
Prepared: 8/20/2010 2:09:45 PM (PST)

Seller Details
Target Name:	Eugene Executive Auto
Business Description:	Used Foreign and Domestic Car Dealership
SIC:	5521 Motor Vehicle Dealers (Used Only)
NAICS:	441120 Used Car Dealers
Sale Location:	Eugene, OR, United States
Years in Business:	40 Number Employees: 2

Source Data
Broker Name:	Wells, Ed
Broker Firm Name:	Oregon Business Properties, Inc.

Income Data
Data is "Latest Full Year" Reported	Yes
Data is Restated (see Notes for any explanation)	No
Income Statement Date	12/31/2000
Net Sales	$4,323,630
COGS	$3,764,262
Gross Profit	$559,368
Yearly Rent	N/A
Owner's Compensation	N/A
Other Operating Expenses	N/A
Noncash Charges	N/A
Total Operating Expenses	$238,468
Operating Profit	$320,900
Interest Expenses	$0
EBT	$320,900
Taxes	$0
Net Income	$320,900

Asset Data
Data is Latest Reported	No
Data is "Purchase Price Allocation agreed upon by Buyer and Seller"	Yes
Balance Sheet Date	4/9/2002
Cash Equivalents	N/A
Trade Receivables	N/A
Inventory	N/A
Other Current Assets	N/A
Total Current Assets	N/A
Fixed Assets	$25,000
Real Estate	$600,000
Intangibles	$72,640
Other Noncurrent Assets	N/A
Total Assets	N/A
Long-term Liabilities	N/A
Total Liabilities	N/A
Stockholder's Equity	N/A

Transaction Data
Date Sale Initiated:	9/6/2001
Date of Sale:	4/9/2002
Days to Sell:	215
Asking Price:	N/A
Market Value of Invested Capital*:	$97,640
Debt Assumed:	N/A
Employment Agreement Value:	$360
Noncompete Value:	$2,000
Amount of Down Payment:	N/A
Stock or Asset Sale:	Asset
Company Type:	S Corporation
Was there an Employment/Consulting Agreement?	No
Was there an Assumed Lease in the sale?	No
Was there a Renewal Option with the Lease?	No

*Includes noncompete value and interest-bearing debt; excludes real estate, employment/consulting agreement values, and all contingent payments.

Additional Transaction Information
Was there a Note in the consideration paid? No
Terms:
Assumed Lease (Months): N/A
Noncompete Length (Months): 60
Employment/Consulting Agreement Description:
Additional Notes:

Was there a personal guarantee on the Note? No

Terms of Lease: N/A
Noncompete Description: N/A

Valuation Multiples
MVIC/Net Sales	0.02
MVIC/Gross Profit	0.17
MVIC/EBITDA	N/A
MVIC/EBIT	0.30
MVIC/Discretionary Earnings	N/A
MVIC/Book Value of Invested Capital	N/A

Profitability Ratios
Net Profit Margin	0.07
Operating Profit Margin	0.07
Gross Profit Margin	0.13
Return on Assets	N/A
Return on Equity	N/A

Leverage Ratios
Fixed Charge Coverage	N/A
Long-Term Debt to Assets	N/A
Long-Term Debt to Equity	N/A

Earnings
EBITDA	N/A
Discretionary Earnings	N/A

Liquidity Ratios
Current Ratio	N/A
Quick Ratio	N/A

Activity Ratios
Total Asset Turnover	N/A
Fixed Asset Turnover	172.95
Inventory Turnover	N/A

Copyright © 2010 Business Valuation Resources, LLC. All rights reserved. www.BVResources.com℠
(888) BUS-VALU, (503) 291-7963

Pratt's Stats® Auto Dealership Report

Pratt's Stats® Transaction Report
Prepared: 8/20/2010 2:09:45 PM (PST)

Seller Details
Target Name:	N/A
Business Description:	Used Car Dealership
SIC:	5521 Motor Vehicle Dealers (Used Only)
NAICS:	441120 Used Car Dealers
Sale Location:	GA, United States
Years in Business:	7
Number Employees:	2

Source Data
Broker Name:	N/A
Broker Firm Name:	N/A

Income Data
Data is "Latest Full Year" Reported	Yes
Data is Restated (see Notes for any explanation)	No
Income Statement Date	12/31/2005
Net Sales	$348,958
COGS	$277,648
Gross Profit	$71,310
Yearly Rent	N/A
Owner's Compensation	$0
Other Operating Expenses	N/A
Noncash Charges	$1,138
Total Operating Expenses	$41,899
Operating Profit	$29,411
Interest Expenses	$0
EBT	$29,411
Taxes	$0
Net Income	$29,411

Asset Data
Data is Latest Reported	No
Data is "Purchase Price Allocation agreed upon by Buyer and Seller"	Yes
Balance Sheet Date	2/21/2008
Cash Equivalents	N/A
Trade Receivables	N/A
Inventory	N/A
Other Current Assets	N/A
Total Current Assets	N/A
Fixed Assets	$83,000
Real Estate	$875,000
Intangibles	N/A
Other Noncurrent Assets	N/A
Total Assets	N/A
Long-term Liabilities	N/A
Total Liabilities	N/A
Stockholder's Equity	N/A

Transaction Data
Date Sale Initiated:	7/12/2006
Date of Sale:	2/21/2008
Days to Sell:	589
Asking Price:	$875,000
Market Value of Invested Capital*:	$83,000
Debt Assumed:	N/A
Employment Agreement Value:	N/A
Noncompete Value:	N/A
Amount of Down Payment:	$865,000
Stock or Asset Sale:	Asset
Company Type:	S Corporation
Was there an Employment/Consulting Agreement?	No
Was there an Assumed Lease in the sale?	No
Was there a Renewal Option with the Lease?	No

*Includes noncompete value and interest-bearing debt; excludes real estate, employment/consulting agreement values, and all contingent payments.

Additional Transaction Information
Was there a Note in the consideration paid? No
Terms:
Assumed Lease (Months): N/A
Noncompete Length (Months): 60
Employment/Consulting Agreement Description:
Additional Notes:
Transaction was submitted by the GABB (5/2008). The reason for selling was relocation. The real estate value of $875,000 was subtracted from the selling price.

Was there a personal guarantee on the Note? No
Terms of Lease: N/A
Noncompete Description: N/A

Valuation Multiples
MVIC/Net Sales	0.24
MVIC/Gross Profit	1.16
MVIC/EBITDA	2.72
MVIC/EBIT	2.82
MVIC/Discretionary Earnings	2.72
MVIC/Book Value of Invested Capital	N/A

Profitability Ratios
Net Profit Margin	0.08
Operating Profit Margin	0.08
Gross Profit Margin	0.20
Return on Assets	N/A
Return on Equity	N/A

Leverage Ratios
Fixed Charge Coverage	N/A
Long-Term Debt to Assets	N/A
Long-Term Debt to Equity	N/A

Earnings
EBITDA	$30,549
Discretionary Earnings	$30,549

Liquidity Ratios
Current Ratio	N/A
Quick Ratio	N/A

Activity Ratios
Total Asset Turnover	N/A
Fixed Asset Turnover	4.20
Inventory Turnover	N/A

Copyright © 2010 Business Valuation Resources, LLC. All rights reserved. www.BVResources.com[SM]
(888) BUS-VALU, (503) 291-7963

Pratt's Stats® Auto Dealership Report

Pratt's Stats® Transaction Report
Prepared: 8/20/2010 2:09:45 PM (PST)

Seller Details
Target Name:	Calcars AB, Inc. and Astra Financial Services, Inc.
Business Description:	Auto Dealerships - Sells Used Vehicles and Finances Customers' Contracts Internally Through its Finance Company
SIC:	5521 Motor Vehicle Dealers (Used Only)
NAICS:	441120 Used Car Dealers
Sale Location:	United States
Years in Business:	N/A Number Employees: N/A

Source Data
Public Buyer Name:	Carbiz Inc.
8-K Date:	10/2/2007
8-K/A Date:	11/29/2007
Other Filing Type:	N/A
Other Filing Date:	N/A
CIK Code:	0001307425

Income Data
Data is "Latest Full Year" Reported	Yes
Data is Restated (see Notes for any explanation)	No
Income Statement Date	12/31/2006
Net Sales	$36,546,000
COGS	$13,172,000
Gross Profit	$23,374,000
Yearly Rent	N/A
Owner's Compensation	N/A
Other Operating Expenses	N/A
Noncash Charges	$576,000
Total Operating Expenses	$27,203,000
Operating Profit	($3,829,000)
Interest Expenses	$1,304,000
EBT	$2,163,000
Taxes	$0
Net Income	$2,163,000

Asset Data
Data is Latest Reported	Yes
Data is "Purchase Price Allocation agreed upon by Buyer and Seller"	No
Balance Sheet Date	7/31/2007
Cash Equivalents	$0
Trade Receivables	$22,469,000
Inventory	$848,000
Other Current Assets	$95,000
Total Current Assets	$23,412,000
Fixed Assets	$871,000
Real Estate	$0
Intangibles	$0
Other Noncurrent Assets	$0
Total Assets	$24,283,000
Long-term Liabilities	$0
Total Liabilities	$21,001,000
Stockholder's Equity	$3,282,000

Transaction Data
Date Sale Initiated:	N/A
Date of Sale:	10/2/2007
Days to Sell:	N/A
Asking Price:	N/A
Market Value of Invested Capital*:	$18,600,000
Debt Assumed:	N/A
Employment Agreement Value:	N/A
Noncompete Value:	N/A
Amount of Down Payment:	$18,600,000
Stock or Asset Sale:	Asset
Company Type:	C Corporation
Was there an Employment/Consulting Agreement?	No
Was there an Assumed Lease in the sale?	No
Was there a Renewal Option with the Lease?	No

*Includes noncompete value and interest-bearing debt; excludes real estate, employment/consulting agreement values, and all contingent payments.

Additional Transaction Information
Was there a Note in the consideration paid? No   Was there a personal guarantee on the Note? No
Terms:
Consideration: Cash in the amount of $18,600,000 (funded by a new line of credit). In addition, the Buyer incurred transaction costs in the amount of $1,225,000 and assumed "immaterial liabilities" of $600,000 (a vehicle replacement program, or vsp, liability and other reserves). Calcars offered a vehicle replacement program ("VSP") where, under certain circumstances, customers may return vehicles and Calcars will provide the customer with a replacement vehicle. Although the Buyer will not offer this program it will honor existing Calcars contracts under this program.
Assumed Lease (Months): N/A   Terms of Lease: N/A
Noncompete Length (Months): N/A   Noncompete Description: N/A
Employment/Consulting Agreement Description:
Additional Notes:
EBT includes other expenses of ($2,510,000) and gain on extinguishment of debt in bankruptcy of $9,806,000.

Allocation of the Purchase Price: Notes receivable, net of reserves $18,500,000, Vehicle Inventory, net of reserves $200,000, Property and Equipment $500,000, Transaction costs $1,225,000, Total purchase price (includes transaction costs and liabilities assumed) $20,425,000.

Calcars operated the fourth largest chain of "buy-here pay-here" auto dealerships in the country with 26 dealerships throughout the Midwest, three of which will be closed by the Buyer. By virtue of the acquisition, the Buyer will operate 23 dealerships in Illinois, Indiana, Iowa, Kentucky, Nebraska, Ohio and Oklahoma, in addition to three dealerships it operates in Florida.

Valuation Multiples
MVIC/Net Sales	0.51
MVIC/Gross Profit	0.80
MVIC/EBITDA	N/A
MVIC/EBIT	N/A
MVIC/Discretionary Earnings	N/A
MVIC/Book Value of Invested Capital	5.67

Profitability Ratios
Net Profit Margin	0.06
Operating Profit Margin	0.09
Gross Profit Margin	0.64
Return on Assets	0.09
Return on Equity	0.66

Leverage Ratios
Fixed Charge Coverage	2.66
Long-Term Debt to Assets	0.00
Long-Term Debt to Equity	0.00

Earnings

Liquidity Ratios

Activity Ratios

Pratt's Stats® Auto Dealership Report

Pratt's Stats® Transaction Report
Prepared: 8/20/2010 2:09:45 PM (PST)

Seller Details
Target Name:	N/A
Business Description:	Used Vehicle Dealer, Service, Parts, and Sales
SIC:	5521 Motor Vehicle Dealers (Used Only)
NAICS:	441120 Used Car Dealers
Sale Location:	Reno, NV, United States
Years in Business:	27
Number Employees:	20

Source Data
Broker Name:	Loftin, Katrina
Broker Firm Name:	BTI Group/ Business Team

Income Data
Data is "Latest Full Year" Reported	Yes
Data is Restated (see Notes for any explanation)	No
Income Statement Date	12/31/2006
Net Sales	$4,902,427
COGS	$3,789,618
Gross Profit	$1,112,809
Yearly Rent	$192,000
Owner's Compensation	$0
Other Operating Expenses	$816,585
Noncash Charges	$0
Total Operating Expenses	$1,008,585
Operating Profit	$104,224
Interest Expenses	$0
EBT	$104,224
Taxes	$0
Net Income	$104,224

Asset Data
Data is Latest Reported	No
Data is "Purchase Price Allocation agreed upon by Buyer and Seller"	Yes
Balance Sheet Date	2/4/2008
Cash Equivalents	N/A
Trade Receivables	N/A
Inventory	$518,067
Other Current Assets	$70,443
Total Current Assets	N/A
Fixed Assets	N/A
Real Estate	N/A
Intangibles	N/A
Other Noncurrent Assets	N/A
Total Assets	N/A
Long-term Liabilities	N/A
Total Liabilities	N/A
Stockholder's Equity	N/A

Transaction Data
Date Sale Initiated:	11/1/2007
Date of Sale:	2/4/2008
Days to Sell:	95
Asking Price:	$600,000
Market Value of Invested Capital*:	$588,510
Debt Assumed:	$0
Employment Agreement Value:	$0
Noncompete Value:	$0
Amount of Down Payment:	$588,510
Stock or Asset Sale:	Asset
Company Type:	LLC
Was there an Employment/Consulting Agreement?	No
Was there an Assumed Lease in the sale?	Yes
Was there a Renewal Option with the Lease?	Yes

*Includes noncompete value and interest-bearing debt; excludes real estate, employment/consulting agreement values, and all contingent payments.

Additional Transaction Information
Was there a Note in the consideration paid? No
Terms:
Consideration: $588,510 in cash.
Assumed Lease (Months): 60
Noncompete Length (Months): 60
Employment/Consulting Agreement Description:
Additional Notes:

Was there a personal guarantee on the Note? No

Terms of Lease: $18,000 per month and three 5-year options
Noncompete Description: Nevada and California

Valuation Multiples
MVIC/Net Sales	0.12
MVIC/Gross Profit	0.53
MVIC/EBITDA	5.65
MVIC/EBIT	5.65
MVIC/Discretionary Earnings	5.65
MVIC/Book Value of Invested Capital	N/A

Profitability Ratios
Net Profit Margin	0.02
Operating Profit Margin	0.02
Gross Profit Margin	0.23
Return on Assets	N/A
Return on Equity	N/A

Leverage Ratios
Fixed Charge Coverage	N/A
Long-Term Debt to Assets	N/A
Long-Term Debt to Equity	N/A

Earnings
EBITDA	$104,224
Discretionary Earnings	$104,224

Liquidity Ratios
Current Ratio	N/A
Quick Ratio	N/A

Activity Ratios
Total Asset Turnover	N/A
Fixed Asset Turnover	N/A
Inventory Turnover	9.46

Copyright © 2010 Business Valuation Resources, LLC. All rights reserved. www.BVResources.com[SM]
(888) BUS-VALU, (503) 291-7963

Pratt's Stats® Auto Dealership Report

Pratt's Stats® Transaction Report
Prepared: 8/20/2010 2:09:45 PM (PST)

Seller Details
Target Name:	N/A
Business Description:	Used Car Dealership
SIC:	5521 Motor Vehicle Dealers (Used Only)
NAICS:	441120 Used Car Dealers
Sale Location:	GA, United States
Years in Business:	10
Number Employees:	3

Source Data
Broker Name:	N/A
Broker Firm Name:	N/A

Income Data
Data is "Latest Full Year" Reported	Yes
Data is Restated (see Notes for any explanation)	No
Income Statement Date	12/31/2006
Net Sales	$199,000
COGS	$85,546
Gross Profit	$113,454
Yearly Rent	N/A
Owner's Compensation	$38,800
Other Operating Expenses	N/A
Noncash Charges	$1,229
Total Operating Expenses	$101,797
Operating Profit	$11,657
Interest Expenses	$2,951
EBT	$8,706
Taxes	$0
Net Income	$8,706

Asset Data
Data is Latest Reported	No
Data is "Purchase Price Allocation agreed upon by Buyer and Seller"	Yes
Balance Sheet Date	2/29/2008
Cash Equivalents	N/A
Trade Receivables	N/A
Inventory	N/A
Other Current Assets	N/A
Total Current Assets	N/A
Fixed Assets	$30,000
Real Estate	$405,000
Intangibles	N/A
Other Noncurrent Assets	N/A
Total Assets	N/A
Long-term Liabilities	N/A
Total Liabilities	N/A
Stockholder's Equity	N/A

Transaction Data
Date Sale Initiated:	4/26/2007
Date of Sale:	2/29/2008
Days to Sell:	309
Asking Price:	$100,000
Market Value of Invested Capital*:	$30,000
Debt Assumed:	N/A
Employment Agreement Value:	N/A
Noncompete Value:	N/A
Amount of Down Payment:	$435,000
Stock or Asset Sale:	Asset
Company Type:	S Corporation
Was there an Employment/Consulting Agreement?	No
Was there an Assumed Lease in the sale?	Yes
Was there a Renewal Option with the Lease?	Yes

*Includes noncompete value and interest-bearing debt; excludes real estate, employment/consulting agreement values, and all contingent payments.

Additional Transaction Information
Was there a Note in the consideration paid? No
Terms:
Assumed Lease (Months): N/A
Noncompete Length (Months): 60
Employment/Consulting Agreement Description:

Was there a personal guarantee on the Note? No

Terms of Lease: option to renew
Noncompete Description: N/A

Additional Notes:
Transaction was submitted by the GABB (5/2008). The reason for selling was relocation. The real estate value of $405,000 was subtracted from the selling price.

Valuation Multiples
MVIC/Net Sales	0.15
MVIC/Gross Profit	0.26
MVIC/EBITDA	2.33
MVIC/EBIT	2.57
MVIC/Discretionary Earnings	0.58
MVIC/Book Value of Invested Capital	N/A

Profitability Ratios
Net Profit Margin	0.04
Operating Profit Margin	0.06
Gross Profit Margin	0.57
Return on Assets	N/A
Return on Equity	N/A

Leverage Ratios
Fixed Charge Coverage	3.95
Long-Term Debt to Assets	N/A
Long-Term Debt to Equity	N/A

Earnings
EBITDA	$12,886
Discretionary Earnings	$51,686

Liquidity Ratios
Current Ratio	N/A
Quick Ratio	N/A

Activity Ratios
Total Asset Turnover	N/A
Fixed Asset Turnover	6.63
Inventory Turnover	N/A

Copyright © 2010 Business Valuation Resources, LLC. All rights reserved. www.BVResources.com^SM
(888) BUS-VALU, (503) 291-7963

Pratt's Stats® Auto Dealership Report

Pratt's Stats® Transaction Report
Prepared: 8/20/2010 2:09:45 PM (PST)

Seller Details
Target Name:	N/A
Business Description:	Auto Sales and Repair (Mercedes Benz and BMW)
SIC:	5521 Motor Vehicle Dealers (Used Only)
NAICS:	441120 Used Car Dealers
Sale Location:	Houston, TX, United States
Years in Business:	N/A Number Employees: N/A

Source Data
Broker Name:	Stabler, Frank
Broker Firm Name:	Certified Business Brokers

Income Data
Data is "Latest Full Year" Reported	Yes
Data is Restated (see Notes for any explanation)	No
Income Statement Date	12/31/2007
Net Sales	$869,963
COGS	$276,327
Gross Profit	$593,636
Yearly Rent	$53,002
Owner's Compensation	N/A
Other Operating Expenses	N/A
Noncash Charges	N/A
Total Operating Expenses	$404,594
Operating Profit	$189,042
Interest Expenses	$0
EBT	$189,042
Taxes	$0
Net Income	$189,042

Asset Data
Data is Latest Reported	No
Data is "Purchase Price Allocation agreed upon by Buyer and Seller"	No
Balance Sheet Date	N/A
Cash Equivalents	N/A
Trade Receivables	N/A
Inventory	N/A
Other Current Assets	N/A
Total Current Assets	N/A
Fixed Assets	N/A
Real Estate	N/A
Intangibles	N/A
Other Noncurrent Assets	N/A
Total Assets	N/A
Long-term Liabilities	N/A
Total Liabilities	N/A
Stockholder's Equity	N/A

Transaction Data
Date Sale Initiated:	6/13/2005
Date of Sale:	5/30/2008
Days to Sell:	1082
Asking Price:	$385,000
Market Value of Invested Capital*:	$385,000
Debt Assumed:	$0
Employment Agreement Value:	N/A
Noncompete Value:	N/A
Amount of Down Payment:	$38,500
Stock or Asset Sale:	Asset
Company Type:	S Corporation
Was there an Employment/Consulting Agreement?	No
Was there an Assumed Lease in the sale?	No
Was there a Renewal Option with the Lease?	No

*Includes noncompete value and interest-bearing debt; excludes real estate, employment/consulting agreement values, and all contingent payments.

Additional Transaction Information
Was there a Note in the consideration paid? No   Was there a personal guarantee on the Note? No
Terms:
Assumed Lease (Months): N/A   Terms of Lease: N/A
Noncompete Length (Months): N/A   Noncompete Description: N/A
Employment/Consulting Agreement Description:
Additional Notes:

Valuation Multiples
MVIC/Net Sales	0.44
MVIC/Gross Profit	0.65
MVIC/EBITDA	N/A
MVIC/EBIT	2.04
MVIC/Discretionary Earnings	N/A
MVIC/Book Value of Invested Capital	N/A

Profitability Ratios
Net Profit Margin	0.22
Operating Profit Margin	0.22
Gross Profit Margin	0.68
Return on Assets	N/A
Return on Equity	N/A

Leverage Ratios
Fixed Charge Coverage	N/A
Long-Term Debt to Assets	N/A
Long-Term Debt to Equity	N/A

Earnings
EBITDA	N/A
Discretionary Earnings	N/A

Liquidity Ratios
Current Ratio	N/A
Quick Ratio	N/A

Activity Ratios
Total Asset Turnover	N/A
Fixed Asset Turnover	N/A
Inventory Turnover	N/A

Copyright © 2010 Business Valuation Resources, LLC. All rights reserved. www.BVResources.com℠
(888) BUS-VALU, (503) 291-7963

Pratt's Stats® Auto Dealership Report

Pratt's Stats® Transaction Report
Prepared: 8/20/2010 2:09:45 PM (PST)

Seller Details
Target Name:	I Trust Motors
Business Description:	Used Car Internet Marketing (competitor of online Auto trader)
SIC:	5521 Motor Vehicle Dealers (Used Only)
NAICS:	441120 Used Car Dealers
Sale Location:	Las Vegas, NV, United States
Years in Business:	3
Number Employees:	17

Source Data
Broker Name:	N/A
Broker Firm Name:	N/A

Income Data
Data is "Latest Full Year" Reported	Yes
Data is Restated (see Notes for any explanation)	No
Income Statement Date	12/31/2005
Net Sales	$645,339
COGS	$361,442
Gross Profit	$283,897
Yearly Rent	$12,100
Owner's Compensation	N/A
Other Operating Expenses	N/A
Noncash Charges	N/A
Total Operating Expenses	$281,751
Operating Profit	$2,146
Interest Expenses	$0
EBT	$2,146
Taxes	$0
Net Income	$2,146

Asset Data
Data is Latest Reported	No
Data is "Purchase Price Allocation agreed upon by Buyer and Seller"	No
Balance Sheet Date	N/A
Cash Equivalents	N/A
Trade Receivables	N/A
Inventory	N/A
Other Current Assets	N/A
Total Current Assets	N/A
Fixed Assets	N/A
Real Estate	N/A
Intangibles	N/A
Other Noncurrent Assets	N/A
Total Assets	N/A
Long-term Liabilities	N/A
Total Liabilities	N/A
Stockholder's Equity	N/A

Transaction Data
Date Sale Initiated:	N/A
Date of Sale:	6/14/2007
Days to Sell:	N/A
Asking Price:	N/A
Market Value of Invested Capital*:	$375,000
Debt Assumed:	$0
Employment Agreement Value:	N/A
Noncompete Value:	N/A
Amount of Down Payment:	$375,000
Stock or Asset Sale:	Asset
Company Type:	LLC
Was there an Employment/Consulting Agreement?	No
Was there an Assumed Lease in the sale?	No
Was there a Renewal Option with the Lease?	No

*Includes noncompete value and interest-bearing debt; excludes real estate, employment/consulting agreement values, and all contingent payments.

Additional Transaction Information
Was there a Note in the consideration paid? No
Terms:
Consideration: Cash in the amount of $375,000.
Assumed Lease (Months): N/A
Noncompete Length (Months): 36
Employment/Consulting Agreement Description: 3 weeks @ 25 hours/week at no charge
Additional Notes:

Was there a personal guarantee on the Note? No

Terms of Lease: N/A
Noncompete Description: 50 mile radius

Valuation Multiples
MVIC/Net Sales	0.58
MVIC/Gross Profit	1.32
MVIC/EBITDA	N/A
MVIC/EBIT	174.74
MVIC/Discretionary Earnings	N/A
MVIC/Book Value of Invested Capital	N/A

Profitability Ratios
Net Profit Margin	0.00
Operating Profit Margin	0.00
Gross Profit Margin	0.44
Return on Assets	N/A
Return on Equity	N/A

Leverage Ratios
Fixed Charge Coverage	N/A
Long-Term Debt to Assets	N/A
Long-Term Debt to Equity	N/A

Earnings
EBITDA	N/A
Discretionary Earnings	N/A

Liquidity Ratios
Current Ratio	N/A
Quick Ratio	N/A

Activity Ratios
Total Asset Turnover	N/A
Fixed Asset Turnover	N/A
Inventory Turnover	N/A

Copyright © 2010 Business Valuation Resources, LLC. All rights reserved. www.BVResources.com℠
(888) BUS-VALU, (503) 291-7963

Pratt's Stats® Auto Dealership Report

Pratt's Stats® Transaction Report
Prepared: 8/20/2010 2:09:45 PM (PST)

Seller Details
Target Name:	M.R.B., Inc. d.b.a. Tomahawk Truck Sales
Business Description:	Retail and Wholesale of Used Transportation Equipment, Primarily Tractors and Trailers
SIC:	5521 Motor Vehicle Dealers (Used Only)
NAICS:	441120 Used Car Dealers
Sale Location:	GA, United States
Years in Business:	8
Number Employees:	N/A

Source Data
Public Buyer Name:	Chancellor Corporation
8-K Date:	2/12/2009
8-K/A Date:	4/13/2009
Other Filing Type:	N/A
Other Filing Date:	N/A
CIK Code:	0000724051

Income Data
Data is "Latest Full Year" Reported	Yes
Data is Restated (see Notes for any explanation)	No
Income Statement Date	12/31/1998
Net Sales	$39,073,588
COGS	$32,752,949
Gross Profit	$6,320,639
Yearly Rent	N/A
Owner's Compensation	N/A
Other Operating Expenses	N/A
Noncash Charges	$39,521
Total Operating Expenses	$5,530,332
Operating Profit	$790,307
Interest Expenses	$449,917
EBT	$344,844
Taxes	$0
Net Income	$344,844

Asset Data
Data is Latest Reported	Yes
Data is "Purchase Price Allocation agreed upon by Buyer and Seller"	No
Balance Sheet Date	12/31/1998
Cash Equivalents	$31,809
Trade Receivables	$374,954
Inventory	$10,721,462
Other Current Assets	$60,452
Total Current Assets	$11,188,677
Fixed Assets	$191,063
Real Estate	$0
Intangibles	$0
Other Noncurrent Assets	$88,090
Total Assets	$11,467,830
Long-term Liabilities	$375,877
Total Liabilities	$11,193,953
Stockholder's Equity	$273,877

Transaction Data
Date Sale Initiated:	N/A
Date of Sale:	1/29/1999
Days to Sell:	N/A
Asking Price:	N/A
Market Value of Invested Capital*:	$6,030,000
Debt Assumed:	N/A
Employment Agreement Value:	N/A
Noncompete Value:	N/A
Amount of Down Payment:	$6,030,000
Stock or Asset Sale:	Stock
Company Type:	S Corporation
Was there an Employment/Consulting Agreement?	Yes
Was there an Assumed Lease in the sale?	Yes
Was there a Renewal Option with the Lease?	No

*Includes noncompete value and interest-bearing debt; excludes real estate, employment/consulting agreement values, and all contingent payments.

Additional Transaction Information
Was there a Note in the consideration paid? No
Was there a personal guarantee on the Note? No

Terms:
Consideration: 4,500,000 shares of the buyer's public company common stock valued at $1.34 per share and $530,000 in transaction costs (not included in the selling price). In addition, an earnout that provides for the payment of 7.5% of the adjusted pre-tax earnings of Tomahawk to each of the selling shareholders. The earnout begins in the fiscal year ended December 31, 1999, and ends in the fiscal year ended December 31, 2004.

Assumed Lease (Months): N/A
Terms of Lease: N/A
Noncompete Length (Months): N/A
Noncompete Description: N/A
Employment/Consulting Agreement Description: Employment agreements for the selling shareholders over a period of five years with minimum base salaries of $200,000 per annum.
Additional Notes:
EBT includes other income of $4,454. Inventories are valued at the lower of cost or market. The cost of vehicles including reconditioning parts and other direct costs is determined using the specific identification method.

Valuation Multiples
MVIC/Net Sales	0.15
MVIC/Gross Profit	0.95
MVIC/EBITDA	7.27
MVIC/EBIT	7.63
MVIC/Discretionary Earnings	N/A
MVIC/Book Value of Invested Capital	9.28

Profitability Ratios
Net Profit Margin	0.01
Operating Profit Margin	0.02
Gross Profit Margin	0.16
Return on Assets	0.03
Return on Equity	1.26

Leverage Ratios
Fixed Charge Coverage	1.77
Long-Term Debt to Assets	0.03
Long-Term Debt to Equity	1.37

Earnings
EBITDA	$829,828
Discretionary Earnings	N/A

Liquidity Ratios
Current Ratio	1.03
Quick Ratio	0.04

Activity Ratios
Total Asset Turnover	3.41
Fixed Asset Turnover	204.51
Inventory Turnover	3.64

Copyright © 2010 Business Valuation Resources, LLC. All rights reserved. www.BVResources.com^SM
(888) BUS-VALU, (503) 291-7963

Pratt's Stats® Auto Dealership Report

Pratt's Stats® Transaction Report
Prepared: 8/20/2010 2:09:45 PM (PST)

Seller Details
Target Name:	N/A
Business Description:	Used Car Sales and Service
SIC:	5521 Motor Vehicle Dealers (Used Only)
NAICS:	441120 Used Car Dealers
Sale Location:	FL, United States
Years in Business:	3
Number Employees:	1

Source Data
Broker Name:	N/A
Broker Firm Name:	N/A

Income Data
Data is "Latest Full Year" Reported	Yes
Data is Restated (see Notes for any explanation)	No
Income Statement Date	12/31/2007
Net Sales	$456,859
COGS	$273,170
Gross Profit	$183,689
Yearly Rent	N/A
Owner's Compensation	$0
Other Operating Expenses	N/A
Noncash Charges	$4,019
Total Operating Expenses	$103,393
Operating Profit	$80,296
Interest Expenses	$814
EBT	$79,482
Taxes	$0
Net Income	$79,482

Asset Data
Data is Latest Reported	No
Data is "Purchase Price Allocation agreed upon by Buyer and Seller"	Yes
Balance Sheet Date	N/A
Cash Equivalents	N/A
Trade Receivables	$0
Inventory	$0
Other Current Assets	N/A
Total Current Assets	N/A
Fixed Assets	$20,000
Real Estate	N/A
Intangibles	$40,000
Other Noncurrent Assets	$0
Total Assets	N/A
Long-term Liabilities	N/A
Total Liabilities	N/A
Stockholder's Equity	N/A

Transaction Data
Date Sale Initiated:	8/12/2008
Date of Sale:	11/14/2008
Days to Sell:	94
Asking Price:	$75,000
Market Value of Invested Capital*:	$60,000
Debt Assumed:	$0
Employment Agreement Value:	N/A
Noncompete Value:	N/A
Amount of Down Payment:	$25,000
Stock or Asset Sale:	Asset
Company Type:	S Corporation
Was there an Employment/Consulting Agreement?	No
Was there an Assumed Lease in the sale?	No
Was there a Renewal Option with the Lease?	No

*Includes noncompete value and interest-bearing debt; excludes real estate, employment/consulting agreement values, and all contingent payments.

Additional Transaction Information
Was there a Note in the consideration paid? No
Terms:
Assumed Lease (Months): N/A
Noncompete Length (Months): 36
Employment/Consulting Agreement Description:
Additional Notes:
Transaction was submitted by the BBF (3/2009). The revenue split is 70% sales and 30% in service. The company is licensed for sales, financing and repairs. There is one lift and parking for about 20 cars.

Was there a personal guarantee on the Note? No

Terms of Lease: $1,590/month, expires 1/11/2011
Noncompete Description: 50

Valuation Multiples
MVIC/Net Sales	0.13
MVIC/Gross Profit	0.33
MVIC/EBITDA	0.71
MVIC/EBIT	0.75
MVIC/Discretionary Earnings	0.71
MVIC/Book Value of Invested Capital	N/A

Profitability Ratios
Net Profit Margin	0.17
Operating Profit Margin	0.18
Gross Profit Margin	0.40
Return on Assets	N/A
Return on Equity	N/A

Leverage Ratios
Fixed Charge Coverage	98.64
Long-Term Debt to Assets	N/A
Long-Term Debt to Equity	N/A

Earnings
EBITDA	$84,315
Discretionary Earnings	$84,315

Liquidity Ratios
Current Ratio	N/A
Quick Ratio	N/A

Activity Ratios
Total Asset Turnover	N/A
Fixed Asset Turnover	22.84
Inventory Turnover	N/A

Copyright © 2010 Business Valuation Resources, LLC. All rights reserved. www.BVResources.com^{SM}
(888) BUS-VALU, (503) 291-7963

Pratt's Stats® Auto Dealership Report

Pratt's Stats® Transaction Report
Prepared: 8/20/2010 2:09:46 PM (PST)

Seller Details
Target Name:	Contra Costa Auto Sales & Service
Business Description:	Used Car Dealer and Automotive Repair Shop
SIC:	5521 Motor Vehicle Dealers (Used Only)
NAICS:	441120 Used Car Dealers
Sale Location:	Concord, CA, United States
Years in Business:	20
Number Employees:	7

Source Data
Broker Name:	Moran, Tony
Broker Firm Name:	Business Team

Income Data
Data is "Latest Full Year" Reported	Yes
Data is Restated (see Notes for any explanation)	No
Income Statement Date	12/31/2003
Net Sales	$916,195
COGS	$0
Gross Profit	$916,195
Yearly Rent	N/A
Owner's Compensation	N/A
Other Operating Expenses	N/A
Noncash Charges	N/A
Total Operating Expenses	$715,130
Operating Profit	$201,065
Interest Expenses	$0
EBT	$201,065
Taxes	$0
Net Income	$201,065

Asset Data
Data is Latest Reported	No
Data is "Purchase Price Allocation agreed upon by Buyer and Seller"	Yes
Balance Sheet Date	12/1/2004
Cash Equivalents	N/A
Trade Receivables	N/A
Inventory	$25,000
Other Current Assets	N/A
Total Current Assets	N/A
Fixed Assets	$100,000
Real Estate	N/A
Intangibles	$310,000
Other Noncurrent Assets	N/A
Total Assets	N/A
Long-term Liabilities	N/A
Total Liabilities	N/A
Stockholder's Equity	N/A

Transaction Data
Date Sale Initiated:	N/A
Date of Sale:	12/1/2004
Days to Sell:	N/A
Asking Price:	N/A
Market Value of Invested Capital*:	$435,000
Debt Assumed:	N/A
Employment Agreement Value:	N/A
Noncompete Value:	N/A
Amount of Down Payment:	$391,500
Stock or Asset Sale:	Asset
Company Type:	N/A
Was there an Employment/Consulting Agreement?	No
Was there an Assumed Lease in the sale?	No
Was there a Renewal Option with the Lease?	No

*Includes noncompete value and interest-bearing debt; excludes real estate, employment/consulting agreement values, and all contingent payments.

Additional Transaction Information
Was there a Note in the consideration paid? No
Terms:
Consideration: $391,500 in cash and a $43,500 promissory note.
Assumed Lease (Months): N/A
Noncompete Length (Months): 60
Employment/Consulting Agreement Description:
Additional Notes:
The reason for selling was retirement.

Was there a personal guarantee on the Note? No

Terms of Lease: N/A
Noncompete Description: 50 mile radius

Valuation Multiples
MVIC/Net Sales	0.47
MVIC/Gross Profit	0.47
MVIC/EBITDA	N/A
MVIC/EBIT	2.16
MVIC/Discretionary Earnings	N/A
MVIC/Book Value of Invested Capital	N/A

Profitability Ratios
Net Profit Margin	0.22
Operating Profit Margin	0.22
Gross Profit Margin	1.00
Return on Assets	N/A
Return on Equity	N/A

Leverage Ratios
Fixed Charge Coverage	N/A
Long-Term Debt to Assets	N/A
Long-Term Debt to Equity	N/A

Earnings
EBITDA	N/A
Discretionary Earnings	N/A

Liquidity Ratios
Current Ratio	N/A
Quick Ratio	N/A

Activity Ratios
Total Asset Turnover	N/A
Fixed Asset Turnover	9.16
Inventory Turnover	36.65

Copyright © 2010 Business Valuation Resources, LLC. All rights reserved. www.BVResources.com℠
(888) BUS-VALU, (503) 291-7963

Pratt's Stats® Auto Dealership Report

Pratt's Stats® Transaction Report
Prepared: 8/20/2010 2:09:46 PM (PST)

Seller Details
Target Name:	N/A
Business Description:	Used Car Sales
SIC:	5521 Motor Vehicle Dealers (Used Only)
NAICS:	441120 Used Car Dealers
Sale Location:	FL, United States
Years in Business:	10
Number Employees:	5

Source Data
Broker Name:	N/A
Broker Firm Name:	N/A

Income Data
Data is "Latest Full Year" Reported	Yes
Data is Restated (see Notes for any explanation)	No
Income Statement Date	12/31/2008
Net Sales	$8,270,257
COGS	$7,837,942
Gross Profit	$432,315
Yearly Rent	N/A
Owner's Compensation	$474,200
Other Operating Expenses	N/A
Noncash Charges	$6,942
Total Operating Expenses	$357,669
Operating Profit	$74,646
Interest Expenses	$44,356
EBT	$30,290
Taxes	$0
Net Income	$30,290

Asset Data
Data is Latest Reported	No
Data is "Purchase Price Allocation agreed upon by Buyer and Seller"	Yes
Balance Sheet Date	N/A
Cash Equivalents	N/A
Trade Receivables	$0
Inventory	$0
Other Current Assets	N/A
Total Current Assets	N/A
Fixed Assets	$90,000
Real Estate	N/A
Intangibles	$295,000
Other Noncurrent Assets	$0
Total Assets	N/A
Long-term Liabilities	N/A
Total Liabilities	N/A
Stockholder's Equity	N/A

Transaction Data
Date Sale Initiated:	9/17/2008
Date of Sale:	1/2/2010
Days to Sell:	472
Asking Price:	$499,000
Market Value of Invested Capital*:	$385,000
Debt Assumed:	$0
Employment Agreement Value:	N/A
Noncompete Value:	N/A
Amount of Down Payment:	$385,000
Stock or Asset Sale:	Asset
Company Type:	Limited Corporation
Was there an Employment/Consulting Agreement?	No
Was there an Assumed Lease in the sale?	No
Was there a Renewal Option with the Lease?	No

*Includes noncompete value and interest-bearing debt; excludes real estate, employment/consulting agreement values, and all contingent payments.

Additional Transaction Information
Was there a Note in the consideration paid? No
Terms:
Assumed Lease (Months): N/A
Noncompete Length (Months): 36
Employment/Consulting Agreement Description:
Additional Notes:
This transaction was submitted by the Business Brokers of Florida.

Was there a personal guarantee on the Note? No
Terms of Lease: N/A
Noncompete Description: 20 mile radius

Valuation Multiples
MVIC/Net Sales	0.05
MVIC/Gross Profit	0.89
MVIC/EBITDA	4.72
MVIC/EBIT	5.16
MVIC/Discretionary Earnings	0.69
MVIC/Book Value of Invested Capital	N/A

Profitability Ratios
Net Profit Margin	0.00
Operating Profit Margin	0.01
Gross Profit Margin	0.05
Return on Assets	N/A
Return on Equity	N/A

Leverage Ratios
Fixed Charge Coverage	1.68
Long-Term Debt to Assets	N/A
Long-Term Debt to Equity	N/A

Earnings
EBITDA	$81,588
Discretionary Earnings	$555,788

Liquidity Ratios
Current Ratio	N/A
Quick Ratio	N/A

Activity Ratios
Total Asset Turnover	N/A
Fixed Asset Turnover	91.89
Inventory Turnover	N/A

Copyright © 2010 Business Valuation Resources, LLC. All rights reserved. www.BVResources.com℠
(888) BUS-VALU, (503) 291-7963

Section 6
BIZCOMPS®
Auto Dealerships Report

Copyright 2010, by BIZCOMPS® reprinted with permission

BIZCOMPS® Transaction Report

Prepared: 8/20/2010 2:13:19 PM (PST) N/A = Not Available

Transaction Details

Business Description	Auto Dealership
SIC	5511 Motor Vehicle Dealers (New and Used)
NAICS	44111 New Car Dealers
Location	West N. Carolina, United States
Number Of Employees	N/A

Transaction Data

Sale Date	12/1/2001
Days On Market	180
Ask Price (000)	$100.0
Sale Price (000) (Excludes Inventory)	$100.0
Percent Down	100.0%
Terms on Outstanding Consideration	N/A

Income Data ($000's)

Annual Gross Sales	$1,000.0
Franchise Royalty	N/A
SDE	$100.0

Asset Data ($000's)

Inventory Value	$0.0
Furniture, Fixtures and Equipment	N/A
Value Of Real Estate	N/A

Operating Ratios

SDE/Annual Gross Sales	0.100
Rent/Annual Gross Sales	N/A

Valuation Multiples

Sale Price/Annual Gross Sales	0.100
Sale Price/SDE	1.000

Copyright © 2010 Business Valuation Resources, LLC. All rights reserved. www.BVResources.com℠
(888) BUS-VALU, (503) 291-7963

BIZCOMPS® Auto Dealerships Report

BIZCOMPS® Transaction Report
Prepared: 8/20/2010 2:13:19 PM (PST) N/A = Not Available

Transaction Details

Business Description	Auto Dealership
SIC	5511 Motor Vehicle Dealers (New and Used)
NAICS	44111 New Car Dealers
Location	Orange County, CA, United States
Number Of Employees	40

Transaction Data

Sale Date	5/7/2001
Days On Market	195
Ask Price (000)	$2,850.0
Sale Price (000) (Excludes Inventory)	$2,150.0
Percent Down	100.0%
Terms on Outstanding Consideration	N/A

Income Data ($000's)

Annual Gross Sales	$12,000.0
Franchise Royalty	No
SDE	$675.0

Asset Data ($000's)

Inventory Value	$450.0
Furniture, Fixtures and Equipment	$225.0
Value Of Real Estate	N/A

Operating Ratios

SDE/Annual Gross Sales	0.056
Rent/Annual Gross Sales	0.100

Valuation Multiples

Sale Price/Annual Gross Sales	0.179
Sale Price/SDE	3.185

Copyright © 2010 Business Valuation Resources, LLC. All rights reserved. www.BVResources.com[SM]
(888) BUS-VALU, (503) 291-7963

BIZCOMPS® Transaction Report

Prepared: 8/20/2010 2:13:19 PM (PST) N/A = Not Available

Transaction Details

Business Description	Internet Used Cars
SIC	5521 Motor Vehicle Dealers (Used Only)
NAICS	44112 Used Car Dealers
Location	Las Vegas, NV, United States
Number Of Employees	N/A

Transaction Data

Sale Date	6/14/2007
Days On Market	N/A
Ask Price (000)	$375.0
Sale Price (000) (Excludes Inventory)	$375.0
Percent Down	100.0%
Terms on Outstanding Consideration	N/A

Income Data ($000's)

Annual Gross Sales	$645.0
Franchise Royalty	No
SDE	($2.0)

Asset Data ($000's)

Inventory Value	$0.0
Furniture, Fixtures and Equipment	N/A
Value Of Real Estate	N/A

Operating Ratios

SDE/Annual Gross Sales	-0.003
Rent/Annual Gross Sales	0.019

Valuation Multiples

Sale Price/Annual Gross Sales	0.581
Sale Price/SDE	

Copyright © 2010 Business Valuation Resources, LLC. All rights reserved. www.BVResources.com℠
(888) BUS-VALU, (503) 291-7963

BIZCOMPS® Transaction Report

Prepared: 8/20/2010 2:13:19 PM (PST) N/A = Not Available

Transaction Details

Business Description	Retail-Used Cars
SIC	5521 Motor Vehicle Dealers (Used Only)
NAICS	44112 Used Car Dealers
Location	Phoenix, AZ, United States
Number Of Employees	N/A

Transaction Data

Sale Date	6/30/2006
Days On Market	N/A
Ask Price (000)	$260.0
Sale Price (000) (Excludes Inventory)	$260.0
Percent Down	N/A
Terms on Outstanding Consideration	N/A

Income Data ($000's)

Annual Gross Sales	$830.0
Franchise Royalty	No
SDE	$150.0

Asset Data ($000's)

Inventory Value	$0.0
Furniture, Fixtures and Equipment	N/A
Value Of Real Estate	N/A

Operating Ratios

SDE/Annual Gross Sales	0.181
Rent/Annual Gross Sales	N/A

Valuation Multiples

Sale Price/Annual Gross Sales	0.313
Sale Price/SDE	1.733

Copyright © 2010 Business Valuation Resources, LLC. All rights reserved. www.BVResources.com[SM]
(888) BUS-VALU, (503) 291-7963

BIZCOMPS® Auto Dealerships Report

BIZCOMPS® Transaction Report
Prepared: 8/20/2010 2:13:19 PM (PST) N/A = Not Available

Transaction Details
Business Description	Used Car Dealer
SIC	5521 Motor Vehicle Dealers (Used Only)
NAICS	44112 Used Car Dealers
Location	Central Illinois, United States
Number Of Employees	4

Transaction Data
Sale Date	12/8/2005
Days On Market	356
Ask Price (000)	$120.0
Sale Price (000) (Excludes Inventory)	$45.0
Percent Down	N/A
Terms on Outstanding Consideration	N/A

Income Data ($000's)
Annual Gross Sales	$1,075.0
Franchise Royalty	No
SDE	$115.0

Asset Data ($000's)
Inventory Value	$5.0
Furniture, Fixtures and Equipment	$45.0
Value Of Real Estate	N/A

Operating Ratios
SDE/Annual Gross Sales	0.107
Rent/Annual Gross Sales	N/A

Valuation Multiples
Sale Price/Annual Gross Sales	0.042
Sale Price/SDE	0.391

Copyright © 2010 Business Valuation Resources, LLC. All rights reserved. www.BVResources.com℠
(888) BUS-VALU, (503) 291-7963

BIZCOMPS® Transaction Report
Prepared: 8/20/2010 2:13:19 PM (PST) N/A = Not Available

Transaction Details
Business Description	Retail-Used Cars
SIC	5521 Motor Vehicle Dealers (Used Only)
NAICS	44112 Used Car Dealers
Location	Georgia, United States
Number Of Employees	6

Transaction Data
Sale Date	5/13/2005
Days On Market	273
Ask Price (000)	$397.0
Sale Price (000) (Excludes Inventory)	$282.0
Percent Down	100.0%
Terms on Outstanding Consideration	N/A

Income Data ($000's)
Annual Gross Sales	$2,133.0
Franchise Royalty	No
SDE	$142.0

Asset Data ($000's)
Inventory Value	$50.0
Furniture, Fixtures and Equipment	$175.0
Value Of Real Estate	N/A

Operating Ratios
SDE/Annual Gross Sales	0.067
Rent/Annual Gross Sales	0.020

Valuation Multiples
Sale Price/Annual Gross Sales	0.132
Sale Price/SDE	1.986

Copyright © 2010 Business Valuation Resources, LLC. All rights reserved. www.BVResources.com[SM]
(888) BUS-VALU, (503) 291-7963

BIZCOMPS® Transaction Report

Prepared: 8/20/2010 2:13:19 PM (PST) N/A = Not Available

Transaction Details

Business Description	Retail-Used Cars
SIC	5521 Motor Vehicle Dealers (Used Only)
NAICS	44112 Used Car Dealers
Location	Florida, United States
Number Of Employees	2

Transaction Data

Sale Date	3/28/2005
Days On Market	228
Ask Price (000)	$99.0
Sale Price (000) (Excludes Inventory)	$98.0
Percent Down	100.0%
Terms on Outstanding Consideration	N/A

Income Data ($000's)

Annual Gross Sales	$240.0
Franchise Royalty	No
SDE	$75.0

Asset Data ($000's)

Inventory Value	$35.0
Furniture, Fixtures and Equipment	$15.0
Value Of Real Estate	N/A

Operating Ratios

SDE/Annual Gross Sales	0.313
Rent/Annual Gross Sales	0.130

Valuation Multiples

Sale Price/Annual Gross Sales	0.408
Sale Price/SDE	1.307

Copyright © 2010 Business Valuation Resources, LLC. All rights reserved. www.BVResources.com℠
(888) BUS-VALU, (503) 291-7963

BIZCOMPS® Auto Dealerships Report

BIZCOMPS® Transaction Report
Prepared: 8/20/2010 2:13:19 PM (PST) N/A = Not Available

Transaction Details
Business Description	Retail-Used Cars
SIC	5521 Motor Vehicle Dealers (Used Only)
NAICS	44112 Used Car Dealers
Location	Georgia, United States
Number Of Employees	1

Transaction Data
Sale Date	11/30/2005
Days On Market	92
Ask Price (000)	$250.0
Sale Price (000) (Excludes Inventory)	$225.0
Percent Down	100.0%
Terms on Outstanding Consideration	N/A

Income Data ($000's)
Annual Gross Sales	$501.0
Franchise Royalty	No
SDE	$107.0

Asset Data ($000's)
Inventory Value	$25.0
Furniture, Fixtures and Equipment	$10.0
Value Of Real Estate	N/A

Operating Ratios
SDE/Annual Gross Sales	0.214
Rent/Annual Gross Sales	0.056

Valuation Multiples
Sale Price/Annual Gross Sales	0.449
Sale Price/SDE	2.103

Copyright © 2010 Business Valuation Resources, LLC. All rights reserved. www.BVResources.com[SM]
(888) BUS-VALU, (503) 291-7963

BIZCOMPS® Transaction Report

Prepared: 8/20/2010 2:13:19 PM (PST) N/A = Not Available

Transaction Details

Business Description	Used Car Dealer
SIC	5521 Motor Vehicle Dealers (Used Only)
NAICS	44112 Used Car Dealers
Location	SW Florida, United States
Number Of Employees	1

Transaction Data

Sale Date	5/15/2001
Days On Market	162
Ask Price (000)	$128.0
Sale Price (000) (Excludes Inventory)	$110.0
Percent Down	33.0%
Terms on Outstanding Consideration	5 Yrs @ 8%

Income Data ($000's)

Annual Gross Sales	$350.0
Franchise Royalty	N/A
SDE	$88.0

Asset Data ($000's)

Inventory Value	$22.0
Furniture, Fixtures and Equipment	$5.0
Value Of Real Estate	N/A

Operating Ratios

SDE/Annual Gross Sales	0.251
Rent/Annual Gross Sales	0.080

Valuation Multiples

Sale Price/Annual Gross Sales	0.314
Sale Price/SDE	1.250

Copyright © 2010 Business Valuation Resources, LLC. All rights reserved. www.BVResources.com℠
(888) BUS-VALU, (503) 291-7963

BIZCOMPS® Transaction Report

Prepared: 8/20/2010 2:13:19 PM (PST) N/A = Not Available

Transaction Details

Business Description	Used Car Sales
SIC	5521 Motor Vehicle Dealers (Used Only)
NAICS	44112 Used Car Dealers
Location	Michigan, United States
Number Of Employees	2

Transaction Data

Sale Date	4/20/2001
Days On Market	15
Ask Price (000)	$45.0
Sale Price (000) (Excludes Inventory)	$40.0
Percent Down	27.0%
Terms on Outstanding Consideration	3 Yrs @ 8%

Income Data ($000's)

Annual Gross Sales	$550.0
Franchise Royalty	No
SDE	$25.0

Asset Data ($000's)

Inventory Value	$0.0
Furniture, Fixtures and Equipment	$15.0
Value Of Real Estate	N/A

Operating Ratios

SDE/Annual Gross Sales	0.045
Rent/Annual Gross Sales	N/A

Valuation Multiples

Sale Price/Annual Gross Sales	0.073
Sale Price/SDE	1.600

Copyright © 2010 Business Valuation Resources, LLC. All rights reserved. www.BVResources.com℠
(888) BUS-VALU, (503) 291-7963

Section 7
Mergerstat
Auto Dealerships
Report

Copyright 2010, by Mergerstat reprinted with permission

Mergerstat Auto Dealerships Report

Factset Mergerstat® / BVR Control Premium Study™ Transaction Report Prepared:
8/20/2010 2:15:44 PM (PST) N/A=Not Available

Transaction Details

	Acquiror	Target
SIC	5511 Motor Vehicle Dealers (New and Used)	5511 Motor Vehicle Dealers (New and Used)
Name	Republic Industries Inc	Cross-Continent Auto Retailers Inc
Business Description	Sells new and used vehicles and provides solid waste collection and recycling services	Owns and operates 7 franchised automobile dealerships
Stock Exchange	New York	New York
Nation	United States	United States

Premiums

2 Month	1 Month	1 Week	1 Day	MergerStat Control Premium
0.542	0.556	0.678	0.662	0.662

Discount

Implied Minority Discount
0.398

Target Stock Prices (per share) (Home Currency)

CUSIP	Target Stock Ticker	Unaffected Price	Announce Day Price	1 Day Price	1 Week Price	1 Month Price	2 Month Price
	XC	6.440	9.500	6.440	6.380	6.880	6.940

Sale Details

Date Announced	9/3/1998
Date Effective	3/20/1999
Deal Value ($mil-US)	$145
Deal Currency	United States Dollar
% of Shares Acquired	100.0
% of Shares Held at Date Announced	N/A
% of Shares Held after Acquisition	100.0
Purchase Price Per Share ($'s-US)	$10.70
Common Shares Acquired (mil)	13.574
Deal Exchange Rate	1.000
Purchase Price/Share (Home currency)	10.70
Consideration	C,L
Attitude	
Form	Acq
Transaction Purpose	Horizontal

Target Financial Data ($mil-US)

LTM Net Sales	564.420
LTM EBITDA	22.530
LTM EBIT	19.030
LTM Net Income	6.360
BV Target Common Equity	-15.090
Target Invested Capital	257.781
Book Value Per Share	-1.110
Common Shares Outstanding (000's)	13.574
Operating Profit Margin	0.034
Net Profit Margin	0.011

Target Pricing Multiples

Implied MVE ($mil-US)	145.241
Price/Sales	0.257
Price/Income	22.837
Price/Book Value	
Target Invested Capital/EBIT	13.546
Target Invested Capital/EBITDA	11.442

Copyright © 2010 FactSet Mergerstat, LLC. All rights reserved.
(888) BUS-VALU, (503) 291-7963

MERGERSTAT®
Global Mergers & Acquisitions Information

Mergerstat Auto Dealerships Report

Factset Mergerstat® / BVR Control Premium Study™
Transaction Report Prepared: 8/20/2010 2:15:44 PM (PST) N/A=Not Available

Transaction Details

	Acquiror	Target
SIC	6081 Branches and Agencies of Foreign Banks	5511 Motor Vehicle Dealers (New and Used)
Name	Royal Bank of Scotland Group PLC	Dixon Motors PLC
Business Description	Foreign bank	Owns and operates car and motorcycle dealerships
Stock Exchange	London	London
Nation	Scotland	England

Premiums

2 Month	1 Month	1 Week	1 Day	MergerStat Control Premium
0.446	0.395	0.172	0.017	0.422

Discount

Implied Minority Discount
0.297

Target Stock Prices (per share) (Home Currency)

CUSIP	Target Stock Ticker	Unaffected Price	Announce Day Price	1 Day Price	1 Week Price	1 Month Price	2 Month Price
	DXM LN	2.110	2.970	2.950	2.560	2.150	2.080

Sale Details

Date Announced	4/22/2002
Date Effective	6/19/2002
Deal Value ($mil-US)	$163
Deal Currency	British Pound
% of Shares Acquired	100.0
% of Shares Held at Date Announced	N/A
% of Shares Held after Acquisition	100.0
Purchase Price Per Share ($'s-US)	$4.48
Common Shares Acquired (mil)	36.460
Deal Exchange Rate	1.492
Purchase Price/Share (Home currency)	3.00
Consideration	C
Attitude	
Form	Acq
Transaction Purpose	Financial

Target Financial Data ($mil-US)

LTM Net Sales	1,219.640
LTM EBITDA	31.980
LTM EBIT	23.670
LTM Net Income	11.210
BV Target Common Equity	106.960
Target Invested Capital	261.090
Book Value Per Share	2.930
Common Shares Outstanding (000's)	36.460
Operating Profit Margin	0.019
Net Profit Margin	0.009

Target Pricing Multiples

Implied MVE ($mil-US)	163.217
Price/Sales	0.134
Price/Income	14.565
Price/Book Value	1.526
Target Invested Capital/EBIT	11.032
Target Invested Capital/EBITDA	8.165

Copyright © 2010 FactSet Mergerstat, LLC. All rights reserved.
(888) BUS-VALU, (503) 291-7963

MERGERSTAT®
Global Mergers & Acquisitions Information

Mergerstat Auto Dealerships Report

Factset Mergerstat® / BVR Control Premium Study™
Transaction Report
Prepared: 8/20/2010 2:15:44 PM (PST) N/A=Not Available

Transaction Details

	Acquiror	Target
SIC	5999 Miscellaneous Retail Stores, NEC	5511 Motor Vehicle Dealers (New and Used)
Name	Jardine Strategic Holdings Ltd	Cycle & Carriage Ltd
Business Description	Operates supermarkets, convenience stores, hotels, restaurants, and distributes motor vehicles	Distributes, retails, and assembles motor vehicles, parts and accessories
Stock Exchange	London	Singapore
Nation	Bermuda	Singapore

Premiums

2 Month	1 Month	1 Week	1 Day	MergerStat Control Premium
-0.048	0.008	-0.021	-0.012	0.013

Discount

Implied Minority Discount
0.013

Target Stock Prices (per share) (Home Currency)

CUSIP	Target Stock Ticker	Unaffected Price	Announce Day Price	1 Day Price	1 Week Price	1 Month Price	2 Month Price
	CNC SP	4.700	4.820	4.820	4.860	4.720	5.000

Sale Details

Date Announced	7/12/2002
Date Effective	11/5/2002
Deal Value ($mil-US)	$137
Deal Currency	Singapore Dollar
% of Shares Acquired	21.1
% of Shares Held at Date Announced	29.1
% of Shares Held after Acquisition	50.2
Purchase Price Per Share ($'s-US)	$2.70
Common Shares Acquired (mil)	50.886
Deal Exchange Rate	0.567
Purchase Price/Share (Home currency)	4.76
Consideration	C
Attitude	
Form	Acq
Transaction Purpose	Horizontal

Target Financial Data ($mil-US)

LTM Net Sales	1,410.330
LTM EBITDA	135.430
LTM EBIT	126.980
LTM Net Income	66.890
BV Target Common Equity	671.720
Target Invested Capital	1,200.447
Book Value Per Share	2.780
Common Shares Outstanding (000's)	241.510
Operating Profit Margin	0.090
Net Profit Margin	0.047

Target Pricing Multiples

Implied MVE ($mil-US)	652.248
Price/Sales	0.462
Price/Income	9.751
Price/Book Value	0.971
Target Invested Capital/EBIT	9.454
Target Invested Capital/EBITDA	8.864

Copyright © 2010 FactSet Mergerstat, LLC. All rights reserved.
(888) BUS-VALU, (503) 291-7963

MERGERSTAT®
Global Mergers & Acquisitions Information

Factset Mergerstat® / BVR Control Premium Study™
Transaction Report
Prepared: 8/20/2010 2:15:44 PM (PST) N/A=Not Available

Transaction Details

	Acquiror	Target
SIC	5511 Motor Vehicle Dealers (New and Used)	5511 Motor Vehicle Dealers (New and Used)
Name	United Auto Group, Inc. (Sytner Group Plc)	William Jacks Plc
Business Description	Owns and operates franchised automobile dealerships	Sells, distributes and provides services to automobiles
Stock Exchange	New York	London
Nation	United States	United Kingdom

Premiums

2 Month	1 Month	1 Week	1 Day	MergerStat Control Premium
-0.590	-0.603	-0.606	-0.606	-0.606

Discount

Implied Minority Discount
-1.538

Target Stock Prices (per share) (Home Currency)

CUSIP	Target Stock Ticker	Unaffected Price	Announce Day Price	1 Day Price	1 Week Price	1 Month Price	2 Month Price
	JCKS	0.635	0.855	0.635	0.635	0.630	0.610

Sale Details

Date Announced	12/12/2005
Date Effective	1/31/2006
Deal Value ($mil-US)	$3
Deal Currency	British Pound
% of Shares Acquired	69.4
% of Shares Held at Date Announced	N/A
% of Shares Held after Acquisition	69.4
Purchase Price Per Share ($'s-US)	$0.43
Common Shares Acquired (mil)	7.660
Deal Exchange Rate	1.730
Purchase Price/Share (Home currency)	0.25
Consideration	C
Attitude	
Form	Acq
Transaction Purpose	Strategic

Target Financial Data ($mil-US)

LTM Net Sales	350.324
LTM EBITDA	5.155
LTM EBIT	3.379
LTM Net Income	0.447
BV Target Common Equity	20.566
Target Invested Capital	6.292
Book Value Per Share	1.863
Common Shares Outstanding (000's)	11.038
Operating Profit Margin	0.010
Net Profit Margin	0.001

Target Pricing Multiples

Implied MVE ($mil-US)	4.779
Price/Sales	0.014
Price/Income	10.692
Price/Book Value	0.232
Target Invested Capital/EBIT	1.862
Target Invested Capital/EBITDA	1.221

Copyright © 2010 FactSet Mergerstat, LLC. All rights reserved.
(888) BUS-VALU, (503) 291-7963

MERGERSTAT®
Global Mergers & Acquisitions Information

Mergerstat Auto Dealerships Report

Factset Mergerstat® / BVR Control Premium Study™
Transaction Report
Prepared: 8/20/2010 2:15:44 PM (PST) N/A=Not Available

Transaction Details

	Acquiror	Target
SIC	5511 Motor Vehicle Dealers (New and Used)	5511 Motor Vehicle Dealers (New and Used)
Name	Pendragon Plc	Reg Vardy Plc
Business Description	Sells new and used motor vehicles	Sells new and used motor vehicles and light trucks
Stock Exchange	London	London
Nation	United Kingdom	United Kingdom

Premiums

2 Month	1 Month	1 Week	1 Day	MergerStat Control Premium
0.531	0.429	0.225	0.134	0.360

Discount

Implied Minority Discount
0.264

Target Stock Prices (per share) (Home Currency)

CUSIP	Target Stock Ticker	Unaffected Price	Announce Day Price	1 Day Price	1 Week Price	1 Month Price	2 Month Price
	VDY	6.620	8.040	7.940	7.345	6.300	5.880

Sale Details

Date Announced	12/5/2005
Date Effective	8/18/2006
Deal Value ($mil-US)	$876
Deal Currency	British Pound
% of Shares Acquired	100.0
% of Shares Held at Date Announced	N/A
% of Shares Held after Acquisition	100.0
Purchase Price Per Share ($'s-US)	$15.57
Common Shares Acquired (mil)	56.253
Deal Exchange Rate	1.730
Purchase Price/Share (Home currency)	9.00
Consideration	C
Attitude	Neutral
Form	Acq-TO
Transaction Purpose	Strategic

Target Financial Data ($mil-US)

LTM Net Sales	3,162.749
LTM EBITDA	453.259
LTM EBIT	441.691
LTM Net Income	409.842
BV Target Common Equity	381.526
Target Invested Capital	990.072
Book Value Per Share	11.736
Common Shares Outstanding (000's)	56.253
Operating Profit Margin	0.140
Net Profit Margin	0.130

Target Pricing Multiples

Implied MVE ($mil-US)	876.083
Price/Sales	0.277
Price/Income	2.138
Price/Book Value	2.296
Target Invested Capital/EBIT	2.242
Target Invested Capital/EBITDA	2.184

Copyright © 2010 FactSet Mergerstat, LLC. All rights reserved.
(888) BUS-VALU, (503) 291-7963

MERGERSTAT
Global Mergers & Acquisitions Information

Mergerstat Auto Dealerships Report

Factset Mergerstat® / BVR Control Premium Study™
Transaction Report
Prepared: 8/20/2010 2:15:44 PM (PST) N/A=Not Available

Transaction Details

	Acquiror	Target
SIC	5511 Motor Vehicle Dealers (New and Used)	5511 Motor Vehicle Dealers (New and Used)
Name	Inchcape Plc	European Motor Holdings Plc
Business Description	Provides retail, finance, lease, insurance, and wholesale services for automobiles	Provides car dealership services
Stock Exchange	London	London
Nation	United Kingdom	United Kingdom

Premiums

2 Month	1 Month	1 Week	1 Day	MergerStat Control Premium
0.077	0.095	0.041	0.024	0.024

Discount

Implied Minority Discount
0.023

Target Stock Prices (per share) (Home Currency)

CUSIP	Target Stock Ticker	Unaffected Price	Announce Day Price	1 Day Price	1 Week Price	1 Month Price	2 Month Price
	EMH	4.703	4.850	4.703	4.625	4.398	4.470

Sale Details

Date Announced	12/15/2006
Date Effective	2/26/2007
Deal Value ($mil-US)	$516
Deal Currency	British Pound
% of Shares Acquired	100.0
% of Shares Held at Date Announced	N/A
% of Shares Held after Acquisition	100.0
Purchase Price Per Share ($'s-US)	$9.42
Common Shares Acquired (mil)	54.767
Deal Exchange Rate	1.957
Purchase Price/Share (Home currency)	4.81
Consideration	C
Attitude	Friendly
Form	Acq-TO
Transaction Purpose	Strategic

Target Financial Data ($mil-US)

LTM Net Sales	1,523.070
LTM EBITDA	51.457
LTM EBIT	42.422
LTM Net Income	25.459
BV Target Common Equity	131.795
Target Invested Capital	516.070
Book Value Per Share	2.406
Common Shares Outstanding (000's)	54.767
Operating Profit Margin	0.028
Net Profit Margin	0.017

Target Pricing Multiples

Implied MVE ($mil-US)	516.070
Price/Sales	0.339
Price/Income	20.271
Price/Book Value	3.916
Target Invested Capital/EBIT	12.165
Target Invested Capital/EBITDA	10.029

Copyright © 2010 FactSet Mergerstat, LLC. All rights reserved.
(888) BUS-VALU, (503) 291-7963

MERGERSTAT®
Global Mergers & Acquisitions Information

Factset Mergerstat® / BVR Control Premium Study™
Transaction Report Prepared: 8/20/2010 2:15:44 PM (PST) N/A=Not Available

Transaction Details

	Acquiror	**Target**
SIC	5012 Automobiles and Other Motor Vehicles	5521 Motor Vehicle Dealers (Used Only)
Name	Copart, Inc. (Copart (UK) Ltd.)	Universal Salvage Plc
Business Description	Provides vehicle disposal services	Collects, stores and sells damaged and discarded vehicles
Stock Exchange	Nasdaq	London
Nation	United States	United Kingdom

Premiums

2 Month	1 Month	1 Week	1 Day	MergerStat Control Premium
0.053	0.122	0.008	0.048	0.048

Discount

Implied Minority Discount
0.046

Target Stock Prices (per share) (Home Currency)

CUSIP	Target Stock Ticker	Unaffected Price	Announce Day Price	1 Day Price	1 Week Price	1 Month Price	2 Month Price
	UVS	1.880	1.955	1.880	1.955	1.755	1.870

Sale Details

Date Announced	4/5/2007
Date Effective	6/15/2007
Deal Value ($mil-US)	$112
Deal Currency	British Pound
% of Shares Acquired	100.0
% of Shares Held at Date Announced	N/A
% of Shares Held after Acquisition	100.0
Purchase Price Per Share ($'s-US)	$3.94
Common Shares Acquired (mil)	28.492
Deal Exchange Rate	2.002
Purchase Price/Share (Home currency)	1.97
Consideration	C
Attitude	
Form	Acq
Transaction Purpose	Strategic

Target Financial Data ($mil-US)

LTM Net Sales	119.213
LTM EBITDA	7.635
LTM EBIT	4.627
LTM Net Income	3.835
BV Target Common Equity	32.243
Target Invested Capital	117.114
Book Value Per Share	1.132
Common Shares Outstanding (000's)	28.492
Operating Profit Margin	0.039
Net Profit Margin	0.032

Target Pricing Multiples

Implied MVE ($mil-US)	112.372
Price/Sales	0.943
Price/Income	29.302
Price/Book Value	3.485
Target Invested Capital/EBIT	25.311
Target Invested Capital/EBITDA	15.339

Copyright © 2010 FactSet Mergerstat, LLC. All rights reserved.
(888) BUS-VALU, (503) 291-7963

MERGERSTAT®
Global Mergers & Acquisitions Information

Factset Mergerstat® / BVR Control Premium Study™
Transaction Report
Prepared: 8/20/2010 2:15:44 PM (PST) N/A=Not Available

Transaction Details

	Acquiror	Target
SIC	6799 Investors, NEC	5521 Motor Vehicle Dealers (Used Only)
Name	IDSP KK	Aucnet, Inc.
Business Description	Operates an investment company	Provides online auctioning of used automobiles
Stock Exchange		Tokyo
Nation	Japan	Japan

Premiums

2 Month	1 Month	1 Week	1 Day	MergerStat Control Premium
0.861	0.797	0.525	0.577	0.577

Discount

Implied Minority Discount
0.366

Target Stock Prices (per share) (Home Currency)

CUSIP	Target Stock Ticker	Unaffected Price	Announce Day Price	1 Day Price	1 Week Price	1 Month Price	2 Month Price
	9669	1,340.000	1,356.000	1,340.000	1,385.000	1,176.000	1,135.000

Sale Details

Date Announced	5/27/2008
Date Effective	7/10/2008
Deal Value ($mil-US)	$202
Deal Currency	Japanese Yen
% of Shares Acquired	95.9
% of Shares Held at Date Announced	N/A
% of Shares Held after Acquisition	95.9
Purchase Price Per Share ($'s-US)	$19.65
Common Shares Acquired (mil)	10.269
Deal Exchange Rate	0.009
Purchase Price/Share (Home currency)	2,112.78
Consideration	C
Attitude	Friendly
Form	Acq-TO-GP
Transaction Purpose	Financial

Target Financial Data ($mil-US)

LTM Net Sales	162.347
LTM EBITDA	28.046
LTM EBIT	16.955
LTM Net Income	7.014
BV Target Common Equity	114.013
Target Invested Capital	221.506
Book Value Per Share	1,144.271
Common Shares Outstanding (000's)	10.713
Operating Profit Margin	0.104
Net Profit Margin	0.043

Target Pricing Multiples

Implied MVE ($mil-US)	210.515
Price/Sales	1.297
Price/Income	30.014
Price/Book Value	1.846
Target Invested Capital/EBIT	13.064
Target Invested Capital/EBITDA	7.898

Copyright © 2010 FactSet Mergerstat, LLC. All rights reserved.
(888) BUS-VALU, (503) 291-7963

Factset Mergerstat® / BVR Control Premium Study™
Transaction Report
Prepared: 8/20/2010 2:15:44 PM (PST) N/A=Not Available

Transaction Details

	Acquiror	Target
SIC	6141 Personal Credit Institutions	5521 Motor Vehicle Dealers (Used Only)
Name	NIS Group Co., Ltd. (NIS1 KK)	Agasta Co. Ltd.
Business Description	Provides consumer loan and financing services	Sells used cars
Stock Exchange	Tokyo	Tokyo
Nation	Japan	Japan

Premiums

2 Month	1 Month	1 Week	1 Day	MergerStat Control Premium
1.505	1.383	1.130	1.076	1.076

Discount

Implied Minority Discount
0.518

Target Stock Prices (per share) (Home Currency)

CUSIP	Target Stock Ticker	Unaffected Price	Announce Day Price	1 Day Price	1 Week Price	1 Month Price	2 Month Price
	3330	11,800.000	11,450.000	11,800.000	11,500.000	10,280.000	9,780.000

Sale Details

Date Announced	6/30/2009
Date Effective	8/25/2009
Deal Value ($mil-US)	$7
Deal Currency	Japanese Yen
% of Shares Acquired	92.3
% of Shares Held at Date Announced	N/A
% of Shares Held after Acquisition	92.3
Purchase Price Per Share ($'s-US)	$259.68
Common Shares Acquired (mil)	0.028
Deal Exchange Rate	0.011
Purchase Price/Share (Home currency)	24,500.00
Consideration	C
Attitude	Friendly
Form	Acq-TO
Transaction Purpose	Strategic

Target Financial Data ($mil-US)

LTM Net Sales	28.097
LTM EBITDA	-1.329
LTM EBIT	-1.463
LTM Net Income	-1.750
BV Target Common Equity	9.547
Target Invested Capital	11.096
Book Value Per Share	304.200
Common Shares Outstanding (000's)	0.031
Operating Profit Margin	-0.052
Net Profit Margin	-0.062

Target Pricing Multiples

Implied MVE ($mil-US)	7.969
Price/Sales	0.284
Price/Income	
Price/Book Value	0.835
Target Invested Capital/EBIT	
Target Invested Capital/EBITDA	

Copyright © 2010 FactSet Mergerstat, LLC. All rights reserved.
(888) BUS-VALU, (503) 291-7963

MERGERSTAT
Global Mergers & Acquisitions Information

Mergerstat Auto Dealerships Report

Factset Mergerstat® / BVR Control Premium Study™
Transaction Report
Prepared: 8/20/2010 2:15:44 PM (PST) N/A=Not Available

Transaction Details

	Acquiror	Target
SIC	6799 Investors, NEC	5521 Motor Vehicle Dealers (Used Only)
Name	Gallop KK	Mitsui & Co. Ltd. / Aucnet, Inc. / J21 KK (Japan Automobile Auction, Inc.)
Business Description	Acquisition vehicle	Engages in car auctions and network auctions
Stock Exchange		Tokyo
Nation	Japan	Japan

Premiums

2 Month	1 Month	1 Week	1 Day	MergerStat Control Premium
0.509	0.457	0.589	0.530	0.530

Discount

Implied Minority Discount
0.346

Target Stock Prices (per share) (Home Currency)

CUSIP	Target Stock Ticker	Unaffected Price	Announce Day Price	1 Day Price	1 Week Price	1 Month Price	2 Month Price
	2394	91,500.000	92,000.000	91,500.000	88,100.000	96,100.000	92,800.000

Sale Details

Date Announced	4/15/2010
Date Effective	6/3/2010
Deal Value ($mil-US)	$133
Deal Currency	Japanese Yen
% of Shares Acquired	95.2
% of Shares Held at Date Announced	N/A
% of Shares Held after Acquisition	95.2
Purchase Price Per Share ($'s-US)	$1,514.94
Common Shares Acquired (mil)	0.088
Deal Exchange Rate	0.011
Purchase Price/Share (Home currency)	140,000.00
Consideration	C
Attitude	Friendly
Form	Acq-TO-GP
Transaction Purpose	Financial

Target Financial Data ($mil-US)

LTM Net Sales	88.823
LTM EBITDA	23.966
LTM EBIT	16.318
LTM Net Income	13.638
BV Target Common Equity	81.131
Target Invested Capital	138.041
Book Value Per Share	84,244.050
Common Shares Outstanding (000's)	0.089
Operating Profit Margin	0.184
Net Profit Margin	0.154

Target Pricing Multiples

Implied MVE ($mil-US)	134.827
Price/Sales	1.518
Price/Income	9.886
Price/Book Value	1.662
Target Invested Capital/EBIT	8.460
Target Invested Capital/EBITDA	5.760

Copyright © 2010 FactSet Mergerstat, LLC. All rights reserved.
(888) BUS-VALU, (503) 291-7963

MERGERSTAT
Global Mergers & Acquisitions Information

Factset Mergerstat® / BVR Control Premium Study™ Transaction Report

Prepared: 8/20/2010 2:16:28 PM (PST) N/A=Not Available

Transaction Details

	Acquiror		Target
SIC	6799 Investors, NEC		5521 Motor Vehicle Dealers (Used Only)
Name	Kelso & Co. LP		Insurance Auto Auctions, Inc.
Business Description	Provides financial services		Processes and sells salvage and total loss vehicles
Stock Exchange			Nasdaq
Nation	United States		United States

Premiums

2 Month	1 Month	1 Week	1 Day	MergerStat Control Premium
0.275	0.276	0.244	0.261	0.261

Discount

Implied Minority Discount: 0.207

Target Stock Prices (per share) (Home Currency)

CUSIP	Target Stock Ticker	Unaffected Price	Announce Day Price	1 Day Price	1 Week Price	1 Month Price	2 Month Price
457875102	IAAI	22.410	27.580	22.410	22.710	22.140	22.160

Sale Details

Date Announced	2/23/2005
Date Effective	5/25/2005
Deal Value ($mil-US)	$335
Deal Currency	United States Dollar
% of Shares Acquired	100.0
% of Shares Held at Date Announced	N/A
% of Shares Held after Acquisition	100.0
Purchase Price Per Share ($'s-US)	$28.25
Common Shares Acquired (mil)	11.862
Deal Exchange Rate	1.000
Purchase Price/Share (Home currency)	28.25
Consideration	C
Attitude	
Form	Acq-GP
Transaction Purpose	Financial

Target Financial Data ($mil-US)

LTM Net Sales	240.179
LTM EBITDA	33.961
LTM EBIT	20.976
LTM Net Income	12.265
BV Target Common Equity	63.410
Target Invested Capital	353.490
Book Value Per Share	5.350
Common Shares Outstanding (000's)	11.853
Operating Profit Margin	0.087
Net Profit Margin	0.051

Target Pricing Multiples

Implied MVE ($mil-US)	334.850
Price/Sales	1.390
Price/Income	27.300
Price/Book Value	5.280
Target Invested Capital/EBIT	16.850
Target Invested Capital/EBITDA	10.410

Copyright © 2010 FactSet Mergerstat, LLC. All rights reserved.
(888) BUS-VALU, (503) 291-7963

Mergerstat Auto Dealerships Report

Factset Mergerstat® / BVR Control Premium Study™
Transaction Report
Prepared: 8/20/2010 2:16:28 PM (PST) N/A=Not Available

Transaction Details

	Acquiror	**Target**
SIC	6799 Investors, NEC	5521 Motor Vehicle Dealers (Used Only)
Name	Solid Acoustics Co. Ltd.	CARCHS Co., Ltd.
Business Description	Provides investment, incubation and business consulting services; produces loud speakers and related acoustic equipments	Operates a chain of used car dealerships and provides related information over the Internet
Stock Exchange		Tokyo
Nation	Japan	Japan

Premiums

2 Month	1 Month	1 Week	1 Day	MergerStat Control Premium
-0.228	-0.168	0.018	-0.189	-0.189

Discount

Implied Minority Discount: -0.233

Target Stock Prices (per share) (Home Currency)

CUSIP	Target Stock Ticker	Unaffected Price	Announce Day Price	1 Day Price	1 Week Price	1 Month Price	2 Month Price
	7602	118.000	126.000	118.000	94.000	115.000	124.000

Sale Details

Date Announced	12/1/2006
Date Effective	1/9/2007
Deal Value ($mil-US)	$99
Deal Currency	Japanese Yen
% of Shares Acquired	51.0
% of Shares Held at Date Announced	N/A
% of Shares Held after Acquisition	51.0
Purchase Price Per Share ($'s-US)	$0.82
Common Shares Acquired (mil)	120.354
Deal Exchange Rate	0.009
Purchase Price/Share (Home currency)	95.70
Consideration	C
Attitude	Neutral
Form	Acq-TO
Transaction Purpose	Financial

Target Financial Data ($mil-US)

LTM Net Sales	332,398.578
LTM EBITDA	208.055
LTM EBIT	205.708
LTM Net Income	-27.768
BV Target Common Equity	191,113.501
Target Invested Capital	3,545.089
Book Value Per Share	809.847
Common Shares Outstanding (000's)	235.988
Operating Profit Margin	0.001
Net Profit Margin	-0.000

Target Pricing Multiples

Implied MVE ($mil-US)	193.746
Price/Sales	0.001
Price/Income	
Price/Book Value	0.001
Target Invested Capital/EBIT	17.234
Target Invested Capital/EBITDA	17.039

Copyright © 2010 FactSet Mergerstat, LLC. All rights reserved.
(888) BUS-VALU, (503) 291-7963

MERGERSTAT®
Global Mergers & Acquisitions Information

Section 8
Valuing Auto Dealerships
July 29, 2010
BVR Webinar

Valuing Auto Dealerships
Business Valuation Resources
July 29, 2010/10:00 a.m. PT

Blake Lyman: Hello and welcome to *Valuing Auto Dealerships*, a BVR webinar featuring Jim Alerding, Kevin Yeanoplos and Carl Woodward. My name is Blake Lyman, Professional Program Manager at BVR.

Today, BVR's Industry Spotlight Series continues with a look at one of the highest profile and most turbulent industries in America. Specifically, today's presentation focuses on the end of the automobile supply chain, the dealership. Over the next 100 minutes, our three experts will lead us through everything you should consider when valuing an auto dealership and a look at what's ahead.

Our moderator today is Jim Alerding who has been actively involved with the valuation of businesses since 1980. In addition to valuing a number of businesses each year, Jim also lectures frequently on the subject of valuations of closely held businesses and has produced a number of treaties and several articles on the subject. A partner with Clifton Gunderson, Jim is the author of *Purchase or Sale of a Closely Held Business* and *Valuation of a Closely Held Business*.

Today we also welcome Kevin Yeanoplos, the Director of Valuation Services for Brueggeman and Johnson Yeanoplos, P.C., a firm with offices in Seattle, Tucson and Phoenix that specializes in the areas of business valuation, financial analysis and litigation support. Kevin has extensive experience having valued over 900 businesses for a variety of purposes including divorce and other litigation, gift and estate taxes, mergers and acquisitions, and ESOPS.

Finally, we are joined by Carl Woodward, a partner with Woodward and Associates, Inc., a specialty firm located in Bloomington, Illinois which serves automobile dealers in all accounting and financial matters. With Woodward and Associates, Carl has consulted with automobile dealers in such areas as tax and estate planning issues, accounting analysis, operations, and dealer transactions. He's also lectured extensively with all of these matters and is the author of *Power Steering*, a national publication with subscribers including automobile dealers and financial institutions.

It is my pleasure to welcome Jim, Kevin and Carl today and you can read much more about them on our webpage for today's webinar.

BVR would also like to thank AccountingWEB and Business Brokerage Press for their support today as co-presenters.

With that, I'll turn it over to Jim Alerding, Kevin Yeanoplos and Carl Woodward. Jim?

James Alerding: Thank you, Blake. We are very pleased to be able to present this webinar to you today and I think that you're going to enjoy the presentation.

We have really great panelists. Kevin Yeanoplos has worked in this area of auto dealerships for quite a while and has done some previous work with BVR on this.

Carl Woodward spends his entire focus on auto dealerships and I've had the pleasure of working with Carl and I think you're going to find his knowledge in the area to be very helpful to all of you who are interested in this industry arena, and as Blake mentioned, it's one of the most volatile and one of the most interesting industry niches that we could deal with today.

We're going to move right into the presentation and I will moderate the panel for us today and try to help out a little bit where I can.

Kevin, an auto dealership is just not selling new cars so can you give us a brief summary of the business lines that make up the traditional auto dealership?

Kevin Yeanoplos: Yes, I'll be happy to do that, and Blake, if you could move to the next slide.

A lot of businesses, we look at the business and it's a little easier to put a value on it because it has one primary focus, one cost structure and the margins may be the same all the way through.

But with an auto dealer, you really, really have to look at it as if it's a number of different businesses. For instance, you'll find obviously, if it is a new car dealership, it's going to have new car sales.

Often, they're going to be selling used car sales.

Now there are some dealers, of course, that only sell used cars. But that, right off the bat, is one of the most important to look at because the margins are different.

If you've got a dealership that sells nothing but new cars, generally speaking, their margins are going to be lower than somebody that would sell nothing but used cars. Now obviously, depending on the brand, that might be something different.

But you do have to look at specifics – the mix of the revenues.

In addition to the car sales, they'll have service and repair, parts, finance and insurance.

The finance and insurance, it's referred to as F&I, that particular business or division of the larger dealership winds up being one of the most profitable because there really aren't that many costs associated with it so the margins are very high with the F&I.

Some dealers will have a body shop.

Some will actually be leasing and renting the automobiles

Fleet sales – as you might expect with fleet sales, the margins there might be lower as well because the whole idea is that you're selling in bulk.

To just swing back around and reemphasize, you really have to look at the revenue mix from one dealer to the next because to make sure you're comparing apples to apples, it's extremely important to understand how much contribution towards the bottom line each one of these separate businesses contributes towards the bottom line.

James Alerding: Carl, do you want to add anything to that?

Carl Woodward: Just a couple of things. On fleet sales, we, when we're valuing, need to look to see if the dealer has much of that and we need to see if the margins are really small, which they usually are, so we don't think we have a dealership with $50 million of sales when $20 million of it is fleet sales with no gross profit margin, so you really have a dealership with $30 million of sales. So you always need to look for that to see if there's a material amount of fleet sales is the one big item I might suggest.

James Alerding: Carl, can you outline some of the specific aspects – and if you could move to the slide over one more there, Blake – of the dealer operations that the analyst needs to recognize and consider when valuing an auto dealership?

Carl Woodward: The rent factor – the rent that's being paid, is it to a related party and is it a reasonable rent factor? If you're doing a valuation for whatever reason, is it a rent factor that would be charged to the next person that bought the dealership. Because you could have a very small or a very large rent factor that would be changed in a sale so you need to allow for either under rent or excess rent to get what we all call normalized profits. That's one biggie.

Another major item at times is what I call diverted income. That's income that the dealership generates but is not run through the books for the dealership and you usually should inquire about this. It might make a material difference on the normalized profits of the dealership.

The third major item is the compensation to the chief executive, the dealer, whoever is there full time running the dealership. There needs to be reasonable compensation to where we might have to make an adjustment up or down when we're trying to normalize the earnings.

Those are the three big ones that come to mind.

James Alerding: In addition to that, of course, are the ones that are on the slide – LIFO inventory, used vehicle valuation adjustments, liability for future chargebacks (finance, insurance and service contracts), dealer reserve accounts, floor plan and other financing issues, impact of discretionary expenses which ties into some of the things Carl was talking about in the compensation area but you've got family use of "demos" and other personal expenses that a lot of times get run through these small businesses, and facility enhancements and franchise dynamics can also enter into the mix.

Blake, the next slide, please.

Kevin, do you want to say something?

Kevin Yeanoplos: Yes, could we go back to that slide?

James Alerding: Sure.

Kevin Yeanoplos: There are a couple of them there that I'd like to emphasize a little bit. One is the LIFO inventory and that can have a particular importance especially if you're using the guideline public company method. We're going to talk about that a little bit later. But often, you'll find that the publicly traded dealers do not use LIFO whereas many of the private dealers use it. So recognizing that that is an issue that needs to be addressed is extremely important especially in terms of again, getting back to the apples to apples.

The other one I wanted to talk about more specifically is the floor plan because over the years, a lot of the questions that I've gotten from people that are doing one of these for the first time has related to the floor plan. Ordinarily, when we look at debt and its interest bearing, we might look at that and consider it part of the capital structure. But with a dealer, the floor plan is almost like a glorified payable. It's a payable that they pay interest on. If you really take a look at it, it's really part of working capital. I think there are a few people that may handle it differently but most people I know handle that floor plan as part of working capital, and that very definitely has an impact on the capital structure issues when you're valuing the company.

James Alerding: That's interesting because you're right, that it can be handled differently because I've actually gone both ways on that. I think if you're doing a weighted average cost of capital, I think there is some rationale for looking at it as part of the capital structure. So I think it could be handled either way.

Back to the LIFO for a minute, I think the other issue that we want to look at with the LIFO is the tax liability on the LIFO so that when you're adding back the LIFO inventory to the asset values, the question becomes whether you book a liability for the tax or not. That, in today's world, could depend on whether it's a pass-through entity, not a pass-through entity, if you're working on a marital dissolution case. It could depend on the state law as to whether you add it back or don't add it back. So it's not clear-cut, and that's something you need to take a look at.

Kevin, can you run us through some of the issues with the economic downturn which, of course, has hit the auto industry likely harder than any other segment maybe than housing? Give us some background on what major events have occurred as a result of the downturn and the ancillary events like the bankruptcy issues and the quality control issues with Toyota and other people.

Kevin Yeanoplos: Sure. I think of a lot of these things that we have on here, unfortunately, people are right in the middle of them because, of course, we're consumers that have been hit with this as much as anybody.

GM and Chrysler went bankrupt and, of course, that has had a significant impact in a number of ways on the industry.

Toyota has had their quality control problems. We've all been watching that kind of unfold. My gut-feel, and as I look at what's happening with Toyota, I really think that they have, I guess, rebounded or they will rebound. For me, as a consumer, and I think for many people, even though there appear to be some – I don't know – elements of a cover-up as things went along, Toyota seems to have handled things very effectively in how they dealt with that. I know that they had a number of incentives to kind of stave off the bad publicity. But that certainly did have an impact on the industry as a whole.

The fact that credit is harder to get for new autos has very definitely hurt them.

We saw fairly recently the Cash for Clunkers program which, on the surface, looked like it was providing a boost to the industry and, of course, it did increase sales. But there were some downsides as well because what it was really doing is stealing from future sales. It just accelerated them, and then, of course, by removing some of the used vehicles from the market, it dried up some of that inventory.

Another thing that isn't here on the slide – and this may be self-evident but I think it's an important thing to consider – as the economy has gone south and we've had to deal with more economic problems, people have been willing and probably more than that, desirous just to hang on to their cars.

When the economy is going well and our businesses and our wages are up, we're more inclined to replace the cars we're driving more frequently.

When the economy is bad, we want to hang on to that and try to make it work for longer.

So there are a number of things that have impacted the industry significantly over the past few years.

James Alerding: Another one that's not on the slide that I think is important – and Blake, I didn't have a chance to check and see if you put the report up there – but the report of the Inspector General on this auto dealership bailout issue was quite critical of the way that companies handled the reduction in a number of dealers – which we'll get into a little bit later – in fact, pretty much just blaming the administration for putting a lot of pressure on the companies to cut dealerships in a way that didn't really make a lot of economic sense but was maybe more politically oriented. That could have some long-term impact.

Carl, I want to go back because we've got a question that's been asked, to give some examples of diverted income. Could you do that for us, please?

Carl Woodward: Yeah, a lot of dealers will have a service contract arrangement with a service contract company where the dealer participates on what's called the back-end profit. In other words, you remit a check to the service contract company. They take their fee out of it. After all the claims are paid, there's some money left. They will share that with the dealer and it's a negotiated item.

We have service contracts, credit life insurance and gap insurance. Things like that are the key ones that I call diverted income.

James Alerding: Just so everybody knows, we've got questions coming in here. Some of them I can see already that we're going to have answers as we go through the process. I would tell you that if you do not get your question answered during the program, you can email, I'm sure, any of the three of us. If you want to email me in particular and if I don't know the answer, I'll send it on to one of these other gentleman or I'll find the answer for you and try and get it back to you. So we're not trying to ignore you but we're trying to stay on time also.

Kevin Yeanoplos: Carl, I've got a question for you. Wouldn't those diverted income amounts that you were just discussing, aren't those the type of things that we would typically see coming in through F&I?

Carl Woodward: No, this is on top of that. It's separate. It's part of the F&I department but it's very common for many dealers to have this. It's generated typically by the F&I department.

The short version of it is, needless to say, the service contract companies are pricing their product to the dealer to hopefully make a profit. Dealers have found that they can say to the service contract company, "If you want my business, I want a share in the profits of what I do with you or I won't use you."

	It's pretty common. I would say a reasonable percentage of my 200 and some dealers have some arrangement like this.
James Alerding:	We're going to get into this subject down the road but I've got two questions already. It's an interesting topic and one that just comes up all the time. I'd like to hear everybody's input on this and I'll give you my thoughts and it may differ from the other, and that is the question about use of rules of thumb in this particular industry in terms of determining goodwill and overall value. Kevin, do you want to take a shot at that first?
Kevin Yeanoplos:	Oh, yeah, sure. You cannot ignore the rules of thumb and I will tell you right now that it's important because they tend to tell you that there might be some blue sky or goodwill there even when it doesn't look like there will be, and so I think that may be one of the most important things. Plus the other reality, the question alludes to the fact that it's used so often. Well, the people that use it are the people that are buying and selling. So I don't think we can ignore it. I personally use it as a point of, I suppose, triangulation because it just seems to me that it shouldn't necessarily be used as a primary way to value it.
James Alerding:	Kevin, that sounds like I wrote your answer for you. Carl, give me your thoughts.
Carl Woodward:	My feeling is that most of those rules of thumb with the multiples, if it gives you a good answer, it's probably due more to luck than anything else because they are not engaged with the real profit of the dealership and you've got to sing quickly. I wrote an article on this, and anybody that would like to have it, all they've got to do is email me and I'll send it to you. You've got regular earnings, reported earnings, normalized earnings, and weighted earnings. Which number do you use in all of those numbers? Then secondarily, what multiple do you use? Be very careful. It's dangerous to rely on it.
James Alerding:	Here's the problem – and I'll be brief here because I don't want to

get us too far off – but let me do a couple of things. If you look at the definition in the International Glossary of Business Valuation Terms, a rule of thumb is "a mathematical formula developed from the relationship between price and certain variables based on experience, observation, hearsay, or a combination of these; usually industry specific."

There are lots of kinds of rules of thumb and they seem to come up often in the auto dealership.

I agree with both what Kevin said and what Carl said.

Let me point out one other thing. If you look at paragraph 39 of the Statement on Standards for Valuation Services for the American Institute, it says, "Although not technically a valuation method, some valuation analysts use rules of thumb or industry benchmark indicators (hereinafter, collectively referred to as rules of thumb) in a valuation engagement. A rule of thumb is typically a reasonableness check against other methods used and should generally not be used as the only method to estimate the value of the subject interest."

Notice in there that the word "generally" appears. I can tell you that I'm the one that put that word in there because I think there are cases – and the auto dealership industry is one of them – where it may be the appropriate value, and that's my opinion.

I think hopefully that will lend some light on that whole issue.

Carl, can you discuss the annual drop in sales?

If you could go to the next slide there, Blake, and yes, it is posted, I see.

Okay, that slide is up, so Carl, could you run us through the slide here in talking about new vehicle sales, how they've dropped, the impact and issues that may be brought up?

Carl Woodward: Yes, I keep track of annual sales nationwide since 1978, and typically the last few years nationwide, new vehicle sales that have been around 17 million units have dropped to 13 million in 2008 and 10 million in 2009 as you can see here on the sheet. So it fell off dramatically. I don't know if it's as dramatic as it shows because I believe a lot of that was fleet sales, but even with the fleet sales allowed for, it fell off the cliff and it's starting to creep back up this year. Every month this year is above the same month from last year and it looks like the trend is going to continue. So we're rebounding now and I don't know what normal will be.

I also did a study, and the scrappage rate, which is the number of vehicles taken to junkyards, I guess, has been a little bit more than the number of units being made. I think we all know that with the population growing, that can't sustain itself so I think we've got good things coming. It's just how long it will take to creep back up to where it might have been before.

James Alerding: Can you move to the next slide, please?

Kevin, can you give us your thoughts also on some of these positive trends and what some of those positive trends might be and how they might be helpful to the dealerships going forward and to the value?

Kevin Yeanoplos: You're actually talking, I think, about the next slide, correct?

James Alerding: Well, that could be. Yeah, let me just finish with this. This kind of finishes Carl's subject. As you can see in line with the number of vehicles that have been going down and the average sales per industry unit has gone done also, there are some positive signs in there, so yes, if you'll move to the next slide now, Blake.

Kevin, maybe you can run through some of these issues for us.

Kevin Yeanoplos: Sure. I'm sure anybody that's ever been asked a question about somebody managing a business – and in fact, any of us on this call that have managed a business know that when something is happening to impact our revenues, we've got to look at our expenses so that we can maintain some desired level of profitability.

The auto dealers are no different. So you see what's happened in response to the decrease in revenue. They've actually cut expenses to fit the new volumes, which makes sense. Any astute business owner would tend to do the same thing. They want to try to maintain those margins as much as possible.

What we see is whereas during the growth years, we had return on equity 25 percent or above, in the middle of this economic downturn and the problems with the auto dealers, that decreased. It basically was cut in half.

Valuing Auto Dealerships, July 29, 2010, BVR Webinar

Lately, 2009 and then going forward into 2010, that rebounded up to about 18 percent as a result of the fact that in response to the decreasing revenues, the dealers have taken a hard look at their expenses. They're just like any business owner. They want to continue to make the money that they want to make. So the margins which dropped off for a while have actually increased.

I think that is an important lesson in effectively managing a business and it's particularly important with the auto dealers because they have tried to respond to the decrease in revenues.

I want to just say this too, I think that that is an important consideration to take a look at because it may mean that we have to be careful if we're focusing too much on the top line – in other words, revenues.

As we will talk later about the market approach, one of the commonly used multiples is the price-to-revenue multiple. We can see that what's happened is as the revenues have dropped, the cost structure may have changed as well in response.

We have to be careful how much focus we're putting on the top line instead of the bottom line and what it may mean now is we need to focus a little bit more on the bottom line, more on the profitability.

James Alerding: Carl, do you want to add some things on this?

Carl Woodward: Just a couple of things. Year-to-date this year reported by the National Auto Dealers, the average dealers' return on equity through April is over 26 percent. So that's a good indicator. It's only four months. But that's getting back to where it used to be. In fact, it's a little higher than the average.

As Kevin had said, good things are happening. Focus more on the profits than the sales is the key.

James Alerding: One of our listeners just emailed in that the NADA May 2010 profit margin was 2.3 percent. So once again, another indication that the expense controls are working and things are going the right direction.

Let's move on to the next slide, if we could.

The dealerships that are remaining, I think, are in a good position. They've cut their expenses, and going forward, I think they're probably in a good position to be very profitable going forward.

Valuing Auto Dealerships, July 29, 2010, BVR Webinar

Carl, can you look and lead us through this slide and talk about the number of dealerships and how they've decreased and what the effects of those decreases might be.

Carl Woodward: Most of the dealership reductions have been what we call "domestics." As everyone knows, a gradual attrition for Ford, Chrysler and GM dealers mainly until the termination and bankruptcy last year would be some real small dealers in rural areas and in metro areas where you had a dealership every four or five miles. Then we lost – I don't know – over 1,000 to 2,000 dealers since the spring of 2009 with the bankruptcy of Chrysler and General Motors though GM did give back several hundred and Chrysler is probably going to end up giving back 100 when they're done.

What that does is we have less dealers with sales going up. So to a certain degree, that's good for the remaining dealers. That's a plus for the remaining dealers but not very good for those that lost their dealership.

James Alerding: Carl, I'm on a subject you touched on previously. What are your sources for the return on equity and profit margins? That's the NADA, isn't it?

Carl Woodward: The NADA publishes something. *The Magazine*, I don't think, has published anymore that you can probably get through a dealer if you don't have access. I also get about 200 financial statements a month so I keep track of this on a regular basis trying to see if what I see matches up with the NADA, though my sample is a lot smaller, and I usually match up real close.

James Alerding: It was mentioned earlier in your introduction but you have a newsletter that can be purchased through your firm, correct, that will give a lot of this information on a monthly basis.

Carl Woodward: I would probably not even charge for it, so if people ever have questions or anything, they're welcome to email me and I field all emails.

James Alerding: Again, just to emphasize, these dealerships' numbers have gone down from 22,300 in 2003 to 18,600 in January 2010. As it says on the slide, more than 100 percent of the total reduction has come from the Big Three. So impliedly in there what that means is that the imports have actually increased the number of their dealerships. So it's an interesting dynamic going on out there.

If you could move to the next slide, please.

Kevin, let's keep this slide up, but I want to ask you another question. Import dealerships have gone up a number as we discussed. The fact that there's a reduction in the numbers of the Big Three, does that make the Big Three dealerships more valuable in your estimation since there are fewer of them?

Kevin Yeanoplos: I don't think there's any question, and part of it, frankly, is if you look behind the reasons for the reduction in the first place, it was with the intent that the remaining dealerships would be more profitable among other things.

There was a very specific reason for reducing the number of dealerships so that the ones that are left are stronger, and if, for no other reason, I would expect them to be more valuable.

Of course, as you reduce the supply, I suppose, and if we just look at economics, then we would expect the dealerships to become more valuable.

Long term, because of the reduction, yes, I would expect them to become more valuable.

James Alerding: Let me flip that over now and talk about the imports. What do you think all this economic situation has had on the going-forward value of the imports? Remember, they're increasing the number of dealerships but they didn't have the turmoil that the Big Three had in terms of their financial status.

Kevin Yeanoplos: For me, that's a little tougher to answer because historically, the values of the imports have been stronger – they just have – for a variety of reasons.

If you look at the top-selling dealerships domestically, they've typically been the imports. There have been, of course, some exceptions in there, the Ford trucks and things like that. But the imports have historically been stronger.

I'm not sure that their values are going to be impacted as much as the domestic dealers, which is kind of an interesting thing because we talked earlier about quality control problems with Toyota.

Carl may know this better because he certainly, day to day, deals with the ins and outs of the auto industry, but my gut-feel with

	Toyota is any change in their value is going to just be a little bit of a blip because as I said earlier, I think they've effectively handled the quality control problems.
James Alerding:	I would agree with you Kevin. Carl, what do you think? I want to get your take on both the Big Three values and the import values.
Carl Woodward:	Ford, right now, is improving for various reasons. General Motors is still not out of the woods to know they're going to succeed but it appears they are.
	The people I deal with, Chrysler, if any of them aren't going to make it, that's the one that might not make it, so we need to at least allow for that issue about Chrysler being the weaker ones.
	Imports – as I say, many dealers before the recession, do I want an import dealer? Well, if I have to pay too much rent and too much blue sky, I might not want, say, a Honda store but something else because if the rent and the expense structure has taken away the way above average profits, does it really matter what franchise I'm buying or valuing? So you have to look at the profit structure because some import dealers have over built and their rent factors are so huge that their profits are below average. It's something for people to consider.
James Alerding:	Very good. Kevin, what impact do you see on the "green cars," that the "green cars" are going to have on both the industry as a whole and on the dealership structure?
Kevin Yeanoplos:	As I've looked at the different things that are impacting the industry, you really need a fantastic crystal ball with some of these things and I think "green cars" may be the most glaring example of that.
	We know right now that there's a tremendous political debate on moving forward "green" initiatives in the auto industry.
	I think it's safe to assume that going forward the auto industry isn't going to be the same as it ever was. We've seen that economically. But from a technology standpoint with discussions on global warming, I think it's definite. We're going to see some changes related to more "green cars" – electric powered, hydrogen has been discussed. So I think it's going to have an impact in a number of areas.
	One of them certainly is, to this point, even with the few "green cars" that we've had like the Prius, for instance, the dealers seem to

have had difficulty getting enough inventory to satisfy the demand. So that's going to be a key issue there. What good is the ability to sell a vehicle if we can't get the inventory? So I think that's one issue that we're going to have to deal with.

Another one – and this certainly might impact the manufacturers more than the dealers – is the technology itself. What are the investments that we have to make in the infrastructure to be able to build these new cars?

James Alerding: I live here in Indiana and we're in an area that's the hotbed of technology and manufacturing for the new "green cars" which is ultimately good for the state. So the impact on the dealers, I think, or the dealerships is going to be interesting because the traditional auto companies are developing "green cars," electric cars. You may have noted in the paper the last couple of days that some of the manufacturers are actually starting to put these out into the rental car companies to get people used to them

But then in addition to that, there are new manufacturers of "green cars," and so the question mark in my mind is – what ultimately is going to happen to those cars? Are they going to wind up setting up their own dealership outlets or are they going to run those through the existing dealership network that's already out there? What impact is that going to have on the value?

For either of you or both, one of the questions that's come through is – one of you guys made the statement that the imports have maybe had traditionally at least the higher values, so based on what for a franchise? Price versus revenues? Price versus cash flows? They're asking for a little more clarification?

Kevin, do you want to jump on that one?

Kevin Yeanoplos: Yeah, I'd say the answer is yes all the way across the board. I suppose whether you're talking about multiples or cash flows, whatever else, I think that the perceived risks, whether rightly or wrongly, have been less with the import dealers.

In addition, you generally have greater volumes. You sell more of those vehicles. They have a higher resale value. They hold their value better. So there are a number of things.

I'm not saying that I prefer one or the other but the practical realities are a lot of people buy imports, and so they've been the more

	popular vehicles, and so it just stands to reason that you would expect higher priced revenue for that particular dealership.

Carl, again, I defer to you with your industry knowledge but that's what I have seen as I have done my valuations over the years. |
| Carl Woodward: | The average import store is bigger than the average of the remaining universal stores so the dollars you're paying will typically be more.

The multiples that I don't like to use – so I'm not suggesting anyone use those – have probably typically been more, but if you were comparing two similar size stores, if you said the multiple for a non-import was 4, the multiple for the import store might be 5 because it's more desirable.

But as I said earlier, once you allow the rent factors to get enough and your costs to creep up where your profits are the same as a domestic, I'm interested in the "green" called money, not "green cars," and there were times where a Chevy store was making so much profit as worth just as much as an import store. You've got to look at the profits. |
| James Alerding: | Let's move on to the next slide, Blake, if we could.

The value drivers essentially are remaining the same as they've traditionally been in the dealership industry, that the economy per se has not changed the value drivers.

The status of the economy is one of those factors, one of those drivers – the status of the industry – we've talked a lot about both of those already.

The brand name and we've now talked some about the brand name issues and how that may impact the value, and add to that now the status of the brand.

The geographic location, and interestingly, that geographic location can cut both ways. You might think, well, it might be better in a high population area but it may not because what's happening with some of the dealership closings is Carl and I are working on one right now where the dealership value is probably – not probably – we think has gone up and it's in a location that is in kind of a smaller town, rural area, and what's happened is that the other dealerships in those brands have gone out of a business as a result |

of the economy, and so our guy's the last guy left standing and has a little bit higher value as a result of that.

Management and financial performance are also important, and of course, management, as you know, as a valuation analyst, that depends on whether that management that may be good or bad is going to be there or not be there after the transition. So that can cut either way on you.

The sales mix, as Carl mentioned before, is an important issue.

Other revenue sources (service department, F&I)

The capital structure – somebody wrote in a question. We'll try and get to that a little bit later about what happens if you've got a dealership with a high cash bank and so they don't have as much floor plan. That's a good question that we'll try and cover before we finish this.

Debt and capital availability, both for the dealership and the customer

Just as a note, one thing that the economy has done is that the real estate values are in trouble because there are lots of empty locations.

Kevin, do you want to add to that?

Kevin Yeanoplos: On which specific one?

James Alerding: On any of them, Kevin, on any of these drivers.

Kevin Yeanoplos: I would say that I do think as you say, the drivers haven't really changed. It's interesting because Carl has said a couple of times that we need to kind of follow the profit and I agree with that. Certainly, the profitability of a business is going to be tantamount as we look at the value.

I do think that all of these factors that we see on this slide ultimately impact the bottom line, and so the focus in what people look at in terms of where the value is in a dealership hasn't changed. It's the actual profitability that's changed.

We talked about the cost structure. I agree, I don't think the value drivers have changed.

	I think ultimately, the variables themselves have changed and that's what's giving rise to the new value metrics, not the drivers themselves.
James Alerding:	Carl, do you want to add anything?
Carl Woodward:	Just one comment. Some people that don't deal in the car industry as much as I do put more emphasis on new, and believe it or not, more gross profits are generated by used parts and service than the new for most dealers, maybe not all imports. So people need to be aware of that when they're doing their valuation.
James Alerding:	One of the questions came in, and you alluded to this, Carl, that Ford has been really doing well, and their question was, of course, is that at least in part because they didn't have to take a bailout.
Carl Woodward:	I've heard from Ford dealers where they got calls from people that bought Chrysler and GM that said, "I'm now coming to buy a Ford product." I think it's a combination, a little bit of that, and a little bit of Ford's got a couple of products – I'm not a product person – but new products that have been very well received. So I think it's a combination of new products and not having the stigma that they had to borrow from the government.
James Alerding:	Okay, so it's really a combination then and not just one thing or the other.
Carl Woodward:	Yes.
James Alerding:	Okay. Let's move on to the next slide, if we can.
	As you can see, the methodologies are the same. Most of the people on the line here, I'm sure, do a lot of valuation work and the asset approach, the income approach and the market approach are still the approaches that we use and the methodologies within those are similar. We've had a lot of questions come through and I don't want anybody to think we won't get to them as to what these rules of thumb might be or where they are today in the marketplace. Both Kevin and Carl, I'm sure, will be able to give us some input on that as we go forward.
	Moving along to the next slide, Kevin, I know that the market approach is one of the areas that you spend a lot of time in and you believe it does have good application to the auto dealership industry, so why don't you lead us through that market approach?

Valuing Auto Dealerships, July 29, 2010, BVR Webinar

Kevin Yeanoplos: Sure. First, I'd like to say that the approaches are the same but I think the actual methods within the approaches might change a little bit. If we look at the income approach, for instance, where before we might be comfortable using some kind of a capitalized cash flow based on historical, we might have to look at a discounted cash flow. I just wanted to throw that out to think about the actual methods may be more focused on forecasts and projections.

The market approach, I will tell you this, if we were sitting there 20 years ago when I just started doing valuation – this probably sounds familiar to everybody – "Well, I know I'm not going to find any comparable companies so I'm not even going to look." Twenty years later now, my preferred method is the market approach if I can find comparables and I think we probably all agree with that. Of course, the difficulty is finding the comparables.

I think that the public comparables that are there for the dealers are some of the best comparable companies that we can find in any kind of an industry. There are only a handful of them. It's easy to get the information.

You can say, "How relevant are those comparables because they're much more diverse, they are much bigger, et cetera."

Well, the reality is valuation, whether it's the market approach or the income approach or the asset approach, is all about reference points. If we have some good reference points, we can adjust for the differences between those reference points and our subject company.

What I'm really swinging back around to say is I think that in the auto industry, those are some of the *most* exact – they're certainly *not* exact – but they may be the closest comparables that we can find in an industry. Those auto dealers are vey comparable except for, as I said, differences in size, diversity and things along those lines. But we can adjust for that. We can adjust the multiples to reflect the differences between the guideline companies and the subject company. So I use it.

Having said that, I don't like to use the private comparables because there's so much noise in them.

James Alerding: One of the questions that was asked – and I'm trying to find it exactly here – Kevin, that I think we ought to maybe talk about is – "Where can we get good transaction comparable data in this industry? Dealerships are bought and sold all the time but the comparable data available is terrible. For example, Pratt's Stats reports 60 transactions but 49 of these are from the 1990s and only five of these occurred in the past three years. Biz Comps is even worse with three reported transactions from 1998 to 2001. The publicly-traded mega dealerships are so big now they don't have to report these acquisitions anymore like they did in the 1990s."

Do you want to talk about that a little bit?

Kevin Yeanoplos: Well, yeah, I will just flat out tell you that recognizing that I'm going to get this question on cross-examination sometime, I don't use private comparables to value companies. If you look at the auto dealer comparables, there are so many problems with private comparables to begin with. I do think it's very useful to use as a sanity check so don't get me wrong and we do look at them. But I'm talking about using them directly to value a company.

The auto dealer comparables, you just alluded to the fact that there aren't that many. The transactions have virtually dried up.

Depending on when you're looking at the comparables, you may have things like during the period of roll-ups where the publicly-traded dealers were buying up private dealers left and right. As you could imagine, in that particular time period, the multiples were very high because there was a consolidation, I suppose. I guess roll-up is a better term but certainly there were a lot of transactions.

The reality is with those private comparables – I talked about the noise – you really don't know what the motivations are of the buyer and the seller. Even with a good source of information like Pratt's Stats, there's really, I think, less information than we need to adequately use those comparables.

Those are my thoughts on the use of private comparables.

James Alerding: I think my own thoughts on this too are that there are good comparables out there in the published data so it may be difficult to use that and that's why people like Carl are so important to know and to get to know because their background, their knowledge and having so much information on these dealerships can be helpful and it's not in data that's normally out there in the public domain.

What do you think, Carl, about this whole issue of these private transactions?

Carl Woodward: As Kevin said, be awful careful. I don't use them and would not touch them with a thousand-foot pole. I own part of a dealership that's sold to a public group a few years ago, and then when I read about the sale, if anybody listening had looked at what was published versus reality, which only I knew, you would come to bad conclusions.

How do you get private data? Usually it's confidential, so if someone gives it to you, they're probably breaking some confidentiality agreement.

So I'm very hesitant to use private data except private data I can obtain.

The public data, sort of like Kevin said, it's dangerous to use it because you might not be getting the real picture.

I do think – and Kevin, you might step in – the public companies have a slightly less expected or required return on their money than most buyers because they're Wall Street and they get higher multiples on that. So I would say the public companies, a requirement for a return is less than the average knowledgeable dealer.

If I were trying to get comparables or do a smell test in what I'm doing, I would to recommend everybody is find some people like Carl Woodward or people in your area that do buy-sells to see what is really going on.

No disrespect to brokers – they'll normally give you a multiple but that's dangerous to use a multiple.

James Alerding: Kevin, I want to flip it back to you just for a minute on this guideline public company method because one of our listeners has asked specifically, "How would you adjust the multiples for public companies to reflect the valuation of a single point dealership?" I think that's something that everybody out there is going to want to know, and you and I, Kevin, have talked about this a little bit. I'm openly not a fan of the guideline public company method in any industry, not just this one, but I kind of have felt the same way myself, that there just aren't enough of these companies that own dealerships, in my opinion, to really get a good handle on it. So Kevin, how do you make those adjustments to come to a good conclusion?

Valuing Auto Dealerships, July 29, 2010, BVR Webinar

Kevin Yeanoplos: How much time do we have?

James Alerding: Not much.

Kevin Yeanoplos: Let me just give you the high points. I think the question might be in any valuation – how do we adjust the market multiple when we're using the market approach?

I think if we step back and look at a multiple to begin with, we've got to realize that the income approach and the market approach are really two peas in the same pod, so a multiple ultimately reflects the risks that the buyer sees in purchasing a particular business.

The short answer is – how do we adjust for it? Well, much like when we are adjusting a discount rate, a market multiple will have components that we can adjust objectively and it's going to have components that we're going to have to adjust subjectively. There's no way of removing the judgment involved in adjusting a multiple. So that's kind of the global answer.

James Alerding: Okay, just to keep us moving here, on that same subject, what are the primary publicly-traded companies that you do rely on for your comparables?

Kevin Yeanoplos: Well, Auto Nation is one. Lithia Motors is another. There are about ten of them and all you need to do is do a search and you can find to get all the information you need.

James Alerding: Okay, that makes sense.

Let's move on to the income approach. Kevin, you've been really setting me up here today in a good way because the first bullet point there is that historical earnings are likely not representative of future earnings in today's dealership world and you mentioned that when you started talking about the market approach. The income approach requires a look at future income.

There are a couple of issues here and we've touched on these a lot already. One of the issues, of course, is that there's been, it looks like, some permanent damage in terms of the number of units that's going to be sold at least in the foreseeable future globally which is going to impact the dealers.

One of our listeners had a question about the margins being lower from the manufacturers, what impact that has. Certainly it's going to have an impact, and so when you're valuing an auto dealership, you need to take a look at that and see what impact it might have.

What I think we're seeing is that the dealers have – and this bears out with the NADA information that shows nice profit trends and returns to traditional margins – adjusted their expense side of their income statement and have been able to make up those differences as what it appears to be.

There's a multitude of factors which we don't have time to go into but that argues very much again using future earnings and/or if you're going to use some earnings from, let's say, the historical, that you might use those in the vane of things appear to be returning to those historical measures of return on equity and net earnings per revenue and things like that as a benchmark.

You do need to take a closer look at what's going to happen in the future.

The DCF method or, if you can't get to the DCF or you want to do it on a shortcut basis, the next year's earnings method is likely the most pertinent to determine a value under the income approach, and either of those might be appropriate depending on your situation.

Blake, next slide.

Carl Woodward: Jim, this is Carl, if I may.

James Alerding: Yeah, sure, go ahead.

Carl Woodward: Dealers have one major expense right now that's extremely low that's expected to change, in my opinion, and that's the floor plan interest expense.

Right now because the LIBOR rate, I think, is not even 1 percent, the interest that dealers are paying on their new vehicle inventory has never been lower, I believe. So when that starts creeping up, I think that's part of the reason we see the profits as high margins right now, is there's an expense that's close to zero that when interest rates start going up – and I think most of the listeners would all agree they're going to go up – we just don't know when and how much – it will make a big difference in profitability. We have an expense now we don't really have that we had before and we will have in the future.

James Alerding: I think that's an excellent point and something that does need to be looked at. Again, as Kevin's touched on and now Carl's touched on and I've touched on a little bit and we've had some questions, this whole concept of floor plan is something that really needs to be looked at when you value this company. As Kevin said, it's oftentimes looked at as part of the working capital. Again, I've looked at it both ways but I would agree that's a good way to look at it and the interest expense can really affect those margins as you go forward.

The income approach might not adequately value the franchise value so that's something to look at and that gets into these rules of thumb because there may value of the franchise, which we'll cover here as we go forward, that's not really reflected in the income approach and the various methods underneath it. That's unusual and that's why I think the auto dealership industry is really unique in terms of looking at it from a valuation standpoint.

In looking at future income, the analyst needs to consider the fact that there are fewer dealers.

Many dealers have adjusted expenses as we talked about to lower volumes.

The dealerships have rebounded more quickly than their sales volume, so in other words, their profits. As Carl mentioned, interest can be part of that.

Since there are fewer dealers, there's less competition.

But as we saw, overall, there are more dealers if you include the imports.

But you need again to look at the brand situation in that because there may be fewer competitors and I mentioned one that Carl and I are working with right now in our rural area where there are no other competitors in that brand area any longer in that market. So there's less competition which is going to be a higher value for that dealership.

Again, imports have not reduced their dealership.

You also need to look, as Carl mentioned, I think, and Kevin, that many times the dealers are locked into leases and other loans on real estate that maybe can't be changed in the short run and that's going to have an impact on it.

Let's move on to the next slide.

The blue sky contains both the franchise rights and the true goodwill. We're still looking on the income approach here.

It's important to separate the value of the franchise rights and the goodwill. Now that hasn't been done traditionally and in some valuations, it maybe still cannot be done.

Franchise rights are tested as an indefinite lived intangible while goodwill is a residual type of an asset. In other words, you look at the total value, you take out the net asset values as adjusted and you take out the specifically identified intangible assets, and if there's a residual, that's truly what's goodwill.

Now one of those things that we need to talk about, because there's a lot of the valuations done in this area and all areas that are in the area of marital dissolution, is are there "personal goodwill" aspects in both the franchise rights and the goodwill.

Let's move on to the next slide, please.

Testing for franchise rights and goodwill – some firms test the value of the franchise using the multi-period excess earnings method. SFAS 141, 142, which I think is now 805 or whatever it is, hasn't had a lot to do with people looking at specific intangibles but it's something we need to talk about.

Others look for the present value of the base profitability for a particular brand in the area where the franchise is located.

Residual earnings, after you take all of those other intermediate excess earnings out, would indicate goodwill.

Then you also need to make qualitative adjustments in order to get to a final conclusion.

Let's go on to the next slide and then I'm going to go back and ask Kevin and Carl to comment on this whole area.

Many dealers are not sophisticated enough to make the split or understand such complex methods.

They may opt for a less precise method and one of the rules of thumb.

Dealers losing money may have no goodwill but still have a positive franchise value, and that's what we're talking about, that the income approach can fool you because there can still be a positive franchise value even though the earnings aren't there.

Kevin, thoughts?

Kevin Yeanoplos: I'm reading this, "Many dealers are not sophisticated enough" … my first thought is many valuation professionals are not sophisticated enough to…

We've been talking about some of the fair value issues. Honestly, that particular area, without question, is one of the most sophisticated, technical, if not the most areas that we deal with in terms of trying to split that out.

I agree with the statement that you can have an intangible asset that's there even if you don't have any goodwill. That's what we've said kind of all the way along, that at least looking at those rules of thumb may lead you to believe that there is an intangible.

I was involved in a case a couple of years ago and it was a dealership. The brand was one that was going through some significant problems at the time. At first glance looking at the dealer, you saw that it was not that profitable. But the reality was there was still somebody that was willing to pay for the franchise. So that's the practical example. It happens all the time.

We've kind of maligned the market approach a little bit but the reality is some of the best information you can get if you're valuing a dealer in a particular city is to try to find information on sales that have occurred within that city. That's information that you're going to have to get somewhere other than one of the databases. So that's important to look at.

James Alerding: Carl, do you want to add anything on that income approach?

Carl Woodward: You need to adjust the income to what you think it's going to be allowing for the rent that you're going to pay. It's common that a dealer will ask for a lot of blue sky and then an exorbitant rent and it's kind of a simultaneous equation. You've got to factor the rent in to the profits before you then do the blue sky computation or you could make a severe mistake and overpay, or if you're the seller trying to do this, if you're not careful, you'll be making a silly request high, drive off the best buyers who are less tolerant of silly

|||||||||||||||||||||||||||||||||||||||||||||||||||||||||||||||||||||||||||||||||||||||||||||||||||||||||||||||

requests, and then you'll end up with a smaller base of potential buyers. So you've got to look at the rent factor along with the blue sky kind of at the same time on the income approach.

James Alerding: I think that's a good point and I think you're partially saying that some of the sellers want to hold on to the real estate and lease it. Is that part of the equation there?

Carl Woodward: Right, and they end up with an unreasonable rent factor because –

James Alerding: Right.

Carl Woodward: Car dealers, since I used to be one, I can say this, have all answers to all questions, many of them do, just ask them, and some of them don't counsel. I'd like to say I want to ask list price but not double list price.

James Alerding: Okay, let's move on to the next slide, and Carl, can you take us through this asset approach starting with this slide and we'll move on from there.

Carl Woodward: What we're seeing here on the asset approach really – and a better word might be book value approach or net worth approach – is step one, is you need to inquire on the balance sheet of the dealership so that you can put all the assets at current values and the liabilities at current values and do a little probing unless it's CPA prepared to find out they've allowed for all the material liabilities.

It's very common that people miss things, they don't add the LIFO reserves back to the net worth of the store – I see once or twice a year – or they don't tax effect it depending on what the divorce laws are in a state, or they miss liabilities because the dealership closes the books out so fast that sometimes they don't have all the material liabilities on there.

The other thing on the asset approach is you need to look at the fixed assets both allowing for leaseholds and not to make sure that the net fixed asset figure is a reasonable number in today's climate when you're doing it so that you do a good job and are not embarrassed later.

The second part of that is what's the intangible value, which is a separate issue from the "clean," as I call it, current value net worth of the business.

Kevin Yeanoplos: Again, looking at this from a practical standpoint, very rarely with an operating business are we using the asset approach.

The main examples of using the asset approach frankly are when we're doing a purchase price allocation.

The difficulty with using an asset approach is simply that there's the risk of missing one of the assets that exists that has value, so we don't use it a lot. It's using either the market approach or the income approach to value a dealer.

James Alerding: Let me jump in if I can because we've had a ton of questions which I've kind of saved to this point and I want Carl to jump in here as to how do you really determine that blue sky or that franchise value and there have been a couple of side issues.

Some people would consider this under the adjusted net asset approach or methodology and others would say it's just part of the income approach, but one of the common ways that dealerships are valued is to value the adjusted net assets and add to it the goodwill, the blue sky, the franchise value, whatever you want to call it.

Carl, what are some of the methodologies that you see out there, and certainly want to know whether you think they're good or bad, these multiples, and what are they multiples of? Give your thoughts on this whole area of franchise value and blue sky.

Carl Woodward: I'll give a couple of these rules of thumb but I do not necessarily subscribe to any of them but you might say the blue sky is some percent of annual sales. If I were using percentages, it might be from zero to 10 percent.

Where do they come with the 10 percent? Until the last couple of years, you could maybe say a dealer might make 2 percent on sales. A 10 percent factor of annual sales might be also looked at as five years at 2 percent a year when 2 percent was not an unreasonable percentage.

Some people take the number of new vehicles sold in a year times the average gross profit margin made on a new vehicle. So let's say you had 1,000 new vehicles and the average gross profit for all gross on a new is, say, $3,000. So 1,000 units times $3,000 would give you a $3 million blue sky figure.

Like I said earlier – and those that request, I'll send you the one-page article – there's a whole bunch of different ways of defining profit or weighted profit/average profit and then what multiple to use. If you go at it that way, the proof of the pudding when you're all done is, "What's my return on my investment?" If it's 5 percent, we know we've overpriced it because I don't know any dealer that would accept that low a percentage, or if it gives you a 50 percent return, we've underpriced it.

There's also the factor that your best buyer might be the dealer next door to you and he might pay a higher premium, shall we say, than the guy that's got to move to the town. But when I'm trying to do a buy-sell for a dealer on selling, I feel the best prospects are the closest ones and then move out on a mileage basis. When you're all done, you need to see that the end result makes sense.

If you haven't done many of these, find someone that's actively involved in buy-sells, not a broker typically, no disrespect, to see that it makes sense what you're doing.

James Alerding: Here's one of the problems with these "rules of thumb," is that – I can just tell from the emails that we've received today – there are lots of theories out there as to what they are. One of the problems is defining what really is the rule of thumb, not so much am I using one, even more so what is it. You can tell from Carl's comments and Kevin's comments and some of my comments there are lots of theories out there or ideas as to what these rules of thumb might even be in the auto dealership industry.

That's an area to be careful in because some people think it might be a multiple of gross profits. Some people think it might be the gross profit per car times the number of cars. Some people think it might be the percentage of revenue. You've got to be careful.

The bottom line is – Kevin stated it well – Carl stated it well – what you have to do is does it make sense and does it make sense in terms of ultimately the buyer being able to realize a proper return on his or her investment when you buy that dealership.

Having said that, I'm of the theory also that you can't just say you take this income approach and if it turns out that when you look at that and you subtract the net asset values you would impliedly get no franchise value or no goodwill value. I don't know that that's a good answer either.

We had that a couple of slides ago where there can be a franchise value, oftentimes may be a franchise value, and it may depend on the timing and the economy and everything else where there aren't necessarily indications of a franchise value under the income approach or the income methods.

Valuing dealerships, I think, is a very complex issue and I would agree with Carl that it's an industry where you really do have to really know something about the industry and it's helpful to consult with somebody that does, I believe. That's why I work with Carl and I work with some other people in the industry because even though I do a fair number of these, I like to get somebody else's thoughts on what's really going on in the marketplace.

I know that's probably not going to be a satisfactory answer for some of you that are on the phone with us today but it's a difficult industry and I think you need to recognize that.

Kevin, do you want to add anything to that?

Kevin Yeanoplos: Well, I just think this, not only the auto dealer industry but a lot of other industries have been struggling and going through hard economic times.

I think the real question that we have to ask is this – all of the things that we've talked about today, all of the changes – what are the changes that are going to be temporary and what are the changes that are going to be permanent? It's important to understand that.

For instance, we saw earlier that some of the changes in the margins themselves were actually temporary because the astute dealers changed their cost structures to maintain their margins.

But there are other changes that we talked about that I look at as being permanent.

A lot of the discussion from the industry leaders and the research that I do tells me that – we alluded to this earlier – there's a new normal in terms of new car sales, that it's going to be less than we've historically seen.

That to me is what I would call a permanent change.

I think that what's happening with the "green cars" and the changes in fuel emissions – that's going to be a permanent change.

We haven't really talked about this but I know it's in one of our slides, the addition of mass transit as a method of dealing with some of the global "green" issues is something else that I think is going to be permanent.

I really think that what we need to do is look at the changes and determine if they're temporary or permanent. If it's a temporary change, we need to address it as such in our methodology, in the income approach, for instance.

James Alerding: Those are great comments, Kevin, and I would agree, and we've had a couple of people send in questions about "how do you factor in the fact what manufacturers now look like" and "yank your franchises at will" and "throw you out of the party," and it's like these other things that you've just been talking about, Kevin. You have to take those into account whether it's the market approach, the income approach or even the "rules of thumb." They all use risk factors. The multiples that you see in these "rules of thumb" may go down because of the increase in the risk factors, and those risk factors, we talk about a whole lot of them here today.

It's the same with the discount rate on a DCF and the same with the multiples that Kevin might use or that we all might use in using the guideline public company methodology. It's like any other business that you value.

I would agree with Kevin, it's not just this industry but certainly this is one that I think has been beat up at least in a higher profile more than others during this period of time.

Let's go ahead on to the next slide, if we may.

I think maybe we've talked about this or answered this but, "What is the value proposition and the formula for determining it in today's environment?"

I think we've gone around and around with that. We've answered a lot of questions, but either Kevin or Carl, do you have anything in particular you want to add to that comment?

Carl Woodward: Let's talk about "green" for a moment. I don't see anything in the next three or four years but General Motors has come out with their, I believe, all-electric car that's priced around $40,000. If they had to sell it for that and didn't have this big tax credit, I don't think they would see too many of those.

I have a couple of clients that are going to be distributors for what they think are going to be these much less expensive electric cars and that puts a big question mark out there five to ten years from now. I don't think anyone's seeing modest priced cars in that area in the next year or so. I understand Nissan is coming out with something late this year. But three, four, five years from now, the electric cars might put a new face on the new car industry. Only time will tell.

James Alerding: Blake has sent me an email here that Doug Twitchell, who publishes some of the BVMarketdata, has indicated that if there are associations that cater to the auto dealer industry, they may be a good source of transaction data.

As Michael points out, many of these aren't reported in SEC filings anymore because the public companies are so large that they don't have to report the details on these sales. So it is getting harder and harder to find that.

We had another question that came up as to, "Where do you find the information to properly value the franchise components since dealers themselves would generally use the rules of thumb?"

Kevin, do you want to take a swat at that?

Kevin Yeanoplos: Yeah, I'll tell ya, I've been thinking about this as we've been discussing the franchise rights, and I may be wrong here but I can't think of a single instance where a person sold just the franchise rights. So it's problematic because the data that we see, even with the private comparables, is going to include everything that's in there. So I don't know of a source that's out there.

The only time it really becomes an issue to me is when, for some reason, we've got to do an allocation, maybe it's for fair value purposes or some income tax reason and we've got to come up with the value of the franchise right.

That being the case, I would be very comfortable using some kind of a relief from royalty method to value the franchise rights. I think it's very common to use it and I think it's a great method, one of the methods within the income approach.

I just don't think that there are any comparable transactions where you're going to find franchise rights. They're so closely intertwined with the dealership, all of the other assets.

Valuing Auto Dealerships, July 29, 2010, BVR Webinar

Carl, I'll again ask you, have you seen any transactions where they've just sold franchise rights?

Carl Woodward: Not really. I don't disagree with you at all. As I've said before, for those people that don't live and breathe like I do everyday, I would have you, after you've done a lot of your work, call somebody like me. I usually will field phone calls, and they're in the charge, just to see about smell tests and what people are thinking and you might get a hold of two or three of those. I do probably as many or more dealership valuations annually as anybody in the United States and I still check with other people that are doing transactions just to see if my thinking is correct.

James Alerding: Kevin, I would agree with you 100 percent. I think probably one of the reasons there aren't any or too many transactions on the franchise value itself is because the manufacturers control the franchise. They really are not tradable per se. So I think that makes it more difficult.

One of our questioners asked, "Do you believe, when using the income approach, that blue sky should be added to the value arrived at under a DCF or a cap earnings method?"

I would say no, but because it's not in addition to if you believe that that method, the DCF or the cap earnings captures your franchise value. I will say again that I don't think it does always, but if you believe that that captures your franchise value and then there's nothing to add.

But if you believe that maybe it doesn't capture it – and it could be because earnings going forward or what you need to look at – it could be for a lot of reasons – but what we've said before is – and I've gotten this information not just from Carl but some other friends of both Carl's and mine that do a lot of this work – that the franchise can still have value even if there's not an indication of such under the income approach. I think that makes it more difficult to value these things but it's something you have to look at.

Another questioner asked that if you had a dealership losing money, you therefore should use a net asset method to value the entire dealership.

I don't know, Kevin or Carl, what you think, but my thought on that is no, not if you're looking at future earnings.

Now if you look at future earnings and they're all losses, then I think you probably do. That comes under the theory of "better dead than alive so let's shoot it and put it out of its misery."

But if you look at the future earnings and say the losses are a temporary situation, then I don't think that you should assume by that that you go right to the net asset or liquidation method and value the company.

Kevin, thoughts?

Kevin Yeanoplos: Yeah, I think there are certainly situations where it would make sense to use it. But as you said, it would be a situation where a company has been losing for five years, and we've seen those, dealerships that have been losing for five years for whatever reason. It may be the brand. It may be management. Generally, it's not going to be the brand, but in a situation like that, yeah, it makes more sense. Only a person that doesn't know what they're doing would continue to throw money in a black hole, so it would make more sense to shut it down and just liquidate.

James Alerding: Carl, any thoughts?

Carl Woodward: Ignoring the last year and a half, typically the sales I see are for two reasons – the dealer is not successful usually due to mismanagement, as Kevin mentioned, or they're deciding they're either older or want to get out of the business.

Where I see those types of dealers and they're making minimal profits or losing, in most cases, again, ignoring the last 24 months, those stores would bring some blue sky franchise value though most of the typical formulas would end up showing zero. You've got to look at expected profits and be able to justify that.

But most dealers that are losing in normal times get blue sky though the standard formulas generally would say no blue sky.

James Alerding: We had a question on the LIFO. I indicated that the tax effect would not be booked on a pass-through entity. Now the question is however, a knowledgeable buyer would pay less for an equity interest because they were assuming they had liability. Well, if it's a pass-through entity, that's true, they might be if the inventory was still there and the LIFO remained. So it depends on the situation. Now you're talking about the specific price.

I was looking more at the value that you might have in a situation where again, what do you do with a pass-through entity.

It's going to be different based on the particular situation that you're looking at and it truly is an issue of saying that the value may be different depending on the purpose of the valuation and that can happen sometimes.

Let's get through these last couple of slides quickly.

I really don't like to keep people on any longer and I thought that was our time break that we were scheduled but I think that all three of us have indicated we're happy to answer questions after the webinar. You can send us your emails. We'll be happy to try and answer. Give us a call or whatever. I think all of us are happy to do that.

Just to wrap up, what's in store for the future?

We've talked about alternative power systems – what's that going to do to the dealership structure?

We've talked about the fact that, at least for the domestics, there are fewer dealers.

We've talked about the fact that – and Kevin mentioned this – mass transit could be an issue way down the future because quite honestly, the mass transit takes a long time to come to fruition, but it could be there in the future.

What will the shift in market share be? Again, that may depend on the location of the franchise.

Now there are more sellers of dealer equipment than buyers so you may have impacts on, if you're looking at asset values, those assets.

The buildings we've talked about have less value. We've talked about the oversupply of buildings and a lot of them are single purpose buildings and so there are some real estate impacts that are occurring.

Then finally unions, at least with the current political situation, are getting a lot of support and there are unions already in some of these dealerships primarily out west, and so you could find that union issues might be an issue in valuation that will come up.

All right, well, I want to thank everybody for listening in today and I hope that it's been helpful, and as I said, if we can help you afterwards, I'm sure we're happy to do so.

Kevin and Carl, great job – I appreciate both of you being on the presentation today. It's been very helpful. I think Kevin and Carl each brought a different perspective to the table which I think was really helpful and hopefully you found was helpful also.

We appreciate you listening and I'll turn it back over to Blake.

Blake Lyman: Thank you, Jim. With that, we'll conclude today's presentation.

BVR would like to thank Jim Alerding, Kevin Yeanoplos and Carl Woodward for their expertise today, all of our listeners for attending, and AccountingWEB and Business Brokerage Press for their support today as co-presenters.

Transcripts and recordings of this and all webinars are available for purchase via our On-Demand Packs. You can find more information on conference On-Demand Packs at *bvresources.com/training*. There you can also find more information on future BVR teleconferences, webinars and live events, as well as the BVR Training Passport, limited access to our webinar series, and the Desktop Learning Center, our new online library of all past webinars. That address again is *bvresources.com/training*.

If you have any questions related to the content or format of this webinar or would like to receive the article Carl mentioned at the beginning of our presentation, please email BVR at *questions@bvresources.com*. That's *questions@bvresesources.com*.

Thank you. You may now disconnect.

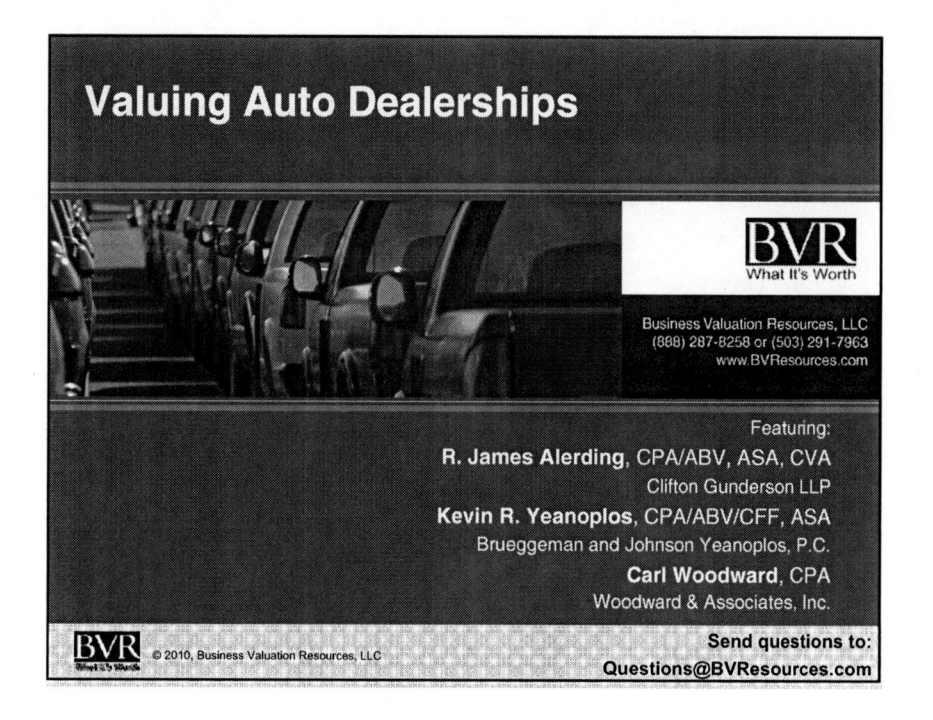

Valuing Auto Dealerships

Featuring:
R. James Alerding, CPA/ABV, ASA, CVA
Clifton Gunderson LLP
Kevin R. Yeanoplos, CPA/ABV/CFF, ASA
Brueggeman and Johnson Yeanoplos, P.C.
Carl Woodward, CPA
Woodward & Associates, Inc.

Business Valuation Resources, LLC
(888) 287-8258 or (503) 291-7963
www.BVResources.com

Send questions to:
Questions@BVResources.com

© 2010, Business Valuation Resources, LLC

Learning Objectives & Ancillary Reading Materials

- Understand the impact of today's economic environment on the value of an auto dealership
- Learn the nuances of valuing auto dealers in today's economic environment
- Discuss special issues relating to auto dealers
- All downloads available at the BVR Teleconference ancillary reading page

"Classic Considerations" in Valuing Auto Dealerships (What you should know)

- An auto dealership is more than selling vehicles
  - New Car sales
  - Used Car sales
  - Service & repair
  - Parts
  - Finance & insurance
  - Body Shop (some dealers)
  - Lease & rental (some dealers)
  - Fleet sales (some dealers)

"Classic Considerations" in Valuing Auto Dealerships (What you should know) (cont'd)

- There are aspects of the dealership operations that the analyst must recognize
  - LIFO inventory
  - Used vehicle valuation adjustment
  - Liability for future chargebacks (finance, insurance and service contracts
  - Dealer reserve accounts
  - Floor plan & other financing issues
  - Impact of discretionary expenses (e.g. family use of "demos", and other personal expenses)
  - Facility enhancements and franchise dynamics as issues

Effect of the Current (and Perhaps the Future) Economy on Auto Dealerships

- The auto industry was hit especially hard in the latest recession
  - GM & Chrysler went bankrupt
  - Toyota has had serious QC problems that have hurt its image
  - GMAC, Chrysler Financial, etc. have had to be bailed out along with their companies
  - The credit "dry up" has stifled new auto sales
  - Cash for Clunkers did no more than accelerate new vehicle sales (i.e. stole from future months sales) and further limited units in the used vehicle market

Effect of the Current (and Perhaps the Future) Economy on Auto Dealerships (cont'd)

- New vehicle sales have dropped significantly in the past five years
  - New unit sales were at just under 17 million per year in 2005
  - By 2009 they had dropped to 10.4 million per year
  - The 2010 estimate run rate through June would indicate up from 2009, but nowhere near the high in 2005
  - At some point in time, the auto industry might be permanently impacted by a new "normal" annual sales figure

Effect of the Current (and Perhaps the Future) Economy on Auto Dealerships (cont'd)

- Average sales per dealership dropped
  - In 2007 they were just under $33 million
  - In 2009 they were down to just under $26 million

Effect of the Current (and Perhaps the Future) Economy on Auto Dealerships (cont'd)

- Profits have begun to adjust to older norms
  - ROE averaged 25% or above during the growth years
  - ROE dipped all the way down to 12.4% in 2008
  - ROE rebounded in 2009 to 18% and is expected to exceed that in 2010
  - Why? Dealers have cut expenses to fit the new volumes
  - Profit margins were at 1.6% (of dealership sales) and above for the growth years, but dropped to 1.0% in 2008
  - They rebounded to 1.5% in 2009, which estimated historical norms
  - Once again, dealer expense cuts are the most likely reasons for the rebound

Effect of the Current (and Perhaps the Future) Economy on Auto Dealerships (cont'd)

- The number of dealerships has also decreased due to the effects of the recession
  - Both GM and Chrysler actively cut the number of dealers
  - Because of political pressure they have had to replace some, but the overall impact is a reduction in dealers
  - The number of dealerships has gone from a peak of about 22,300 in 2003 to 18,600 in January of 2010
  - More than 100% of the total reduction has come from the "Big Three" in the past two years

Effect of the Current (and Perhaps the Future) Economy on Auto Dealerships (cont'd)

- What impact will "green cars" have on the economy and on the individual dealers now in existence?
- The auto industry is *still* being hit hard and is likely to encounter some unknowns future period

How does the effect of the economy impact valuations of auto dealers?

- The value drivers remain essentially the same
    - Status of the economy
    - Status of the industry
    - Brand name – add to that now the "status" of the brand
    - Geographic location
    - Management & Financial Performance
    - Competition (brand & market related)
    - Sales mix (new vs. used)
    - Other revenue sources (e.g. Service Dept. and F & I dept.)
    - Capital Structure
    - Debt and capital availability, both for the dealership and for the customer
    - Real estate values in trouble, tons of empty properties

How does the effect of the economy impact valuations of auto dealers? (cont'd)

- **Methodologies are the same**
    - Asset Approach
    - Income Approach
    - Market Approach

How does the effect of the economy impact valuations of auto dealers? (cont'd)

- The market approach is the most difficult to use:
  - Guideline companies should be considered for valuation of the individual dealership just as they are in other industry valuations.
  - Guideline companies should be adjusted
  - Because of the current economic upheaval market transactions are likely not representative of current values

How does the effect of the economy impact valuations of auto dealers? (cont'd)

- Income Approach
  - Historical earnings are likely not representative of future earnings
  - The income approach requires a look at **future** income to determine a value
  - The DCF method or the "next year's earnings" capitalization method are likely the most pertinent to a determination of value under the income approach

How does the effect of the economy impact valuations of auto dealers? (cont'd)

- The income approach might not adequately value the Franchise Value
- In looking at future income the analyst should consider
  - Fewer dealers
  - Many dealers have adjusted expenses to lower volume
  - Dealerships have rebounded more quickly than their sales volume
  - Since there are few dealers, there is less competition
  - HOWEVER – imports have not reduced the number of dealers
  - Many times dealers are locked into leases and/or loans on real estate

How does the effect of the economy impact valuations of auto dealers? (cont'd)

- Blue sky contains both the franchise rights and the true goodwill
  - It is important to separate the value of the franchise rights and the goodwill
  - Franchise Rights are tested as an indefinite lived intangible
  - Goodwill is a residual
  - Query: Are there "personal goodwill" aspects in both the franchise rights and the goodwill

How does the effect of the economy impact valuations of auto dealers? (cont'd)

- Testing for franchise rights and goodwill
  - Some firms test the value of the franchise rights using the multiperiod excess earnings method
  - Others look for PV of base profitability for a particular brand in the area where the franchise is located
  - Residual earnings would indicate goodwill
  - Qualitative adjustments are also needed

How does the effect of the economy impact valuations of auto dealers? (cont'd)

- Many dealers are not sophisticated enough to make the split or understand such complex methods
  - They may opt for a less precise method
  - Dealers losing money may have no goodwill but positive franchise value

How does the effect of the economy impact valuations of auto dealers? (cont'd)

- Asset Approach
  - Book Value
  - Adjusted Book Value
    - Needs to take into account intangible value
    - Franchise Value is added to the adjusted asset values
  - Liquidation Value

How does the effect of the economy impact valuations of auto dealers? (cont'd)

- What is the Value Proposition and the formula for determining it in today's environment?

What is in store for the future?

- Focus on alternative power systems
- What will this do to the current dealership structure?
- Fewer dealers
- HOWEVER – imports have increased their dealership numbers
- What will the impact of mass transit be and when?
- What will the shift in the market share be?

What is in store for the future? (cont'd)

- There are more sellers of dealer equipment than buyers
- In certain areas of the country there are often union workers in dealerships – what is the impact of obligations to unions when a dealership is sold?
- Buildings have less value because they are generally single purpose buildings

Conclusion

What are the challenges for increasing the value of an auto dealership in the future?

Section 9
Data Sources

Data Sources

BVR
What It's Worth

About Business Valuation Resources, LLC

www.bvresources.com

Every top business valuation firm depends on BVR for authoritative market data, continuing professional education, and expert opinion. Rely on BVR when your career depends on an unimpeachable business valuation. Our customers include business appraisers, certified public accountants, merger and acquisition professionals, business brokers, lawyers and judges, private equity and venture capitalists, owners, CFOs, and many others. Founded by Dr. Shannon Pratt, BVR's market databases and analysis have won in the courtroom—and the boardroom—for over 15 years.

To learn more about any of the sources cited in the Industry Transaction & Profile Report, please contact our Sales Department at sales@bvresources.com or 503-291-7963 ext. 2.

***Industry Transaction & Profile Report* Data Sources:**

Pratt's Stats®—No BV practitioner can be without Pratt's Stats®—the leading private company deal database. This searchable online database, available only through Business Valuation Resources, boasts the most complete financial details available anywhere on nearly 16, 000 private companies, with up to 88 data points that include 6 valuation multiples and 13 financial ratios. Each Pratt's Stats® transaction includes detailed data vital in applying the market approach, deriving a selling price, or performing a fairness opinion analysis. You'll find notes on each transaction – even data on non-compete agreements – not available in any other database. (*Subscription includes online access with unlimited searches and quarterly newsletter: Pratt's Stats Private Deal Update*™)

BIZCOMPS®—The most thorough—and most accurate—online database for financial details on "main street" private companies (median selling price is $159,000). In the past, trustworthy data on the sale price of small businesses was virtually non-existent. BIZCOMPS® removes marketplace uncertainty with access to meaningful financial information on 12,500+ actual transactions. (*Subscription includes online access with unlimited searches*)

Factset Mergerstat®/BVR Control Premium Study™—This online database, available exclusively through BVR, delivers empirical support for quantifying control premiums, implied minority discounts and public company valuation multiples. Quickly and easily search 7,450+ transactions that detail the control premium, the implied minority discount and up to five valuation multiples for each transaction. Plus, free quarterly data summaries are available in a printer friendly version. (*Subscription includes online access with unlimited searches and quarterly online Control Premium Study report*)

BizMiner/BVR Industry Financial Reports—BizMiner is the most compelling source of current industry specific data available. BizMiner's extensive–and cost effective–in-

Data Sources

dustry and geographic comparable data covers 16,000 lines of business in 300 U.S. markets. No other source reports at this level of detail. Our unfettered subscription packages feature unlimited access, unlimited searches, and unlimited downloads of every report. BizMiner helps business appraisers by offering better data and lower costs. (*Subscription includes unlimited online access*)

First Research Industry Profiles & State Profiles—Provides detailed industry analysis and state economic analysis. In a matter of minutes you can gain key insights into your industry or state. Each Industry Profile includes sections on: critical issues, quarterly industry update, industry overview, credit and business risk issues, business trends, and industry growth forecasts. Each State Profile includes sections on: the big picture, employment data, major industry update, local real estate summary, and website resources. (*Purchase includes reports in PDF format delivered via email*)

Other BVR Products Include:

BVUpdate™—BVU has been the voice of the valuation profession since its inception. To keep you current, you'll receive the monthly BVU, weekly news updates (via BVWire) and all historical issues of the Business Valuation Update™. You'll get the latest news on new approaches, professional news, the leading conferences, publications of interest, new court decisions, changes in regulations and professional standards—everything you need to know to stay on top of the business valuation profession. (*Subscription includes online access and monthly print newsletter*)

BVLaw™—Appraisers and attorneys alike turn to the exclusive **BVLaw™** collection of close to 3,000 cases and case abstracts concerning economic damages, lost profits, estate and gift tax, divorce, shareholder oppression, partnership dissolution, securities litigation—and more. **BVLaw™** has been locating, indexing and analyzing BV-specific cases for over 15 years. BVR's team of legal analysts continuously track published decisions form the courts in all 50 U.S. states and federal jurisdictions (including Delaware Chancery Court and the U.S. Tax Courts) guaranteeing to keep you current on the latest valuation law, with new cases added everyday. (*Subscription includes online access with unlimited searches and monthly alerts on new case law and case abstracts*)

BVResearch™—Searchable database of business valuation research papers, articles, industry surveys, key court case abstracts, first generation content, webinar transcripts and other invaluable material from the most respected sources and experts in the profession. Valuation analysts, attorneys, and other experts use *BVResearch™* every day to keep current with the most important trends and topics related to business valuation – and to save hours of research time. (*Subscription includes online access with unlimited searches*)

Public Stats™—Searchable database with 2,680+ transactions that detail the 100% sale of publicly-held companies. It features up to 64 data points and 5 valuation multiples on each transaction, making it a natural extension to Pratt's Stats®. It allows you to easily compare your target company to public company transactions. Public Stats™ is widely applied with the market approach in order to determine fair market value and to perform financial research on comparable company pricing, supporting conclusions of fair value for financial reporting, or solicit approval for an acquisition. (*Subscription includes online access with unlimited searches*)

Factset Mergerstat® Review—The annual Mergerstat® Review, available exclusively through BVR, is the must-have source for data and analysis of the M&A market. The

Data Sources

Mergerstat® Review delivers data on transactions in which buyer or seller was a U.S. based company and covers privately held, publicly traded and cross-border transactions. It also analyzes unit divestitures, management buyouts and certain asset sales. The Factset Mergerstat® Monthly Review (a monthly PDF included with your purchase of the Mergerstat® Review) delivers the most valuable M&A statistics and analysis, including the latest activity, deal data by industry – ideal for adding insight and impact to valuation reports, pitch books, client presentations, market overviews and competitive reports. (*Purchase includes hard cover copy of current edition and monthly Factset Mergerstat® Monthly Review in PDF format*)

Pitchbook/BVR Guideline Public Company Comps Tool—This searchable tool provides financial statements, ratios, valuation multiples and more for specific public companies. Perform a search a get all 10Q and 10K filings (from EDGAR) and valuation date-specific public market prices for public comps that match your subject company. This Tool will save you hours, if not days, of research time. (*Subscription includes online access with unlimited searches*)

The FMV Restricted Stock Study™—Available exclusively through BVR, this all-inclusive online database provides empirical support to determine discounts for lack of marketability. Now with over 590 total transactions, the database is built upon hard data – not reported averages or arbitrary rules of thumb. Search results export directly into Excel with up to 65 data fields and verifiable details on each restricted stock transaction. Appraisers save countless hours by relying on The FMV Restricted Stock Study™. (*Subscription includes online access with unlimited searches*)

Valuation Advisors Lack of Marketability Discount Study™—Turn to this resource when you need to defend your discounts for lack of marketability. This online database includes 4,560+ transactions in pre-IPO private stock and options. It is the largest and most up-to-date pre-IPO database for lack of marketability discounts. Defend your conclusion with the most convincing data available. (*Subscription includes online access with unlimited searches*)

Butler Pinkerton Total Cost of Equity (TCOE) and Company-Specific Risk Calculator™

This cutting-edge, web-based tool, available exclusively through BVR, objectively quantifies Total Risk using real-time market observations. The Butler Pinkerton Calculator™ (BPC) offers empirical data for TCOE and company-specific risk premiums (CSRP) – a first for the business valuation industry. Impeach your opponent's cost of capital. Excel with the Calculator while your competition relies on subjective guesses devoid of empirical evidence. (*Subscription includes unlimited online access*)

ktMINE/BVR Royalty Rate Comparables & License Agreements—BVR now offers valuation analysts hands-on access to the most comprehensive source of royalty rate data available anywhere through our relationship with ktMINE. This interactive database provides direct access to royalty rates, actual license agreements and detailed agreement summaries and statistical analysis. With precise search functionality and robust data mining capabilities, ktMINE lets you quickly find and analyze market comparables from over 7,600 non-redacted IP license agreements and over 26,000 royalty rates, along with documents culled from the recesses of the SEC from 1975 to present day. (*Subscription includes online access*)

Data Sources

Duff & Phelps Risk Premium Report—Authored by Roger Grabowski, this resource offers defensible cost of capital measures, particularly for small target companies. Duff & Phelps presents historical equity risk premiums (ERPs) and size premiums for 25 size-ranked portfolios using 8 alternative measures of company size. The rate of return figures are also adjusted for factors that skew other ERP studies, including the presence of distressed securities in the database, and the impact of firms that de-list. Based on Standard & Poor's Compustat database, the Duff & Phelps Risk Premium Report is now regarded as the single best source for cost of capital data. Leading experts confirm that Duff & Phelp's use of historical returns since 1963 produces market risk premia that are more consistent with current estimates than a starting point of 1926. (*Purchase includes reports in PDF format delivered via email*)

Economic Outlook Update™—This quarterly report and forecast of the national economy provides excellent support for the economic outlook section of a valuation report or for your own background information. It includes general economic indicators, GDP, consumer prices and inflation rate, interest rates, unemployment, consumer spending, the stock and bond markets, construction, manufacturing, future outlook, the real estate market, and more. It also contains an abundance of tables and charts, ready-to-use in your next valuation report. It includes complete citations to all original source materials. (*Subscription includes online access to current and historical issues with downloadable PDF, Word, and Excel formats available*)

The BVR/DVA 123R Compliance & Employee Stock Option Calculator™—Developed by Derivative Valuation Associates, LLC, this tool simultaneously calculates the value of Employee Stock Options (ESOs) and the underlying company stock based on user inputs. While the valuation of ESOs has been a central issue in numerous tax cases and matrimonial disputes, the courts have not historically scrutinized the option pricing and methodologies. However, FASB's release of Statement of Financial Accounting Standards (SFAS) No. 123R and regulations pertaining to IRC Section 409A by the U.S. Treasury has clearly raised the bar. Unless your option valuation model can adjust for the dilutive aspect of ESO and simultaneously allocate values to stocks and ESOs, it will yield incorrect ESO and stock values. Ensure the accuracy of your calculation with this ground-breaking online resource. (*Subscription includes unlimited online access*)

BVR Guides & Books by Expert Authors - Available in both print and electronic format.

- AHLA / BVR Guide to Healthcare Valuation (Mark Dietrich, ed.)
- BVR' Business Valuation in Divorce Case Law Compendium*
- BVR's Business Valuation Sourcebook (Bill Sipes, ed.)
- BVR's Comprehensive Guide to Lost Profits Damages (Nancy J. Fannon, ed.)
- BVR's Guide to Business Valuation Issues in Estate & Gift Tax (Linda Trugman, ed.)
- BVR's Guide to Discounts for Lack of Marketability (John Stockdale, Sr.)
- BVR's Guide to Fair Value in Shareholder Dissent, Oppression, and Marital Dissolution (Adam Manson, ed.)
- BVR's Guide to Intellectual Property Valuation (Michael Pellegrino)

Data Sources

- BVR's Guide to Personal v. Enterprise Goodwill (Adam Manson and David Wood, eds.)
- BVR's Guide to Physician Practice Valuation (Mark Dietrich, ed.)
- BVR's Guide to Restaurant Valuation (Ed Moran)
- BVR's Guide to the Use and Application of the Transaction Databases (Nancy Fannon and Heidi Walker)
- BVR's Guide to Valuations for IRC 409A Compliance (Neil Beaton)
- BVR's Industry Transaction & Profile Report
- Business Reference Guide Online {Business Brokerage Press}
- The Lawyer's Business Valuation Handbook: Understanding Financial Statements, Appraisal Reports, and Expert Testimony {Shannon Pratt and Alina Niculita, - American Bar Association}
- Standards of Value: Theory & Application {Shannon Pratt, William Morrison and Jay Fishman - Wiley}
- Buy-Sell Agreements {Chris Mercer - Peabody Publishing}

* Available only in CD format

For more information about the Business Valuation Resources, LLC product portfolio, contact our Sales Department at sales@bvresources.com or 503-291-7963 ext. 2.